Global Media, Biopolitics a

Global Media, Biopolitics and Affect shows how mediations of bodily vulnerability have become a strong political force in contemporary societies. In discussions and struggles concerning war involvement, health care issues, charity, democracy movements, contested national pasts, and climate change, performances of bodily vulnerability are increasingly used by citizens to raise awareness, to create sympathy, to encourage political action, and to circulate information in global media networks. The book thus argues that bodily vulnerability can serve as a catalyst for affectively charging and disseminating particular political events or issues by means of media. To investigate how, when, and why that happens and to evaluate the long-term social impacts of mediating bodily vulnerability, the book offers a theoretical framework for understanding the role of bodily vulnerability in contemporary digital media culture. Likewise, it presents a range of close empirical case studies in the areas of illness blogging, global protests after the killing of Neda Agda Soltan in Iran, charity communication, green media activism, online war commemoration, and digital witnessing related to conflicts in Sarajevo and Ukraine.

Britta Timm Knudsen is Associate Professor in the Department of Aesthetics and Communication at Aarhus University, Denmark. Her previous books include *Enterprising Initiatives in the Experience Economy* (co-edited with Dorthe Refslund Christensen, and Per Blenker, 2014) and *Re-investing Authenticity, Tourism, Place and Emotions* (co-edited with Anne Marit Waade, 2009).

Carsten Stage is Associate Professor in the Department of Aesthetics and Communication, ARTS at Aarhus University, Denmark. His previous publications include 'Online A-liveness', a chapter in *Mediating and Re-Mediating Death* (2014), and 'Contagious Bodies' (co-authored with Knudsen) in the journal *Emotion, Space and Society*. He is co-editor of *Conjunctions. Transdisciplinary Journal of Cultural Participation*.

Routledge Studies in New Media and Cyberculture

Global Media, Biopolitics and Affect

Politicizing Bodily Vulnerability

**Britta Timm Knudsen and
Carsten Stage**

Routledge
Taylor & Francis Group

LONDON AND NEW YORK

First published 2015 by Routledge

2 Park Square, Milton Park, Abingdon, Oxfordshire OX14 4RN

711 Third Avenue, New York, NY 10017

*Routledge is an imprint of the Taylor & Francis Group,
an informa business*

First issued in paperback 2018

Library of Congress Cataloging-in-Publication Data
Timm Knudsen, Britta.
  Global media, biopolitics, and affect : politicizing bodily vulnerability /
by Britta Timm Knudsen, Carsten Stage.
    pages cm. — (Routledge studies in new media and cyberculture ; 27)
  Includes bibliographical references and index.
  1. Human body in mass media. 2. Human body—Political aspects.
3. Mass media—Political aspects. 4. Communication in politics—
Technological innovations. 5. Biopolitics. I. Stage, Carsten.
II. Title.
  P96.B64T56 2014
  302.23—dc23
  2014032637

ISBN: 978-1-138-01906-5 (hbk)
ISBN: 978-1-138-54864-0 (pbk)

Typeset in Sabon
by Apex CoVantage, LLC

Contents

Figures

Acknowledgements

We began the collaboration that led to this book in 2009. Throughout the project we have had the support of colleagues from all over the world, and we are very grateful for their helpful comments and inspiring discussions.

First of all, we would like to thank colleagues from our research unit on Affect and Methodological Challenges at the Department of Aesthetics and Communication, Aarhus University, with whom we have discussed these matters: Christoffer Leiding Kølvraa, Camilla Møhring Reestorff, Jonas Fritsch, Jette Kofoed, Dorthe Staunæs, Frederik Bøhling, Lise Dilling-Hansen, and Mikkel Rytter. Our colleagues from the Culture and Media and Event Culture section, Bodil Marie Stavning Thomsen, and Dorthe Refslund Christensen, as well as colleagues from diverse sections at Aarhus University, Dan Ringgaard, Mads Krogh, Mads Daugbjerg, Louise Fabian, Anne Marit Waade, and Rivka Syd Eisner, who have also been important discussion partners.

A special thank you goes to Christian Borch, and Katherine Gibson for reading parts of the manuscript. Warm thanks also to Celia Lury, Anna Gibbs, Joanne Garde-Hansen, Lisa Blackman, John Protevi, Tony Sampson, Jenny Sundén, Nigel Thrift, Brian Massumi, Erin Manning, John Urry, David Crouch, Tim Edensor, Frederik Tygstrup, Karen Hvidtfeldt Madsen, and Devika Sharma for their comments, for sharing thoughts, and for the discussions we have had on the subject of affect at various events. We also thank Emma Waterton, Steve Watson, Christina Smith, and Szilvia Gyimóthy for proposing and joining panels that served as platforms for fruitful discussions on heritage, affects, and emotions. All of our analyses have been tried out on our students, and thanks to their questions and enthusiasm we improve every day. We are also grateful to Claire Neesham and Lucy Seton-Watson from the Language Service, Faculty of Arts, for proofreading our texts.

Some chapters of the book have been published previously. We therefore would like to thank the publishers, editors, and reviewers of the journals *Memory Studies*, *Distinktion*, and *Culture Unbound* as well as Dorthe Refslund Christensen and Kjetil Sandvik as editors of *Mediating and*

Remediating Death, published by Ashgate, who reviewed and commented on earlier versions of the chapters.

Chapter 1 on illness blogging and crowds is a slightly amended version of the article 'The Online Crowd: A Contradiction in Terms?' (2013), published in *Distinktion: Scandinavian Journal of Social Theory*, 14(2), 211–226 (http://www.tandfonline.com). Chapter 2 on Neda and assemblages is a heavily amended version of 'Thingifying Neda' (2011) in *Culture Unbound*, 3, 419–438. Chapter 5 is an extensively revised version of 'Online War Memorials' (2012) published in *Memory Studies*, 13, 418–436, and this is also the case with chapter 6, part of which is adapted by permission of the publishers from 'The Besieged City in the Heart of Europe: Sniper Alley in Sarajevo as Memorial site on YouTube' (2014) in *Mediating and Remediating Death*, eds. Dorthe Refslund Christensen and Kjetil Sandvik (Farnham: Ashgate), 111–132, copyright © 2014. The Introduction, Chapter 3 on charity and seduction, and Chapter 4 on green activism and the sublime were written for this book exclusively.

We would also like to thank Allana Beltran, Paula Slater, Reza Deghati, and Shaun Walker for giving us permission to use pictures and to Winifred Hunton-Chan and Julia Butterfly Hill for their help in the process. Regarding the photo of Neda Agda Soltan (Figure 2.3) best efforts have been made to obtain permission for this particular photo.

For their continuous love, support and understanding we end by thanking our respective families—Jan, Elise, Nina and Signe, August, and Marius. Without you nothing would be worth it.

Introduction
Politicising Bodily Vulnerability

The political is, and always has been, a bodily, affective affair. It is felt in the surface of our skin when we feel indignation over injustice, enthusiasm to take part in positive change, or fear of political marginalisation. But such an understanding of the political is at odds with the ideal of political space as inhabited solely by liberal (and somehow bodiless) subjects engaged in rational contestation—a space that needs shielding from the instability caused by too much affect and too much bodily investment. As Nigel Thrift (2008) and Chantal Mouffe (2000b) have argued, the ideal of "cool politics" is not only wrong but also politically problematic. It detaches affect from the contemporary progressive agenda, handing it over as an all-too-powerful tool to the opponents of that agenda. In the case studies we present in this book, in which vulnerable, fragile bodies are engaged in affective political mobilisation, a further important objection is that today's new digital-media technologies have made affect one of the most democratic micro-political tools available to ordinary citizens. Affect offers individuals the opportunity to bypass institutional hierarchies by evoking new social connections through media-aesthetic appeals to the sympathy or indignation of other bodies. It is not our goal, however, to argue for a political ecology devoid of rational decision and informed discussion. Rather, we wish to show how affect under the right circumstances, rather than a threat, can be a catalyst for attractions and connections that have the capability to establish new assemblages of bodies, technologies, and objects, with their own capacity for political change (Anderson et al., 2012).

Our main argument in this book is that bodily vulnerability is becoming an increasingly important part of contemporary media processes, in two respects. First, bodily vulnerability is increasingly used to mobilise awareness and political action and to circulate information about global injustice. Second, bodily vulnerability has become a key theme in discursive struggles over, for example involvement in war, contested national pasts, and the legitimacy of political protest against climate change. We argue that bodily vulnerability has become a strong social force, both in the collective processes of discursively defining the proper past and future of a given society in media and as a catalyst for affectively charging and disseminating particular political events or issues by means of media. To investigate these processes, the book offers, first, a theoretical framework in which to understand and evaluate the mediatised, affectively mobilising, and discursively fragmenting role of bodily vulnerability in contemporary digital media culture. Second, it presents a range of close empirical case studies in the areas of illness blogging (Chapter 1), a global assemblage protest (Chapter 2), charity communication (Chapter 3), green media activism (Chapter 4), online war commemoration (Chapter 5), and digital witnessing (Chapter 6). The book thus serves as a detailed analytical deployment of contemporary theoretical interest in affect and its socially transformative or (bio)political potential, and contributes to the developing field of research in the areas of media affect and contagious communication (Boltanski, 1999; Gibbs, 2008; Featherstone, 2010; Grusin, 2010; Blackman, 2012; Sampson, 2012).

This introduction outlines the aim and focus of the book, our general methodological considerations, and a theoretical framework developing a particular understanding of global media, biopolitics, and affect, which are important concepts in our case studies. The first three chapters focus primarily on bodily vulnerability as a social force of mobilisation, online 'crowding', and media circulation. The last three chapters focus more on differing discursive struggles over how to integrate particular 'vulnerable bodies' (Nature as victim, the dead soldier, the civilian victims of war, ethnic groups) into competing social-victimisation narratives. The chapters thus move from cases in which the legitimacy of bodily vulnerability is relatively uncontested, to cases in which it is highly contested. In this way we show that affect motivated by the spectacle of bodily vulnerability is a powerful way of attuning both spectators and, at the same time, an unruly force that creates discursive ruptures and conflicts.

In the book the topic of bodily vulnerability and its mobilising political potential is researched mostly in the field of digital communication but with a general interest in the constant dynamic interrelationship between mediated and material environments and between online and offline actions and phenomena. The book touches on three main academic areas: first, digital culture and communication studies; second, vulnerability studies in the areas of politics, globalisation, environmentalism, and memory studies; and, third, affect studies itself. In relation to these areas the book attempts to offer an interdisciplinary approach that links close readings with sociocultural levels, and that develops the relationship between vulnerability, global media, affective processes, and the mediated (bio)political body.

VULNERABILITY AND VICTIMHOOD

All the cases of the book involve some element of bodily/organic weakening, dying or death, mediated or represented in various ways (e.g. a terminally ill blogger, civilians killed during war or protest, soldiers dying in combat, citizens suffering as a result of famine and poverty, and Nature dying as a result of pollution). Mediation is used to engage the receiver in otherwise 'untold stories' (Garde-Hansen and Gorton, 2013: 12) about the suffering and/or death of human or non-human organisms, and thus to motivate experiences of 'feeling like' the suffering body by producing affective experiences of shared vulnerability. Mediation is used to connect the event of suffering and death to a human capacity for ethical self-transgression via affective responses making bodies permeable to each other (Blackman, 2012). In relation to our case-studies vulnerability seems to function as either (or both) (1) an *energiser* that directs attention towards certain bodies and stimulates an urge to respond (positively/negatively), repeat, imitate, accumulate, or circulate—a function that can be used more or less strategically—or (2) an *event (of the virtual)* that helps the involved to bypass current hindrances by offering a motivation to imagine a world that handles vulnerabilities in better ways.

The academic field on mediated suffering and morality is a growing one (Boltanski, 1999; Sontag, 2003; Butler, 2004; 2009; Chouliaraki, 2006; Silverstone, 2007; McCosker, 2013). Our understanding of mediated vulnerability is particularly inspired by Judith Butler's recent work, which in turn draws on and discusses the philosophy of Emmanuel Lévinas. We thus claim that the act of mediation, be it visual, audiovisual or written, tries to enable the experience of a '"common" corporeal vulnerability' (Butler, 2004: 41) between the mediated/mediating body and the receiving body. According to Butler, vulnerability is the shared existential condition of all humans: No human being is simply autonomous, but each is always dependent on the care, support, and recognition of others. And in this sense, the self is always somehow situated outside itself, due to our 'primary sociality' (Butler, 2004: 28; see also Butler, 2009: 53).

The concept of vulnerability is nevertheless a complex one, because 'vulnerable' is a quality that is not only shared by all bodies but also ascribed (more or less rightly) to some bodies and not to others according to the distribution of recognition and non-recognition, inclusion and exclusion in specific contexts. Vulnerability can thus be integrated or denied in processes of political thinking and solution making. In this sense, vulnerability is not only an ontological condition of human life, but also an ideal that we can use to 'critically evaluate and oppose the conditions under which certain human lives are more vulnerable than others, and thus certain human lives are more grievable than others' (Butler, 2004: 30).

As we show in this book, mediation can modulate, block, and support the acknowledgement of vulnerability. Sometimes mediation is lacking, so that vulnerability goes relatively unnoticed by a global audience; sometimes mediation converts vulnerability into something else (e.g. cultural deviance, self-inflicted violence); and sometimes mediation succeeds in establishing moments of shared vulnerability between mediated and receiving bodies (Butler, 2004: 142). In the following chapters, we focus on the mediated uses of vulnerability and on the social consequences of actual spectacles of bodily suffering.

Political scientist Joseph S. Nye Jr. has introduced a typology of two different forms of power: 'hard power', where institutions get others to act according to their wishes by means of either negative or positive transactions (e.g. military coercion or economic sanctions or reward), and 'soft power', where institutions 'shape the preferences of others' (2004: 5) by attracting or seducing them by means of cultural products, values, and foreign policies that come across as desirable. '[S]oft power is attractive power' (Nye, 2004: 6). Soft power is at work if 'my behaviour is determined by an observable but intangible attraction', as Nye (2004: 7) puts it. In this book we are particularly interested in the soft power of mediated bodily vulnerability—or rather, in the type of soft power we want to ambiguously term *vulnerable power*. Just as hard power can be sub-categorised as 'military' and 'economic' power according to Nye (2004: 31), throughout this book, we investigate how 'vulnerable power', as a subcategory of soft power, is used both by individuals via practising and staging their own bodily vulnerability to reach a certain goal and by others via representations of bodily vulnerability to attract attention and willingness to act towards a given social/political cause.

Part of our investigation is to understand under which conditions mediated vulnerability has the potential to mobilise and/or democratise. To understand this, we have to take a closer look at the adjoining concept, victimhood. The two concepts are linked, although not in a straightforward way, in our case studies. In one case victimhood is avoided, which makes the acknowledgement of vulnerability more powerful (Chapter 1); in another, victimhood is simply ascribed to the mediated body without question (Chapter 2). What the two scenarios have in common is that the social construction of victimhood does not block or complicate the soft power of mediated vulnerability. In Chapters 4 through 6, the articulation of vulnerability as one element of narratives of victimhood becomes increasingly complicated, as the act of ascribing victimhood is also treated as suspicious, as potentially strategic, and thus as a social position in need of verification and/or contestation (Dean, 2010). In these later chapters, vulnerability is either manufactured by activists who put themselves in danger to highlight Nature as victim, or connected to groups who claim some sort of collective justification of victimhood in politically heated contexts. These features clearly make the narrative and juridical construction of 'justified victim' versus 'indefensible perpetrator' more difficult to establish, thereby turning the relation between mediated vulnerability and social victimhood into a field of discursive struggle and affective dissonances or 'emotional noise' (Garde-Hansen and Gorton, 2013: 1).

In this sense, vulnerability as a resource for empathy and political mobilisation is acknowledged or blocked or changed—or simply 'politicised' by inscribing vulnerability in the political antagonisms between different sensual-somatic articulations of the social (Ranciére, 2000; Panagia, 2009; Protevi, 2009)—through these highly historical and context-dependent processes of victimisation and de-victimisation. This underlines that the soft influence of vulnerable power is thus vulnerable in two ways: First, because it more or less strategically invests mediated vulnerability in the political distribution and redistribution of the social and, second, because it is not strong (or 'hard') enough to determine how it may be historicised, contextualised, politicised and moulded by established discourses or semantic ecologies. Vulnerability can attune and awaken publics, and can appeal to a transindividual acknowledgement of shared vulnerability; but it cannot control the specific practices or effects of this awakening. For that reason, the use of mediated vulnerability is not to be condemned or praised in itself; rather, it should be discussed in relation to the specific processes of political mobilisation that it shapes.

METHODOLOGY

The criterion for selection of the cases investigated in the book is their cultural resonance: All those selected have motivated a high degree of reaction and dissemination. The empirical material analysed in the book is embodied data (Walkerdine, 2010), which means that it bears witness to the bodily states of affect of various social actors. Each chapter provides the exact methodological reasons, choices, and delimitations for data collection in relation to the specific case. However, we would like to make some general statements about how we collected the data and how we identify affect in online audiovisual material. Finally, we offer a more normative framework for politically evaluating the mediated exposure of bodily vulnerability.

Our primary material is audiovisual or written textual material produced (1) in the heat of affective experiences, (2) while remembering or recollecting affects via textual production, or (3) with the intention of evoking affect around vulnerable bodies. Our main textual sources are various types of online archives such as YouTube, blogs, and websites. In some chapters we add more quantitative material generated by the media platforms themselves (e.g. viewing statistics; Rogers, 2013: 5). As argued by Adi Kunstman, Garde-Hansen, and Gorton, and, in the quotation that follows from Tova Benski and Erin Fischer, the internet is a particularly interesting source of material for affect research:

> The internet offers a unique place to study emotions, not only for empirical and theoretical reasons, but for methodological reasons as well. It can be thought of as a unique laboratory for the study of emotions for two key reasons. First, the internet is a fertile ground for a huge diversity and amount of communication of all sorts and from a large and diverse group of people. Much of that communication is emotional,

reflecting immediate feelings, sometimes, as they occur—most use of social media such as Facebook and Twitter is now occurring on mobile devices. Second, these communication acts are all registered.

(Benski and Fisher, 2014: 6)

Kunstman also stresses the immediacy and spontaneous character of much internet communication and how it can be approached as offering us access to 'archives of feeling' (drawing on Ann Cvetkovich's work), registering impulses 'once vibrant, but now "saved as"' (drawing on the work of Garde-Hansen, Hoskins, and Reading; Kuntsman, 2012: 6–7).

To identify affective processes in our textual archives, we make use of a range of analytical strategies focusing either on how affects become visible through the temporal characteristics of the material (how rhythms, repetition, and difference in time motivate/are motivated by certain affects), in content (what do people say/write about their affects), and formal dimension (how affects create breakdowns or instabilities in normal communication patterns). More specifically, in Chapter 1 we analyse crowdings on the online blog of Eva Markvoort based on love and empathy by focusing on articulated and formal traces of affective sameness and collective imitation. In Chapter 2 we focus on following new connections and assemblage building in relation to the killing of Neda Agda Soltan, where sadness and indignation function as a motivation to contribute both to an assemblage and to what holds the assemblage together. In Chapter 3 we investigate articulations showing how affects motivated by global inequality pose a seductive challenge that generate affects both as a reward (the joy of making a difference) and as a desire for change (the thrill of seeing that the future can be different) in relation to the Kibera project and students' production of charity videos. In the fourth chapter on the green creative activism of Julia Butterfly Hill and Alana Beltran, we take special interest in moments of enthusiasm expressed during/after sublime experiences that open the possibility for transgression of the given obstacles to create a more sustainable future. In Chapter 5 and 6 on war commemoration of Danish soldiers and the digital witnessing of conflict zones in Sarajevo and Kiev, national pride, but also anger, disgust, and fear, respectively, are investigated. We detect these affects through textual and audiovisual ruptures pointing at the affective heatedness of debates and 'chora sites' (gestures, outbursts, broken language, redundancy, shakings) and perform a rhythmanalysis of memorial videos and live streaming images from Kiev in relation to reactions and subsequent commentaries (see the chapter outline at the end of this introduction).

All our cases thus attempt to give a vulnerable body a voice through mediation, first, by defining something or someone as vulnerable (e.g. the sick body, the political victim, distant sufferers, nature, soldiers and citizens of conflict zones) and, second, by identifying the social agencies that carry either a historical and/or a present political responsibility for this. This raises the dilemma of how analysts are to discuss the politically transformative potential of various forms of mediated vulnerabilities—especially when exposing bodily vulnerability becomes a widespread strategy. To be able to qualify such a discussion we first focus on the quantifiable effects of the mediation of vulnerability in the cases analysed—or rather, their measurable cultural resonance and spreadability (Jenkins et al., 2013). Such effects could be determined by the number of comments, views, shares, and likes that each instance of mediated vulnerability creates; the specific geographical way it spreads in online media networks; the further media attention it creates (e.g. coverage by mainstream media); the economic output it mobilises (e.g. via donations); and the type of public it mobilises (e.g. parliamentary, offline/online, national/global publics). These features are of course not in themselves a clear indication of the transformative or sustainable character of the political processes enabled. A video showing suffering a long way away can for example be disseminated very intensely online without ever generating concrete change for the sufferers. Therefore, we also need a more normative framework to evaluate the political potential of each case in question.

To enable such a discussion, we use the following five questions to consider the qualitative character of political mobilisation present in the empirical material in the book: (1) *Voice or cultural reproduction:* Do the less privileged actually acquire a voice and achieve social inclusion through the specific spectacle of vulnerability, or does the spectacle in fact reproduce established patterns of cultural recognition, exclusions, and power? (2) *Agonism or antagonism:* Does the exposure of bodily vulnerability lead to the creation of agonistic relationships based on an acceptance of political differences or of antagonistic relationships characterised by hostile and aggressive non-acceptance (Mouffe, 2000a)? (3) *Action or passivity:* Does mediated bodily vulnerability motivate political actions, or, rather, passive spectatorship? (4) *Long-term or short-term involvement:* Are investments concerning the elimination of unjust vulnerability of a long-term or short-term character? (5) *Structural or individualised political solutions:* Do the political interventions focus on structural changes or on emotional investments in individual cases, or both? By posing these particular questions in the context of our cases, we implicitly affirm the creation of *voice, agonism, action, long-term involvement,* and *structural solutions* as valuable characteristics of a constructive and viable process of mobilisation involving mediated vulnerability.

BODILY VULNERABILITY AND MEDIA GLOBALISATION

One argument in the book is that globalisation processes have affected the cultural life of the vulnerable body in two different ways: first, thematically, as representations of and performances by the vulnerable body are increasingly linked to issues of acute, even life-threatening global risks (e.g. climate change, global terrorism, global capitalism, famine). In other words, bodily vulnerability is conceptualised as standing for or as imitating the destructive consequences of globalisation processes, in order to promote reflection on the future risks of being and having a body. When life itself is threatened, the carrier of life, the body, receives more attention. Second, the vulnerable body is increasingly used as a soft-power vehicle of intensive image and visual spectacle, with the ability to circulate in global media networks. Exposing one's own (or others') vulnerable body has become a way to capture the interest and political attention of the global public sphere: to make information move more swiftly through global media networks.

Global media networks that are based on satellite and internet communication are important catalysts for the 'complex connectivity'—based on flows of people, information and objects and leading to intensified cycles of cultural de- and re-territorialisation (Tomlinson, 1999)—that lies at the heart of globalisation as a concrete, empirical change in contemporary life (Hjarvard, 2003; Jansson, 2004; Lull, 2007; Castells, 2009). Contrary to the arguments of cultural/economic homogenisation and cultural essentialism (Huntington, 2006), the cultural consequences of this increased connectivity across geographical distances are multidimensional. The complex cultural state of 'globalisation', we would argue, includes all of the following tendencies: new cosmopolitan publics, and ethical relations (Silverstone, 2007); new power geometries between movers and dwellers and new legal zones mediating the relationship between nation states and global flows (Tellmann et al., 2012); new participatory knowledge and/or do-it-yourself (DIY) communities (Lévy, 1997; Jenkins, 2006; Bruns, 2008; Gauntlett, 2011); new global media events, and new ways of witnessing catastrophes and wars (Christensen, 2008; Andén-Papadopoulos, 2009); new affective economies of fear, empathy, and vulnerability (Ahmed, 2004; Chouliaraki, 2006); new types of digitised work (Terranova, 2000; Gregg, 2011); new forms of pollution and risk production (Beck, 2004); new social movements and protest cultures focused on global crises and challenges (Porta, 2008); new green everyday technologies and practices (Marres, 2011); new intertwinements of consumption, charity, and corporate social responsibility (Arvidsson and Peitersen, 2013); and new patterns of migration, cultural hybridity, cultural war, ethnocentrism, and identity politics (Appadurai, 2006).

Two important media concepts in this book related to these sociological changes are 'immediacy' and 'participation'. Both concepts are crucial for understanding how global media, bodies, and affective processes have become increasingly intertwined. According to John Tomlinson (2007), we are currently facing an era of increased immediacy, with the gap between departure and arrival either diminishing or even closing in relation to a range of everyday practices. Many bodies carry digital technologies (or 'terminals' according to Tomlinson) around with them with which they can connect to friends via Skype, buy books on Amazon, watch movies and series on Netflix, communicate with the workplace via e-mail, listen to music on Spotify, witness distant events on news media outlets, and learn about various issues on Wikipedia—spontaneously or instantaneously and according to cognitive and affective desires. This logic of immediacy is supplemented by increasingly frequent opportunities for user participation, defined in the broadest sense, in which 'participation concerns collective actions that form something larger so that those involved become part of and share the entity created' (Kelty et al., 2014: 5)—via digital communication (Benkler, 2006; Jenkins, 2006; Carpentier, 2011). That non-professionals can participate in media production and dissemination processes means that they also become better able to express vulnerability in global media networks, to share images of vulnerability, to create states of vulnerability among receivers, and to collectively develop affective processes around mediated vulnerability among media produsers (Kuntsman, 2012; Benski and Fisher, 2014).

'Media are affective tools, and online media present a number of networked tools that can be used by emotion agents to transmit affect', according to Joanne Garde-Hansen and Kristyn Gorton (2013: 4. In an investigation of the affective relationship among globalisation, media, and the body in terms of changed cultural states of 'immediacy' and 'participation', the following are all important features: the increasing mobility of digital technologies, the opportunity of sensual liveness with distant events, processes of peer production and sharing, the constant availability of certain types of information and interaction, and the increased opportunity to act according to a logic of propensity (Thrift, 2008b). The result is the production of new forms of globally connected embodiment that are constantly intertwined with digital technologies, thereby making it possible to create more quasi-synchronised relations of attraction and repulsion between bodies, or organisms, across vast geographical distances. In this way, globalisation, often described as stretched relations and flows, can also motivate processes of bodily intensification by offering more sensually complex environments, by making available the affective stimulation that suits the singular body, and by enabling more global processes of affective hyping and crowding.

Scott Lash argues in *Intensive Culture* that with globalisation the world has become both more extensive and more intensive at the same time: 'We thus live in a culture that is at the same time extensive and intensive. Indeed, the more globally stretched and extensive social relations become, the more they simultaneously seem to take on this intensity' (2010: 3). Following Lash, the stretching of social relations, movement (migration and tourism) and consumption across the globe do not mean that life has become less intense locally. Global connectivity and the site-specific complexity that it creates have not diminished intensive living. Rather, they seem to work against low-intensity environments and consumers waiting, being 'forced' to watch media products that they find boring, or having to break up intense social relationships because of distance.

This line of thinking concerning the connection between globalisation, media, and affective embodiment is anticipated in Marshall McLuhan's seminal work of 1964, *Understanding Media*, on how electronic media extend the human senses and nervous system:

> In the electronic age, when our central nervous system is technologically extended to involve us in the whole of mankind and to incorporate the whole of mankind in us, we necessarily participate, in depth, in the consequences of our every action. It is no longer possible to adopt the aloof and dissociated role of the literate Westerner.
>
> (McLuhan, 1987: 4)

In this sense electronic media are treated as technologies that change what a body is and what it can do by adding new qualities and sensibilities to it (Thacker, 2004). Electronic media are also treated here as intrinsically intertwined with the emotional dimensions of the body (see e.g. Vincent and Fortunati, 2009).

Following Jay David Bolter and Richard Grusin, the body (see also Thacker, 2004; Angel and Gibbs, 2006) is already in itself a medium or carrier of 'special cultural messages', sometimes intentionally and sometimes not, via clothes, accessories and body shapes (Bolter and Grusin, 2003: 239). According to Bolter and Grusin, 'the body both remediates and is remediated' (2003: 238). A female bodybuilder is an example of how the body remediates itself by challenging older versions of what the female body is supposed to look like. We claim in our analyses that digital media also remediate the vulnerable body as a communicative medium, by giving it new qualities that transform it into a soft-power or biopolitical tool. Once remediated through digital media, the vulnerable body can become both a globalised, viral source of imitation (Tarde, [1895] 1903; Sampson, 2012) and a socially visible, politically powerful, contagious and socially mobilising body. The specific quality added by new digital media (as opposed to e.g. television) is the fact that everyday citizens can now participate in these processes when, for instance, making commemoration videos or blogs about their own or another's vulnerabilities. In other words, the soft-power potential of the mediated vulnerable body has been democratised because participatory technology now allows for user-generated production and dissemination of media material on a global scale.

Every remediation is to some extent a 'frontal assault on the problem of representation' in offering new experiences of full presence, according to Bolter and Grusin (2003: 236). The assault is nevertheless never completely successful, as every remediation can create both a lack of media awareness (immediacy) and increased media awareness (hypermediacy). Following this, our cases attempt to make the vulnerable body fully present to the receiver by remediating the body as a medium, to give it new qualities and powers. But they do not always succeed, because focus on the mediated and strategic character of vulnerability is also motivated. Broadly speaking, mediated vulnerability is successful as a biopolitical, soft-power tool when moments of experiential presence are created.

The remediation of the human body challenges traditional notions of what a body is in the first place. In our investigation we take a particular interest in the political potentials of the human body, but we situate ourselves theoretically in a framework that not only stresses the relational and decentred character of the body, but also introduces non-human actors such as Nature, materiality, and technology into the study. Our understanding of what a body is and what it can do is primarily inspired by recent developments in theories of affect and social contagion (Brennan, 2004; Clough, 2007; Gibbs, 2008; Thrift, 2008a; Borch, 2009; Blackman and Venn, 2010; Featherstone, 2010; Henriques, 2010; Blackman, 2012). Here, the role of bodies in immaterial processes and exchanges—for instance being touched, feeling aversion and attraction, being contaminated by moods and atmospheres, being attached in certain ways to objects and spaces—are at the centre of attention. These developments in affect theory oppose the traditional biomedical understanding of the body as a purely human, delimited, biochemical entity. Our multidimensional understanding of the body thus follows Lisa Blackman's description of how certain affective theories develop a more complex, dynamic or 'assemblaged' understanding of the body: as a process, as specific 'brain–body–world entanglements' (Blackman, 2012: 1), as not strictly human, as intertwined with both technologies and cultural resources, as having a strong immaterial and mimetic component, and as existing in a tension between networked multiplicity and personal singularity. This complex, multidimensional understanding of the body is relevant in our cases in several ways. Primarily, the immaterial power of human vulnerability only becomes present and possible to communicate via the complex intertwinement between human bodies and non-human actors and technologies (media, objects, machines, etc.). Similarly, the body's ability to come across as vulnerable is also dependent on the context in which discourses shape for instance when and how a certain life is perceived as something to be grieved over or something that is dispensable.

BODILY VULNERABILITY AND BIOPOLITICS

The most important epistemological context for the power of human vulnerability is what Michel Foucault (1976) coined 'the biopolitical age'. In the first volume of *The History of Sexuality,* Foucault describes the biopolitical age, evolving in the seventeenth eighteenth century, as the story of how biology comes to be directly reflected in politics as it begins to address the vital biological processes of human existence in themselves. Throughout the classical age, the dominant form of power is the *sovereign* power (which exerts its power over life by its legitimate right to kill) and the *disciplining* power (which manages and governs populations' bodies through the institutions and architectures of power, such as schools, armies, prisons, and factories). Modernity's biopolitical power over life, by contrast, unfolds in two ways, both as a continuation of the disciplining of bodies and as a regulation of populations. On one hand, we have an anatomical–political disciplining of the human body, itself perceived as a machine: The body is controlled, dressed, tamed, and enhanced. On the other hand, biopolitical power directly regulates the biological processes themselves: birth and death (e.g. eugenics), health and disease, reproduction and sexuality. Here it is 'life itself' rather than political rights that has become pivotal for politics, even though politics is often articulated through rights claims such as the right to life, to the body, to health, to happiness, to children, and so on (Foucault, 1976: 191).

As we also know, power has to be exchanged and practised in order to work. Because it comes 'from below' as well as 'from above', power is pervasive throughout the whole network of the social. The exercise of power goes through a 'conduct of conduct' (Foucault, [1982] 1994: 341), meaning that power in the form of governmentality presupposes the liberty and agency of the one over whom power is exercised. 'To govern, in this sense, is to structure the possible field of action of others', to quote Foucault lecturing at the Collège de France in 1978–1979 (Foucault, [1982] 1994: 341). One scholar who has used the concept of governmentality in relation to media's biopolitical power over audiences' bodies and affects is Richard Grusin (2010), whose book *Remediation, Affect and Mediality after 9/11* sketches a scenario in which governmental power is produced and reproduced through media at several levels. Using the shift from a disciplinary society to a control society (as outlined by Gilles Deleuze in his 1990 *Postscript to Control Societies*) and connecting the biopolitical system of domination to digital information technology, Grusin points to how media work in concert with the state by communicating and 'vitalising' it, as well as to how informal media, social media such as blogs, YouTube, and Twitter participate in governmental processes. His example is the Abu Ghraib photographs that circulated in 2006, showing Western soldiers torturing Iraqi prisoners by staging them in obscene and humiliating 'installations' which they subsequently photographed and disseminated. Grusin argues that the dissemination of the Abu Ghraib photos is a showcase of how governmental power is not just 'from above', but was echoed and reinforced 'from below' through the everyday practice of the soldiers sharing the photos. The very dissemination of the Abu Ghraib photos shows both how the state has power over the soldiers' bodies and how it influences the soldiers' conduct towards the prisoners.

Let us now turn to theories that investigate biopolitics through concepts such as sympathy, imitation, empowerment, disruptive events, and re-politicisation. Nigel Thrift pursues the relationship between affect and politics in his writings. With Deleuze and Massumi, Thrift states that biopolitical power over bodies is exerted by 'a neo-authoritarian new deal whose main interest is in accelerating innovation' (Thrift, 2008a: 222). As a biopolitical answer to this he searches for ways of 're-materialising democracy' that take biology seriously. Thrift argues in favour of a re-enchantment of modernity that makes possible a politics oriented to the medial conditions of the present moment: 'Most of the time Western democratic cultures tend to be disengaged, but they can be "switched on" by particular issues with high affective resonance' (Thrift, 2008a: 240). Following this, he suggests focusing more on sympathy as a trans-individual way of relating to others that challenges an asymmetrical domination–resistance relationship. For Thrift, the biopolitical tool is our bodies and their ability to move in synchronised ways with other bodies.

To Negri and Hardt, biopolitics focuses more on subjective agency enacted by the power *of* (not *over*) life to determine an alternative production of subjectivity. Negri and Hardt articulate the biopolitical act par excellence as an event that disrupts the normative system expressing an act of freedom: 'Events of resistance have the power not only to escape control but also to create a new world' (Hardt and Negri, 2009: 61). The very distinction between power over life (biopower) and the power of life (biopolitics) can bring us further toward qualifying what forms the power of life take as a biopolitical tool. Spectacles of human vulnerability thus have to become events in order to be able to point to a possible new world.

The combination of vulnerability and empowerment (loaded with immanent power to empower others) is also present in Banu Bargu's work on human shields and the weaponisation of life. Human rights activists in Iraq, Palestine, and Turkey, for instance, place themselves in or around combat targets to deter combatants from attacking in order to protest against current political affairs. In September 2004, for instance, a group of 25 activists from Diyarbakir in south-east Turkey went to Gabar to protest against security operations by the Turkish military against the Kurdish population of Turkey and northern Iraq (Bargu, 2013). Other activists followed them, and by December a group of 750 individuals had formed a human chain stretching over 3 kilometres. The human chain action continued until summer 2005. Human shields expose the precarious distinction between 'civilian' and 'combatant', but they incarnate an alternative, non-violent form of radical political participation for civilian actors (as opposed to suicide bombers, for example). According to Bargu, human shields pose a critique of the humanisation of warfare and give substance to biopolitics in three ways. First, they *re-politicise* the political meaning and value of human life; secondly, they act as *moral agents,* taking the responsibility for protection upon themselves; and thirdly, they reassert the *materiality of bodies* as human shields, making the suffering of others more visible (Bargu, 2013: 13–14). What is particularly interesting in Bargu's analysis of human shields is that bodies become a biopolitical tool that presents a moral alternative to current power geometries.

This line of thinking is also present in Brian Doherty's interesting work on protest techniques among eco-activists, including body lock-ons, walkways, tripods, and tunnels. All of these aim at 'manufacturing vulnerability', for instance slowing down tree-felling machines or staging a dramatic and media-friendly clash between the hard power of businesses and the system and protesters' moral commitment as expressed in their willingness to risk injury (2000: 70). Last, but not least, we briefly mention Jonathan Darling's development of Giorgio Agamben's work on 'homo sacer' and 'bare life' (Agamben, 1998) as a form of radically excluded subjectivity without rights. According to Agamben this is increasingly produced via contemporary forms of biopower, which normalise a camp-like state of exception and reduce the inhabitants' lives to bare existence, stripped of all political status (1998: 171). Darling, taking a critical-reformist position, criticises Agamben for only theorising a radical and unconditional hospitality as the political alternative to the production of bare life. Instead, Darling argues (citing Edkins and Pin-Fat) that public performances by asylum-seekers in Britain with the status of non-citizens staging their 'becoming bare life' via for example lip-sewing protests that actually exemplifies how 'bare life makes an ethical demand on others, to be attentive and, above all, to respond. The key mechanism here becomes that of establishing a relation and a response' (Darling, 2009: 655). Like Bagu and Doherty, Darling thus describes the re-politicisation of vulnerability, or bare life, as a strategy that can be used by disenfranchised subjects to connect to and morally mobilise a wider public. What we would like to add to this observation is the importance of affect in the mobilisation process.

BODILY VULNERABILITY AND AFFECTIVE CONTAGION

As a consequence of the biopolitical age in which we live which intertwines biology and sociality, and because of the prominence of the body and its post-human prosthetic connectedness to digital, locative, and mobile media networks, the affective turn has been noticeable in the humanities and social sciences for some time. Many scholars have already offered various genealogies of the theories of affect (Thrift, 2008a; Gregg and Seigworth, 2010; Blackman, 2012), as well as multiple explorations of the potential of affect in such disciplines as sociology, heritage and memory studies, cultural studies, geography, media theory, psychology, learning, aesthetics, political theory, and philosophy.

One group of prominent contemporary affect theorists including Massumi, Thrift, Brennan, and Clough focuses on affect as a reaction to a stimulation, which somehow hits the body and then (a little) later is processed by the cognitive apparatus. According to Brennan, the very concept of affect is placed among *drives* (hunger, sex, aggression, fear, and self-preservation), *emotions* and *feelings*, which Brennan for example characterises as the way sensory information is processed, understood, and interpreted by a system of reception. In other words: 'Feelings are sensations that have found the right match in words' (2004: 5). Affects are placed between drives and feelings. Brennan puts particular effort into the distinction between affects and feelings because she conceptualises affect as belonging to a bodily sphere that is prior to and often disrupts or disturbs established cognitive/discursive patterns. For Brennan, affects are in close contact with the vital processes of the body and often occur at the moment of emotional activation, that is in the moment of a dynamic shift or change. Affect theorists inspired by materialist philosophers such as Deleuze and Guattari seem fascinated by the vitality affects and their ability to change attention, awareness, and self-perception. An affective *shock* 'is nothing less than the perception of one's own vitality, one's sense of aliveness, of changeability (often signified as 'freedom')' (Massumi, 2002: 36).

Another group including Sarah Ahmed, Ruth Leys, Margaret Wetherell, Judith Butler, and Lisa Blackman problematises these inherent dichotomies of mind and matter, body and cognition, biology and culture, the physical and the psychological. For this group, these concepts are intermingled and are impossible to distinguish sharply from one another. For the first group, affect is beyond (or before) cognitive categorisation, and therefore, any analytical strategy must necessarily focus on semantics and semiotics as distorted traces of affect, not a medium for it. For the second group, affects can be intertwined, channelled, and even motivated by discourses. Language would thus be considered capable of expressing affects, as there would be no inherent contradiction between the categories of language and the categories taking part in the social shaping of bodies. The dilemma seems to be whether human beings are living a life as bodies to be touched or shocked *before* (or *underneath*) the constraints of cultural discourses or whether these bodies are always already sensing via these very same discourses.

As our intention is to look at the social impacts of the display of vulnerability in global media, we cannot avoid the cultural schemes that humans use in evaluating the affective quality of vulnerability. We therefore agree with those in the second group, especially Wetherell and Leys, who point to the necessity of insisting on the discursive-affective messiness of 'the empirical', something that many famous affect theorists seem unable and unwilling to engage with in consistent and useful ways (2012: 76). On the other hand, we align with Thrift in his very general claim about the relationship between affects and cognition: 'Without affects, cognitive systems collapse: nothing is affectively neutral because emotions provide vital information about every bit of information. They are a key element of all decisions' (2008a: 228).

The 'affective turn' has motivated a preoccupation with understandings of the social focused on momentary constellations of forces, energies, transmissions, rhythms, and atmospheres. In this endeavour, theories in this field often draw on the materialist-relational accounts of the social to be found in the materialist philosophy of Deleuze and Guattari, in post-human feminist theories, in actor-network theory, and in the early-period sociology of for example Gabriel Tarde and Gustave Le Bon. We believe that in the exploration of affective mobilisation, this early-period sociology and its renewed actuality are constructive for the understanding of both intensity/affect and collectives (e.g. gatherings, crowds, publics, communities, and swarms) motivated by digital media (Gibbs, 2008; Borch, 2012; Sampson, 2012).

Le Bon's and Tarde's theories of the social attempt to develop an epidemical model of society, based on passions transmitted through semiconscious, automatic, and involuntary processes of imitation (Thrift, 2008a: 230), and highlighting concepts such as crowds, prestige, imitation, and sympathy. Le Bon's crowd psychology is also relevant when trying to understand the collective affective potential of digital communication. The crowd is described by Le Bon as an affectively synchronised and de-individualised gathering which is 'little adapted to reasoning', 'quick to act', and 'a single being' or 'mental unity' (1895: xi, 2). It is impulsive, irritable, and susceptible to leaders with a talent for suggestion, exaggeration, affirmation, and repetition (Le Bon, 1895: 11, 23). In his famous essay 'The Public and the Crowd', Tarde distinguishes between the crowd as 'a collection of psychic connections produced essentially by physical contacts' (1901: 278) and the public as a 'dispersion of individuals that are physically separated and whose cohesion is entirely mental' (1901: 277). We wish to challenge this distinction. The speed, immediacy, intimacy, and multimodality of online communication seem to situate bodily connections and reactions at the centre of this type of mediated exchange. These features blur the clear boundaries between a mediated public and an unmediated crowd, between private sphere and public life, between geographical distance and perceptual proximity, between the body as an entity and the collective life of bodies.

Tony Sampson likewise identifies a rather straightforward line between offline crowding in an earlier age and contemporary networked, mediatised crowding: 'Just as Canetti's premodern crowd, on hearing and seeing music and dance, joins in and remains fixed within the neighbourhood, today, the millions of consumers who cluster around Lady Gaga and Barak Obama on Twitter and Facebook perhaps do so in part because of a similar tendency to become fascinated by intoxicating glories' (Sampson, 2012: 168). Sampson thus stresses that the suggestive transmissions between bodies cannot be reserved for 'unmediated' spaces, as the 'distinction between being offline and online is now a redundant concept' (2012: 164). He argues that the increased connectivity enabled by network media technologies has also increased the possibility of spreading contagious affects, feelings, and emotions. In this way, the internet has transformed the affective infrastructure and possibilities of intersubjective contagion in contemporary network societies. Sampson reads Tarde as key to understanding the affective fabric—or virality—of network culture. He suggests that whereas Tarde himself saw urban space as the pivotal site for intense contagion, today this space has been supplemented with the internet (Sampson, 2012: 31): 'The internet now provides what Thrift calls a novel 'prosthetic impulse', or vector, for social imitative encounters' (Sampson, 2012: 57); 'social media can speed up and intensify the crowd's desire to fight oppressors by encouraging them to share images of burning martyrs and downtown riots, which quickly spread contagions from region to region' (Sampson, 2012: 164). Tarde is thus used by Sampson to understand the networkability and accidental status of contemporary events generated on- and offline, and to describe 'how small, unpredictable events can be nudged into becoming big, monstrous contagions without a guiding hand' (Sampson, 2012: 6), which he calls the power of 'vibratory events'. We argue that mediated vulnerability is a possible trigger for such vibratory events.

The role of the leader in crowds and masses is quite well known, especially since Freud's famous analysis in *Group Psychology and the Analysis of the Ego* ([1922] 1983) of the relation between the leader and the individual in a crowd or mass as being one of identification, in which crowd members take the leader as their ego-ideal and connect to him through love (Freud, [1922] 1983). For Tarde, the social bond is prior to imaginary relations of the kind that Freud describes between a leader and the mass. What is a society? asks Tarde, and his answer is that it is imitation (Tarde, [1895] 1903: 146). The imitation takes place at semiconscious levels, which is why he characterises members of society as hypnotised and as somnambulists. The imitation at stake here is not an imaginary mirroring such as the expression of a desire for identification that gives direction and meaning for the one who desires to be like the other; rather, it is instinctive, semiconscious, biological, and having to do with the social as a nervous system (as Tarde often describes it).

An (online) crowd leader has the (often unintended) ability to move, mobilise, intensify, and transmit the affective processes that motivate crowd formation. In order to do this the leader must have *prestige*, a concept that both Tarde and Le Bon use to qualify leadership: A leader is the one the others imitate. For Tarde, prestige is a unilateral relation (the leader does not imitate members of the crowd), but he suggests a more advanced form of imitation that is mutual, namely *sympathy* in the sense used by Adam Smith (Tarde, [1895] 1903: 139). In his *Theory of the Moral Sentiments*, Adam Smith describes sympathy as the generic fellow feeling per se: 'Pity and compassion are words appropriated to signify our fellow-feeling with the sorrow of others. Sympathy, through its meaning was, perhaps, originally the same, may now, however, without much impropriety, be made use of to denote our fellow-feeling with any passion whatever' (2009: 15). And he goes on: 'In every passion of which the mind of man is susceptible, the emotions of the bystander always correspond to what, by bringing the case home to himself, he imagines should be the sentiments of the sufferer' (Smith, [1790] 2001: 15). As Smith and Tarde show, sympathy is distinguished from empathy and pity by being a fellow feeling generated out of the sameness of bodies, a sameness that could be striven for, via spectacles of vulnerability.

BODILY VULNERABILITY, DISCOURSE, AND EVENT

Our book shares a range of interests with Anthony McCosker's (2013) recent book *Intensive Media*, which deals with the mediation of pain, in relation to disaster, torture, illness, masochism, salvation, and war. In his work pain is an intensifier that 'both resists communication and operates as a highly generative conduit for media production, circulation and attention' (McCosker, 2013: 2). We, however, differ from McCosker's work on a range of other points as he focuses solely on (1) pain images, whereas we are interested in a range of affects (e.g. love, indignation, anger, fear); (2) on various forms of visual representation (movies, painting, TV, photography), whereas we focus primarily on visual and written online communication; and (3) on theorising affect—through a Massumian line of thinking—as pre-individual and pre-discursive, whereas we are interested in the conceptual difference between affect and discourse in maintaining an affective-discursive messiness as a constructive analytical point of departure and in the discursive impact of affects.

Defining who is or was vulnerable (e.g. historical victims), who caused or did not cause the production of vulnerability (e.g. the state or terrorists), and who or what should be protected on the grounds of vulnerability has motivated fierce discursive struggles in some of our cases. Certain spectacles of public vulnerability nevertheless seem to attract more discursive struggles than others. Exposing voluntary, momentary vulnerability (through e.g. hunger strikes or tree sitting) is politicised and contested more rapidly than involuntary, lasting vulnerability (in e.g. terminal illness). Not surprisingly, it seems that bringing private suffering perceived as authentic and involuntary to the public eye is less politically fragmenting than the exposure of self-inflicted vulnerability. In the book, it thus becomes clear that certain types of affect that are created by mediated vulnerability are more aligned with established contextual discourses than others, and that mediated vulnerability can stir and intensify affect in relation to existing political battles, but that affects can also help to negotiate and transform discourses.

As already mentioned, the relationship between affect and discourse has been a key discussion in 'the affective turn', which at least in its earlier phases was often conceptualised as breaking with more linguistic- or discourse-oriented approaches, giving signification and representation too much attention at the expense of embodied experience (Leys, 2011; Wetherell, 2012). To quote Margaret Wetherell, 'for a large number in the social sciences, the most interesting thing about affect is that it is not discourse' (2012: 52). The meaningfulness of such a claim—that affect is non- or pre-discursive—depends very much on the definition of 'discourse'. Norman Fairclough's narrow, linguistic definition of discourse as a type of social practice to be studied in 'spoken or written language use' (1992: 62) renders the relationship to the affective quite differently from accounts which focus on discourse as more general systems in which knowledge shapes and is shaped by social practices across modalities (e.g. visuality, writing, sound, materiality, flesh; Butler, 1993; Kress and Leeuwen, 2001; Laclau and Mouffe, 2001). In other words, the discourse/affect relationship cannot be discussed without careful definition of discourse. Is discourse to be understood as language influencing an extra-discursive reality/body (as claimed by Fairclough), or is it a term describing the cultural and social norms, ideals, and constraints that shape not only social signification but also the construction of social and bodily identities, thereby making the idea of a purely non-discursive reality, body, or identity illusionary. We will argue that affect can actually be described as 'pre-discursive', 'partly discursive', and 'partly non-discursive', depending on the definition of discourse.

(1) *Affect as pre-discursive (using a narrow understanding of discourse):* Following a narrow, linguistic definition of discourse, it is uncontroversial to describe affect as 'pre-discursive' because experiences of affect often arrive prior to explicit language categorisation; that is the body can sense something and perhaps not initially be able to put it into words and can experience that a certain term (e.g. happy, fearsome, enthusiastic) does not grasp the complexity of the experience. Or the contrary can be the case: that language completes and intensifies the affective dimensions of an event by finding 'just the right words' to explain and share it with others. In this sense, affect can be described as pre-discursive if this simply means 'experiences not yet put into words' (rather than 'pre-cognitive bodily sensing').

(2) *Affect as partly discursive (using a broad understanding of discourse):* That affect is often a highly mediated and culturally produced phenomenon is evident. The most obvious example would be how different food cultures can motivate very different affective responses of either attraction or repulsion to the same food object (e.g. an insect or pig meat). Here pre-existing discourses shape how body and object come into contact and the affective relation that is created (Ahmed, 2004). As Wetherell argues, the human senses actually take in far more stimulations from the world than human consciousness can process, which supports Thrift and Massumi's break with purely representational theories. This, however, cannot be used to make a clear-cut division between bodily non-representational living and conscious representational cognition, because these dimensions constantly intertwine. The brain, for instance, starts to prepare conscious action before it is actively initiated by the body (Wetherell, 2012: 63), it layers information without being consciously aware of it (see priming experiments and bodily automatism; Wetherell, 2012: 64), and the body constantly seems to draw on non-conscious interpretative work, while acting out habits or routines and preparing for future decisions.

Sara Ahmed describes how affects 'stick' to particular objects as a result of prior histories of contact between bodies and objects (see also Kofoed and Ringrose, 2012), and Ahmed thus develops the historically or discursively produced side of affect: 'emotions are the very "flesh" of time . . . Through emotions, the past persists on the surface of bodies' (2004: 202) as she puts it. For Ahmed, affective and emotional responses simply involve historically produced bodily knowledge (2004: 7). New experiences, creating new histories of contact between bodies and objects (or other bodies), would nevertheless be able to shape the bodily knowledge of the person in a different way. This focus on the body's capacity to rearrange its bodily knowledge—or internalised/objectified discourses—leads us to the final clarification of the relationship between discourse and affect: that affect is also a non-discursive force based on the body's ability to sense the world in ways that do not simply reproduce its discursive pre-understandings of it.

(3) *Affect as partly non-discursive (using a broad understanding of discourse):* We argue that the body can be discursively positioned and perceptually open at the same time, which implies that we can both avoid overstating the role of discourses in the production of affect and yet acknowledge that there is no such thing as immediate being bypassing discourse or representation completely. The body can, however, be affected in complex ways depending on how experiences interact with, are challenged by or intertwined with discourses: Sometimes affects simply reproduce or strengthen discourses, sometimes they open possibilities for future changes, and sometimes they motivate discursive crisis. And the individual body response will, of course, be highly influenced by contextual factors such as individual histories, social status, the time and place of stimulation, and so on. Judith Butler describes this complex relationship between affect and discourse in the following way:

> That the body invariably comes up against the outside world is a sign of the general predicament of unwilled proximity to others and to circumstances beyond one's control. This 'coming up against' is one modality that defines the body. And yet, this obtrusive alterity against which the body finds itself can be, and often is, what animates responsiveness to that world. That responsiveness may include a wide range of affects: pleasure, rage, suffering, hope, to name a few. Such affects, I would argue, become not just the basis, but the very stuff of ideation and of critique. In this way, a certain interpretative act implicitly takes hold at moments of primary affective responsiveness. . . . Because such affective responses are invariably mediated, they call upon and enact certain interpretative frames; they can also call into question the taken-for-granted character of those frames, and in that way provide the affective conditions for social critique.
>
> (2009: 34–35)

We follow this by arguing that while affects are always discursively filtered, they are not fully determined by discourses and are capable of opening up spaces of discursive invention. This line of thinking is already present in the phenomenology of perception by Maurice Merleau-Ponty according to which perception does not happen 'in my head' but happens nowhere else than in my body which is a thing in the world (1964: 25). But perception—that, for Merleau-Ponty, happens through sight—is intertwined with a gaze that encompasses cultural pre-understandings and frames that familiarise the onlooker with unfamiliar sceneries. Humans thus understand the world through a dialectics or chiasm between perceiving/sensing the world from inside the body and gazing at the world from outside with all the cultural schemes and files at hand (Merleau-Ponty, 1964: 177). In this book we show that although the spectacles of mediated vulnerability can create highly historical or discursively produced responses, by simply repositioning the body in an already acquired subject position, they can also open spaces for discursive renegotiation. This happens when mediated vulnerability succeeds in creating 'dislocating' body events that do not entirely fit established frameworks and thus perhaps succeeds in creating 'floating signifiers' for political interaction about topics otherwise hegemonised by other discourses (Laclau and Mouffe, 2001). For that reason we prefer to talk about affect that has a 'partly non-discursive' rather than 'pre-discursive' force being able to motivate momentary 'gaps between affective experience and hegemonic cultural narratives' (Wetherell, 2012: 71).

We argue that, under the right circumstances, mediated vulnerability can have a dislocating function. Laclau connects 'the dislocation of the structure' with the concept of the event (Laclau, 1990: 42). Prominent events theorists such as Jacques Derrida, Alain Badiou, Claude Romano, and Martin Jay investigate how something that happens can become an important event to someone whether it is minor or major in scale. An event 'does not belong to a fact's actuality, but to its possibility, or better, to the possibility of making possible, to *possibilization*' (Romano, 2009: 43). If a body event has to qualify as a dislocative event, it has to promise potential new futures. The first important characteristic of events as producers of affectedness is thus that they give access to a not-yet-there world that make publics dream and imagine other possibilities. Understood as glimpses of the not-yet-there world, events are in that sense a source of engagement, empowerment, and discursive renegotiation. Badiou even claims that: 'Events as truth is experienced as a 'hole' in established knowledge' (2007: 58). To sum up, affect is here understood as a type of bodily sensation-response that is intertwined with, but can also sometimes be in opposition to, established discourses.

CHAPTERS

All chapters focus on empirical cases that can be approached analytically through the abovementioned concepts—vulnerability, global media, biopolitics, and affect—but in various ways. Chapter 1, 'Illness Blogs and Online Crowding', turns to early-period sociology in order to understand the relationship between digital media and affect motivated by the display of the suffering female body. It consists of a case study of Eva Markvoort's illness blog,

65 Red Roses, and of how her terminally sick body became a catalyst not only for global outbursts of empathy and support but also for political agenda setting and for mobilisation of new organ donors in Canada. The chapter claims that new types of affectively charged collectivities that are created via spontaneous interaction on various media platforms can be understood through Gustave Le Bon's concept of the 'crowd'. It is argued that Eva Markvoort's exposure of her vulnerable body enabled collective affective processes that can be identified in the responses on the blog and that she therefore functions as a crowd facilitator, motivating both linguistic and bodily imitation through her personal prestige and her image-producing embodiment of an abstract disease and problem. Linked to the normative questions outlined previously, this case study shows how voice can be given to less fortunate persons (the terminally ill), and how long-term and structural change becomes possible through the prestige of the ill person as affective transmitter.

Chapter 2, 'Global Assemblages of Suffering and Protest', focuses on how the construction of new global relations between technologies, human bodies and materiality challenge or 'decode' established hierarchies and social formations (like a state) by transforming the capacities of singular components (e.g. the vulnerable and dying body). It takes its point of departure in a case study of the global dissemination of YouTube videos of the death of Iranian protester Neda Agda Soltan, who became an icon for the national and international protests against the re-election of President Mahmoud Ahmadinejad in June 2009 after she was shot while taking part in a demonstration. The chapter takes a special interest in how Neda became an 'affective transmitter' in different local contexts outside Iran motivating all sorts of participatory productivity or 'assemblage building' (e.g. media production, masks, statues, etc.) and draws its conclusions with reference to the neo-assemblage theory of Manuel DeLanda. The case study shows how a reaction against political injustice is stimulated in the short term, but perhaps only in the short term and only in a way that is likely to reproduce Western understandings of Iran (as e.g. a culture of martyrdom).

Chapter 3 discusses a paradox: How come affect seems to be thriving as a political force in a range of social fields, while it seems to be retreating in the area of charitable giving? (see the discussion of 'compassion fatigue' or a 'crisis of pity' in relation to suffering a long way away and the rise of consumption-based charitable giving that is not dependent on spectacles of suffering.). The chapter argues that affects are not disappearing from this field but are taking on new forms, as global inequality prompts people to seek ways to actively help than donating money. The cases analysed are Danish boarding school students' production of YouTube videos in response to a national TV event, and the Kibera project, through which musicians donate instruments to fellow or future musicians in Kenya. Via these examples, we argue that the field of charity is facing 'a productive turn', where affect is created through an experience of seduction that 'challenges' the fortunate to act on global inequality and vulnerability.

Chapter 4 contributes to the overall structure of the book by examining political activism, which deploys vulnerable-power strategies within the most important contemporary area of human vulnerability: climate change and environmental risks following the anthropocene. We analyse two cases—one from the US and one from Australia—in which activists manufacture and stage their own bodily vulnerability as a political weapon intended to motivate adequate political responses. It is argued that activists' manufactured vulnerability seems to consist of a time-splitting performance in which a virtual disastrous version of the future is staged on the activists' bodies in the present. Finally, it is discussed whether contemporary activism should be evaluated for to its ability to build institutions or, alternatively, for its ability to create sublime visual events, which through their dissemination and circulation on various platforms are able to evoke political enthusiasm, and a desire for transgressing existing hindrances, and to create new belongings through excessive visual repertoire. The chapter furthermore discusses the circumstances in which activists run the risk of reproducing inadequate cultural patterns (e.g. non-reflexive preservation discourses).

Chapter 5 deals with bodily vulnerability, war, and affective rhythms. Through Henri Lefebvre's concepts of 'arrhythmia' it highlights the democratic potentials of social media platforms such as YouTube through an examination of affective rhythmic strategies of particular videos, designed to create a common pulse through music, and how comments to these representations of bereaved soldiers disturb the attempt to create collective entrainment. The analysis presents a case study of 28 tribute videos posted on YouTube for fallen Danish soldiers in the Afghanistan and Iraq wars. It focuses on the strategic attempt to transform the deceased soldier-body into a national object of grief, as well as the political 'agonism' expressed in the commentaries. We likewise examine the new types of commemorative practice that the specific media space of YouTube enables. Unlike the nation state's traditional war-memorial monuments, the online war memorial is marked by explicit differences of opinion and affective dissonance concerning the status and legitimacy of the war. It is argued that the tribute videos of YouTube establish a more democratic situation, characterised by public commemorative 'arrhythmia'.

Chapter 6 also deals with bodily vulnerability and war, examining affective reactions to and the cultural implications of contemporary witnessing of conflict zones in Sarajevo and Ukraine where sniper attacks on civilians have taken place. Looking at DIY YouTube videos made by witnesses Julia Kristeva's concept of 'chora', is used to analyse how the spaces being mediated have an unfinished and open-ended character due to the atrocities that have happened or are happening. The conflict site as chora both motivates continuous affective investments of fear, sympathy, and fascination and discursive struggles or 'antagonisms' over who counts as a legitimate victim of the conflicts that these videos document or narrate. The chapter cites Sarajevo and the sites of the Ukrainian protests as non-closed 'chora' sites and analyses the close relationship between the formal characteristics of the videos (what kind of footage, witnessing in time and space, perspective, and modes) and the reactions evoked in the comments posted. The chapter thus discusses the extent to which the videos produce antagonistic reactions and are culturally reproductive of nationalist hatred and stereotyping, as well as how the chora sites keep on motivating new attempts to mediate and witness present and past injustices.

REFERENCES

AGAMBEN, G. 1998. *Homo Sacer: Sovereign Power and Bare Life*, Palo Alto, Stanford University Press.

AHMED, S. 2004. *The Cultural Politics of Emotion*, Edinburgh, Edinburgh University Press.

ANDÉN-PAPADOPOULOS, K. 2009. US Soldiers Imaging the Iraq War on YouTube. *Popular Communication*, 7, 17–27.

ANDERSON, B., KEARNES, M., MCFARLANE, C. & SWANTON, D. 2012. On Assemblages and Geography. *Dialogues in Human Geography*, 2, 171–189.

ANGEL, M. & GIBBS, A. 2006. Media, Affect and the Face: Biomediation and the Political Scene. *Southern Review*, 38, 24–39.

APPADURAI, A. 2006. *Fear of Small Numbers. An Essay on the Geography of Anger*, Durham, Duke University Press.

ARVIDSSON, A. & PEITERSEN, N. 2013. *The Ethical Economy: Rebuilding Value after the Crisis*, New York, Columbia University Press.

BADIOU, A. 2007. The Event in Deleuze. *Parrhesia*, 2, 37–44.

BARGU, B. 2013. Human shields. *Contemporary Political Theory* [Online], 12. Available at: http://www.academia.edu/4777379/_Human_Shields [Accessed 1 November 2013].

BECK, U. 2004. *Risikosamfundet—på vej mod en ny modernitet*, København, Hans Reitzels Forlag.

BENKLER, Y. 2006. *The Wealth of Networks*, London, Yale University Press.

BENSKI, T. & FISHER, E. 2014. *Internet and Emotions*, London, Routledge.

BLACKMAN, L. 2012. *Immaterial Bodies. Affect, Embodiment, Mediation*, London, Sage.

BLACKMAN, L. & VENN, C. 2010. Affect. *Body and Society*, 16, 7–28.

BOLTANSKI, L. 1999. *Distant Suffering. Morality, Media and Politics*, Cambridge, Cambridge University Press.

BOLTER, J.D. & GRUSIN, R. 2003. *Remediation*, London, MIT Press.

BORCH, C. 2009. Body to Body: On the Political Anatomy of Crowds. *Sociological Theory*, 27, 271–290.

BORCH, C. 2012. *The Politics of Crowds: An Alternative History of Sociology*, Cambridge, Cambridge University Press.

BRENNAN, T. 2004. *The Transmission of Affect*, Ithaca, Cornell University Press.

BRUNS, A. 2008. The Future Is User-Led: The Path towards Widespread Produsage. *Fibreculture* [Online], 11. Available at: http://eleven.fibreculturejournal.org/fcj-066-the-future-is-user-led-the-path-towards-widespread-produsage/ [Accessed 20 June 2011].

BUTLER, J. 1993. *Bodies that Matter. On the discursive limits of 'sex'*, New York, Routledge.

BUTLER, J. 2004. *Precarious Life. The Powers of Mourning and Violence*, London, Verso.

BUTLER, J. 2009. *Frames of War. When Is Life Grievable?*, London, Verso.

CARPENTIER, N. 2011. *Media and Participation: A Site of Ideological-democratic Struggle*, Bristol, Intellect.

CASTELLS, M. 2009. *Communication Power*, Oxford, Oxford University Press.

CHOULIARAKI, L. 2006. *The Spectatorship of Suffering*, London, Sage.

CHRISTENSEN, C. 2008. Uploading Dissonance: YouTube and the US Occupation of Iraq. *Media, War and Conflict*, 1, 155–175.

CLOUGH, P. T. 2007. Introduction. *In:* CLOUGH, P. T. (ed.) *The Affective Turn*, Durham, Duke University Press.

DARLING, J. 2009. Becoming Bare Life: Asylum, Hospitality, and the Politics of Encampment. *Environment and Planning D: Society and Space*, 27, 649–665.

DEAN, C. J. 2010. *Aversion and Erasure. The Fate of the Victim after the Holocaust*, Ithaca, Cornell University Press.

DOHERTY, B. 2000. Manufactured Vulnerability. *In:* SEEL, B., PATERSON, M., & DOHERTY, B. (eds.) *Direct Action in British Environmentalism*, New York, Routledge.

FAIRCLOUGH, N. 1992. *Discourse and Social Change*, Cambridge, Polity.

FEATHERSTONE, M. 2010. Body, Image and Affect in Consumer Culture. *Body and Society*, 16, 193–221.

FOUCAULT, M. 1976. *Histoire de la Sexualité, 1, La Volonté de Savoir*, Paris, Gallimard.

FOUCAULT, M. [1982] 1994. The Subject of Power. In: FAUBION, J.D. (ed.) *Michel Foucault Power*, New York, The New York Press.

FREUD, S. [1922] 1983. Masse-psykologi og jeg-analyse. *In: Metapsychology 2*, København, Hans Reitzel.

GARDE-HANSEN, J. & GORTON, K. 2013. *Emotion Online. Theorising Affect on the Internet*, Basingstoke, Palgrave.

GAUNTLETT, D. 2011. *Making Is Connecting*, Cambridge, Polity.

GIBBS, A. 2008. Panic! Affect Contagion, Mimesis and Suggestion in the Social Field. *Cultural Studies Review*, 14, 130–145.

GREGG, M. 2011. *Work's Intimacy*, Cambridge, UK; Malden, MA, Polity Press.

GREGG, M. & SEIGWORTH, G. J. (eds.) 2010. *The Affect Theory Reader*, Durham: Duke University.

GRUSIN, R. 2010. *Premediation: Affect and Mediality After 9/11*, New York, Palgrave Macmillan.

HARDT, M. & NEGRI, A. 2009. *Commonwealth*, Cambridge, Harvard University Press.

HENRIQUES, J. 2010. The Vibrations of Affect and their Propagation on a Night Out on Kingston's Dancehall Scene. *Body & Society*, 16, 57–89.

HJARVARD, S. (ed.) 2003. *Media in a Globalized Society*, Copenhagen, Museum Tusculanum.

HUNTINGTON, S. 2006. *Civilisationernes sammenstød?*, København, Informations Forlag.

JANSSON, A. 2004. *Globalisering—kommunikation og modernitet*, Lund, Studentlitteratur.

JENKINS, H. 2006. *Convergence Culture: Where Old and New Media Collide*, New York, New York University Press.

JENKINS, H., FORD, S. & GREEN, J. 2013. *Spreadable Media: Creating Value and Meaning in a Networked Culture*, New York, New York University Press.

KELTY, C., PANOFSKY, A., ERICKSON, S., CURRIE, M., CROOKS, R., WOOD, S., GARCIA, P. & WARTENBE, M. 2014. Seven Dimensions of Contemporary Participation Disentangled. *Journal of the Association for Information Science and Technology*. Advanced online publication. Available at http://onlinelibrary.wiley.com/doi/10.1002/asi.23202/ful [Accessed 2 October 2014].

KOFOED, J. & RINGROSE, J. 2012. Travelling and Sticky Affects: Exploring Teens and Sexualized Cyberbullying through a Butlerian-Deleuzian-Guattarian lens. *Discourse: Studies in the Cultural Politics of Education*, 33, 5–20.

KRESS, G. & LEEUWEN, T.V. 2001. *Multimodal Discourse. The Modes and Media of Contemporary Communication*, London, Arnold.

KUNTSMAN, A. 2012. Introduction: Affective Fabrics of Digital Cultures. *In:* KUNTSMAN, A. & KARATZOGIANNI, A. (eds.) *Digital Cultures and the Politics of Emotion*, New York, Palgrave.

LACLAU, E. 1990. *New Reflections on the Revolution of our Time / Ernesto Laclau; Translated by Jon Barnes*, London; New York, Verso.

LACLAU, E. & MOUFFE, C. 2001. *Hegemony and Socialist Strategy. Towards a Radical Democratic Politics*, London, Verso.

LASH, S. 2010. *Intensive Culture: Social Theory, Religion and Contemporary Capitalism*, London, Sage.

LE BON, G. 1895. *The Crowd. A Study of the Popular Mind*, New York, Dover Publications, Inc.

LÉVY, P. 1997. *Collective intelligence: Mankind's Emerging World in Cyberspace*, New York, Plenum Trade.

LEYS, R. 2011. The Turn to Affect: A Critique. *Critical Inquiry*, 37, 434–472.

LULL, J. 2007. *Culture-On-Demand*, Oxford, Blackwell.

MARRES, N. 2011. The Costs of Public Involvement: Everyday Devices of Carbon Accounting and the Materialization of Participation. *Economy and Society*, 40, 510–533.

MASSUMI, B. 2002. *Parables for the Virtual*, Durham, Duke University Press.

MCCOSKER, A. 2013. *Intensive Media. Aversive Affect and Visual Culture*, New York: Palgrave.

MCLUHAN, M. 1987. *Understanding Media. The Extensions of Man*, London, Ark.

MERLEAU-PONTY, M. 1964. *Le Visible et l'Invisible*, Paris, Gallimard.

MOUFFE, C. 2000a. *The Democratic Paradox*, London.

MOUFFE, C. 2000b. Politics and Passions: The Stakes of Democracy. *Ethical Perspectives*, 7, 146–150.

NYE, J.S. 2004. *Soft Power: The Means to Success in World Politics*, New York, Public Affairs.

PANAGIA, D. 2009. *The Political Life of Sensation*, Durham, Duke University Press.

PORTA, D.D. 2008. Eventful Protest, Global Conflicts. *Distinktion: Scandinavian Journal of Social Theory*, 9, 27–56.

PROTEVI, J. 2009. *Political Affect. Connecting the Social and the Somatic*, Minneapolis, University of Minnesota Press.

RANCIÉRE, J. 2000. *The Politics of Aesthetics. The Distribution of the Sensible*, London, Continuum.

ROGERS, R. 2013. *Digital Methods*, Cambridge, MIT Press.

ROMANO, C. 2009. *Event and World*, New York, Fordham University Press.

SAMPSON, T. 2012. *Virality. Contagion Theory in the Age of Networks*, Minneapolis, University of Minnesota Press.

SILVERSTONE, R. 2007. *Media and Morality: On the Rise of the Mediapolis*, Cambridge, Polity.

SONTAG, S. 2003. *Regarding the Pain of Others*, New York, Picador.

SMITH, A. [1790] 2001. *The Theory of Moral Sentiments*, New York, Penguin Books.

TARDE, G. [1895] 1903. *The Laws of Imitation*, New York, Henry Holt and Company.

TARDE, G. 1901. The Public and the Crowd. *In: Gabriel Tarde. On Communication and Social Influence*, Chicago, Chigaco University Press.

TELLMANN, U., OPITZ, S. & STAEHELI, U. 2012. Operations of the Global: Explorations of Connectivity. *Distinktion: Scandinavian Journal of Social Theory*, 13, 209–214.

TERRANOVA, T. 2000. Free Labour: Producing Culture for the Digital Economy. *Social Text*, 18, 33–58.

THACKER, E. 2004. *Biomedia*, Minneapolis, University of Minnesota Press.

THRIFT, N. 2008a. *Non-Representational Theory*, London, Routledge.

THRIFT, N. 2008b. Pass It On: Towards a Political Economy of Propensity. *Emotion, Space and Society*, 1, 83–96.

TOMLINSON, J. 1999. *Globalization and Culture*, Cambridge, Polity.

TOMLINSON, J. 2007. *The Culture of Speed. The Coming of Immediacy*, London, Sage.

VINCENT, J. & FORTUNATI, L. 2009 (eds.) *Electronic Emotion. The Mediation of Emotion via Information and Communication Technologies*, Berlin, Peter Lang.

WALKERDINE, V. 2010. Communal Beingness and Affect: An Exploration of Trauma in an Ex-industrial Community. *Body & Society*, 16, 91–116.

WETHERELL, M. 2012. *Affect and Emotion*, London, Sage.

1 Illness Blogs and Online Crowding

Our claim is in this chapter that new forms of illness communication—in which the ill blogger becomes a social mobiliser of crowds and empathy and a creator of social or economic value to the benefit of causes such as organ donation or cancer research—can be treated as interesting sites for politicising bodily vulnerability (Stage, 2014).[1]

Contemporary illness practices, and not least the social visibility of illness and dying, have been transformed by the internet through the proliferation of new arenas for creating and building relationships, offering support, and sharing knowledge on these issues (Sharf, 1997; Hardey, 2002; Kimby, 2007; Walter et al., 2011). Social media platforms such as blogs offer an opportunity for vulnerable and sick bodies to circumvent the normal social sequestration of illness. Recent research literature on online illness communication has tended to focus on its consequences for the individual (both positive and negative, psychological and relational) as well as the risks inherent in privatising the disease-fighting process through exposing personal struggles (Pitts, 2004: 55; Orgad, 2005: 142; Heilferty, 2009: 1541). A rare exception is McCosker's interest in 'affective labour' or 'shifting boundaries between work, illness and self' on cancerblogs (McCosker, 2013: 140). Our focus on the mobilising potential of online illness communication therefore offers a relatively unexplored perspective. We argue that, transcending the sphere of the individual, online illness communication can engage in affecting social structures/discourses and mobilising citizens around social causes. It can do this by offering the opportunity of affective attachment to these causes through the vulnerable and ill body.

To investigate how the ill body can become a force for social and political mobilisation, we analyse and discuss the blog *65 Red Roses* by Eva Dien Brine Markvoort (1984–2010). Eva Markvoort's blog is a clear example of mediated vulnerability, which, in certain instances, is capable not only of building affective sameness among receivers but also of mobilising *the receivers*' bodies around a political cause via biopolitical soft power from below. We conduct this analysis through the lens of crowd psychology, with a special focus on Gustave Le Bon's late-nineteenth-century conceptualisation of the crowd. We have chosen Le Bon because his description of the crowd—despite its race-based explanations, its problematic later history, and its too clearly drawn dichotomies (Laclau, 2005: 40)—can accommodate the idea of crowd formations that do not share a physical space. The reason for applying Le Bon's crowd concept to an online setting is precisely that it can highlight how digital media alter the formation of publics and crowds (Olofsson, 2010) yet also allow for moments of intense mediated affect in relation to specific online events and spaces. The crowd concept thus helps to sharpen our understanding of various types of online practice in general, and a certain type of affective clustering around certain sites at specific moments in particular. This dimension cannot be properly described either by the more general term *public* or by notions of communities based on shared identities or cognitive imaginations of a common space and time (such as Benedict Anderson's 'imagined communities'). These concepts have an underdeveloped understanding of the bodily affective qualities of the media collective that we want to investigate.

THREE TYPES OF CROWDS

A crowd is not just many people gathered at the same spot. It is a particular type of affectively synchronised and therefore de-individualised gathering which is 'little adapted to reasoning', 'quick to act', and 'a single being' or 'mental unity' (Le Bon, 1895: xi, 2). It is the 'disappearance of conscious personality and the turning of feelings and thoughts in a definite direction' that constitute the crowd (Le Bon, 1895: 2). The crowd is impulsive, irritable, and susceptible to leaders with a talent for suggestion, exaggeration, affirmation, and repetition (Le Bon, 1895: 11, 23). Thus, the crowd is a way of being together in which the personal dispositions and the rationality of the individual are subsumed under the unpredictable energy of the collective mind and the psychology of the crowd. In other words, the crowd works according to a logic of contagion and suggestibility: a particular disposition to act is transmitted to a composite of (no longer) individuals (Le Bon, 1895; Borch, 2006; 2009).

Overall three conceptions of the crowd, distinguished by its relationship with media publics, can be identified: (1) A traditional understanding of the crowd underlines the importance of physical co-presence or being together 'body to body' (Canetti, 1960: 18; Borch, 2009) in the formation of crowds. Gabriel Tarde, for example in his 1901 essay 'The Public and the Crowd', distinguishes between a *crowd* as 'a collection of psychic connections produced essentially by physical contacts' (1901: 278), and a *public* as a 'dispersion of individuals that are physically separated and whose cohesion is entirely mental' (1901: 277). In this understanding the crowd and the public are contradictory social formations. (2) This is to a lesser degree the case in the work of Stephanie Alice Baker. Baker explicitly connects digital media and the concept of the crowd with her term 'the mediated crowd'.

This describes 'an interactive community that both traverses and intersects geographical public space and the virtual public sphere' (Baker, 2011) (see also Olofsson's [2010] description of 'the traversing crowd'). For Baker, crowd studies analysts need to put more effort into understanding the role of communication technologies in the formation of crowds; they need to acknowledge that many contemporary crowds coordinate, and are to some degree created (practically and emotionally), through technological tools and environments, as was the case for the August 2011 riots in Britain. (3) Baker, although open to the possibility that mediation and crowd formation are not mutually exclusive, seems to uphold the notion that mediated crowds still have to meet somewhere in a geographical space to become an actualised crowd. Interestingly, it may be Le Bon who among the crowd theorisers is the most willing to suspend physical co-presence as a prerequisite for the formation of crowds. Le Bon describes the crowds primarily as a composite of de-individualised individuals sharing a common space and time. Nevertheless, in a few passages he stresses that co-presence is not indispensable for the creation of crowd characteristics:

> Disappearance of conscious personality and the turning of feelings and thoughts in a definite direction, which are the primary characteristics of a crowd to become organized, do not always involve the simultaneous presence of a number of individuals on one spot.
>
> (Le Bon, 1895: 2)

And later, he states, 'For individuals to succumb to contagion their simultaneous presence on the same spot is not indispensable. The action of contagion may be felt from a distance under the influence of events which give all minds an individual trend and the characteristics peculiar to crowds' (Le Bon, 1895: 78). Here he seems to be saying that people can become a crowd—or at least just like a crowd—without offline co-presence, if they are oriented towards the same event and collectively contaminated by a particular mental state.

Taking Le Bon into the digital age, we follow Lisa Blackman's idea for reconfiguring the crowd in the light of digital media technologies (2012: 27). Blackman argues that the 'improvised crowd' and a 'temporary and transient public' are no longer mutually exclusive, and that an offline existence is not a precondition for crowds. Few academic studies, however, have focused directly on the online crowd. Christian Russ is an exception, defining the online crowd as a social formation of individuals who 'gather virtually, behave and act collectively and produce effects and phenomena which would not be possible without the internet' (Russ, 2007: 65). Russ's main interest here (in contrast to ours in this chapter) is in how online crowds 'can be actively formed for promising business models' and how 'decision makers and providers will be better capable to predict and promote successful online communities and services' (Russ, 2007: 65). As noted in the

Introduction, Tony D. Sampson also discusses Le Bon in the context of the study of online communication (e.g. viral marketing), but he concentrates on discussing the larger differences between the contagion theories of Le Bon and Tarde. Like Sampson, we acknowledge that Le Bon's theory of contagion overemphasises a conservative criticism of the irrational, hypnotised, and hallucinatory character of the crowd (Sampson, 2012: 89). But we still maintain that Le Bon is relevant in the study of affective crowding online because—unlike Tarde—he describes crowd formation freed from the constraints of unmediated bodily encounters in physical space.

Crowds and publics can co-exist, for example, when online publics share, discuss, and circulate media text in such a way that they also share a certain, in this instance textually mediated, event in a synchronised online space (Warner, 2002). But a shared online event or space alone is not a sufficient condition to define a crowd. To become an online crowd a public must be characterised by intense affective unification. Following this, the term *online crowd* is used here to describe a certain type of online behaviour where the participants of a public simultaneously (1) share affective processes and (2) come together on certain online sites (e.g. in relation to a blog post). In other words, *online crowding* refers to *the affective unification and relative synchronisation of a public in relation to a specific online site*. We have thus established three different conceptions of the crowd, assigning differing degrees of importance to co-presence: (1) the 'body to body crowd' of Tarde (and most often also Le Bon), based on physical proximity; (2) the 'mediated crowd' of Baker, based on the technological augmentation of offline crowds; and (3) the 'online crowd', based on the idea of a contagious process that turns 'feelings and thoughts in a definite direction' among a collective of online media users (Le Bon, 1895: 2).

EVA MARKVOORT'S *65 RED ROSES*

From July 2006 to late March 2010, Eva Dien Brine Markvoort communicated about her life with the life-threatening lung disease cystic fibrosis (CF) on her blog *65 Red Roses* (Figure 1.1). On 27 March 2010, Eva Markvoort died, having shared her life with her many readers in a very intimate and disclosing way. The blog clearly had several purposes over time, including creating social relations with other people suffering from CF, and promoting both a political cause (creating awareness of CF and of the need for more people to sign up for organ donation) and other related projects (such as the documentary made about Eva Markvoort, *65_Redroses*, 2009, by Phillip Lyall and Nimisha Mukerji).

The development of the blog from 2006 to 2010 can be divided into three phases. The first phase ranges from the initial entry on 15 July 2006 to the end of October 2007. It consists of Eva Markvoort's descriptions of life with CF and the worsening of her condition, leading to her double lung

Figure 1.1   Picture of Eva for the #4Eva campaign

Artist: Eva Markvoort. Photo: Cyrus McEachern. Courtesy of 65RedRose.com #4Eva.

transplant. The second phase, from late October 2007 to the end of August 2009, follows the improvement of her condition after the transplant and the public screening of a documentary film about her. The last phase begins on 30 August 2009 with an entry in which Eva Markvoort explains that she cannot breathe as well as before and ends on 27 March 2010 with her death. Today, the blog serves as a place for the family to post information about Eva Markvoort's projects and campaigns and as a space for commemoration of and tribute to her. The blog (and the documentary) were highly effective in raising national and global awareness of CF and of organ donation. Our explanation for the blog's significant ability to mobilise both global attention and local action is its powerful mediation of vulnerability as a catalyst of interbodily affective involvement and activation.

METHODOLOGY

Our approach to the affects in this material is based on a kind of methodological 're-electrification' of the material so that we can focus on the processes and energies that motivated and shaped the production of communicative objects (composites of letters, pictures, and sounds). Our primary analytical strategy is to investigate symptoms of temporally synchronised affective sameness in the comments of the blog. We include both primary text written by Eva Markvoort and tertiary texts produced by the users (Fiske, 1987), so as to empirically ground the exchanges of affect and imitation in relation to the blog. Our primary examples from the blog are (1) a coughing video and the user comments that it generated (to highlight the transmission of affect from blogger to followers), (2) a farewell video and its approximately 2,500 comments (to focus on a clear instance of online crowding), and (3) the memorial event, 'Eva's Celebration of Life', an event which was both online and offline (to look into the complex intertwining of different types of crowds in relation to the blog). In addition to these examples, we refer more briefly to other blog posts and textual material about Eva Markvoort for further empirical grounding.

Following Catherine Heilferty's review of ethical research practices in relation to illness blogs, we have approached the blog as 'creative work intended for a public audience' (Heilferty, 2011: 950). The analysis of this kind of illness blog does not raise the same kind of ethical dilemmas as studies of cancer forums or other restricted illness forums, for instance, where the users are looking for personal relationships and support more than public awareness. Eva Markvoort clearly wanted to raise awareness and public debate, as underlined by her performance on broader mainstream media outlets (in newspapers, on radio, in the documentary). And as the family left behind has continued to use the online platform she created, her death has not changed the explicitly public nature of the communicative practices on the blog.

The blog also has analytical and theoretical limitations. As described by Robert Glenn Howard, 'vernacular' voices online—often perceived as personal, 'bottom-up' contributions—regularly intertwine with institutional and commercial voices (Howard, 2008). This also applies to Eva Markvoort, who was blogging not only as a private person, but also as a campaigner to raise CF awareness and additionally as the main character of a documentary film. She thus had multiple coexisting, but not necessarily contradictory, agendas. This relates to a general problem in the analysis of online relations: How do we know that articulated vernacular intentions are authentic and truthful, rather than institutional and strategic? An additional consideration is that quite a lot of research maintains that computer-mediated communication is increasingly used to augment media users' ordinary lives by confirming or creating new networks, rather than as a sphere of inauthenticity or semi-fake relations (Baym, 2010). Following this—and taking into account Eva Markvoort's performances across a range of media platforms (e.g. on TV and in newspaper interviews), her ability to motivate offline actions (e.g. signing up for organ donation), and the size of the blog's public—concerns about communicative inauthenticity seem less acute in relation to this particular case. That said, because there is a possible disconnect between online and offline subjects, text-based studies of online practices should continuously evaluate the authenticity of their empirical material.

ONLINE CROWDING ON *65 RED ROSES*

Eva Markvoort sometimes seems to want to use her body to create micro-shocks. One of the clearest examples of this is a video entry from 18 January 2008. This is a three-minute close-up of Eva Markvoort having a severe coughing attack.[2] She uploads the video at a later point when she is getting better and alerts the receiver: 'I warn you, if you don't have CF, its not easy to see and is probably not work or child-safe'.[3] According to Eva Markvoort, the video serves as an 'honest glimpse' of life with cystic fibrosis. There is no narrative or speech—only Eva Markvoort continually coughing, her face tormented with pain. The sound of the rattling lungs and Eva Markvoort looking directly at the camera makes the video almost unbearable to watch. As her quotation shows, Eva Markvoort is well aware of the affective power of the video, which seems to transmit the bodily state of her pain to the body of the receiver via an affective response of co-suffering.

One of the comments made on the day of the video upload seems to confirm that an affective body-to-body transmission has taken place. The response states,

> It was for the eyes for me too . . . damn those eyes . . . they hurt. The first few coughs I felt / in my chest. I felt your fear . . . my fear . . . wow. / Damn girl, we need to go out and change the world . . . cure cf, and while we're waiting make people donors . . . / because no one should hurt like that. / HUGS! / :) and a smile because I can right now.[4]

Following Massumi (2002), this comment can be understood as an emotional qualification, 're-registering' an already felt affective sensation in the body ('the first few coughs I felt / in my chest'). It can also be seen as a very condensed example of how mediated vulnerability can motivate sympathy and experiences of bodily sameness ('I felt your fear . . . my fear . . . ') and of how this can mobilise an urge to act. After the initial re-registering, the response thus re-establishes a narrative logic ('we need to go out and change the world . . . cure cf, and while we're waiting make people donors'). For us, this is a clear example of the affective transmissions enabled by Eva Markvoort's blog and of the vitalising, mobilising, and discursively rupturing character of affect. The post is not an example of online crowding, however: the video attracts very little online attention and almost no evidence of users 'clustering' around it (with e.g. many comments or views). However, we can identify here an affective transmission between Eva Markvoort and the user who wrote the comment cited earlier.

An example where crowding is identifiable is the video *Farewell*, uploaded on 11 February 2010. This shows Eva Markvoort in a hospital bed with her father, mother, and sister at her bedside.[5] In the video, Eva Markvoort explains that her 'life is ending' (00.00.57) as the doctors can no longer find effective treatment. Despite this dramatic information, Eva Markvoort is remarkably calm and remains focused on the positive dimensions of her situation and life—that she has loved and been loved more than you can expect—and on the support she has received during her illness (showing e.g. the 'wall of love' in her hospital room: letters and pictures sent by blog readers and supporters). Her bodily weakness is reflected not only in the content of her words, accepting that she will soon die, but also in her rusty voice, and the way she sometimes leans on her family to find rest. The affective power of her words is directly transmitted to the faces of her family (00.00.57).

The video attracted what we would term an online crowd: one that is clearly taking part in a contagious process, turning feelings and thoughts in a definite direction after their affective attunement by the video. The 2,000-plus comments (and more than 170,000 views on YouTube) can be considered lasting imprints of online-crowding behaviour, in which people dispersed around the world momentarily 'become one' via entering the affective gathering that is trying to support Eva Markvoort. The affective mobilisation of the receivers is expressed in various ways in the linguistic traces left behind by the online crowd. In the video, Eva Markvoort is very much focused on love and loving—a focus that is contagiously transmitted and imitated by most of the receivers, who also declare their love and sympathy for her. Following are three examples showing the contagious character of her message of love:

> Lovelovelovelovelovelovelovelovelovelovelovelovelovelovelovelove lovelovelovelovelovelovelovelovelovelovelovelovelovelovelovelovel ovelovelovelovelovelovelovelovelovelovelovelove.
> (12 February 2010)

> I love you.I love you.I love you I love you I love you.
> (12 February 2010)

> LOVE LOVE LOVE LOVE LOVE LOVE LOVE LOVE LOVE LOVE LOVE LOVE LOVE LOVE.
> (12 February 2010)

Following Massumi (2002), we see the redundant passages as a consequence of language functioning as the dampener of affect rather than as the creator of narratives or structures. The redundancy expresses a certain bodily state of empathy or 'hole in time;' similarities in the specific type of redundancy deployed in the comments—'love'—show a particular behaviour becoming contagious and spreading. The redundancy also underlines that not all crowds are to be characterised as destructive or destabilising, as so often in the crowd literature (Canetti, 1960: 19). Following Le Bon, '[w]ithout a doubt criminal crowds exist, but virtuous and heroic crowds, and crowds of many other kinds, are also to be met with' (Le Bon, 1895: xiii).

If a crowd is a gathering that shares affect and behaves in a unified way, we would argue that the people 'swarming' around Eva Markvoort's blog can be described as an online crowd. Approximately 2,000 of the comments were written between 10 and 15 February, underlining that the blog served as a virtual gathering-point for a (slightly de-synchronised) crowd. In the online crowd related to the farewell video, social position such as economic, cultural, or social capital plays no role (Canetti, 1960: 29): All comments are equally important, and all have the same status and visual output. Established identities, in other words, seem cancelled out by a more bodily logic of collectively moving towards the same online site to experience and share affects of empathy and compassion. In that sense, the online public momentarily *becomes* an online crowd, by gathering around an event in time and space to express (according to the comments) unified affective responses. Following Sara Ahmed, it is of course possible that the crowd only looks unified from the outside, with individual experiences of such practices (or, in this case, word choice) differing significantly in intensity and content (Ahmed, 2010: 43). To get around this, Ahmed proposes that it is suggestion that spreads when crowds form, rather than exactly the same affective quality across bodies. Identifying an online crowd would then imply finding symptoms of a shared suggestive quality (here represented as 'love') among a group of media users, rather than verifying the exact identical affective state in everybody involved (Ahmed, 2010: 39; see also Knudsen and Stage, 2012).

A further type of crowd—the technologically augmented or mediated crowd—is also relevant to this case, as Eva Markvoort's family created a combined online and offline memorial service to honour her after her death. The commemorative event, 'Eva's Celebration of Love', was held on 30 April 2010 at Massey Theatre, New Westminster, Canada, and was live-streamed on the blog, thus creating a complex assemblage of online and offline 'event publics'.[6] Before the livestream began, Eva Markvoort's father gave an introduction that helped to synchronise online and offline participation and conflated the online and offline presence: 'We're at the theatre now and the livestream will commence at 3:30 pst. / we will see you there / bill / eva's dad'.[7] The memorial service was an open event: According to a Canadian newspaper it mobilised more than 2,000 participants.[8] The event lasted just over two hours and consisted of various tributes to Eva Markvoort, including personal speeches (by her mother, her brother and sister, and her best friends), musical and theatrical performances (e.g. by her father and her ex-boyfriend), and an audiovisual slideshow of private pictures of Eva Markvoort.

As an offline and online event, the memorial service established a quite multifaceted type of crowd, combining a large physically present crowd with a much larger online audience, all sharing the same highly affectively charged experience. Traditionally, both offline and online gatherings would be defined as publics, whereas following Baker, the offline audience would be characterised as a mediated crowd. The argument of this chapter is that the online gathering united around the livestream—synchronised, according to the comments, by an affective media experience in real time[9]—can also be characterised as an online crowd. Unlike Eva Markvoort's online and offline memorial service, an online crowd is usually only relatively synchronous, because different users access the event a little out of sync but still close enough to be part of a shared movement towards the site. The memorial service intensifies this synchronicity, because of the live character of the online media experience.

Additionally, the memorial service is another example of a rather private experience being made into a public event: an event which makes it onto the mainstream news coverage. This makes her an even more likely crowd-facilitator, because of the affective potential represented by shared privacy and bodily authenticity. The memorial service also participates in the larger social de-privatisation of illness and death resulting from new media technologies (Walter et al., 2011). This, of course, raises a more principled question about the political and social transformations of public spheres, if illness, death, and dying act as triggers for crowding. Following Laurent Berlant, we see this trend as partaking in creating an increasingly intimate public sphere, where an exaggerated focus on victimhood leads to a 'privatisation of citizenship' (1997: 3) and the collapsing of 'the political and the personal into a world of public intimacy' (1997: 1). This tendency is problematic, according to Berlant, as it could end up re-routing 'the critical energies of the emerging political sphere onto the sentimental spaces of an amorphous opinion culture' (1997: 3). In other words, an overload of public intimacy associated with affective crowding could transform critical and structural engagement in political change into individual short-term investments rather than into structural long-term solutions (Hess, 2009).

Eva Markvoort's blog is genuinely political, in the sense that an otherwise marginalised individual (the weak and sick person) and the crowd surrounding her succeed in pushing the boundary between private and public in order to make her life conditions into an object of public political concern. In this process the blog, so to speak, remediates the sick body (Thacker, 2004), in allowing it to become socially powerful and viral regardless of its organic weakness and vulnerability. According to Seyla Benhabib (1992), it cannot really be claimed that certain issues are too private to become an issue of public contestation. The women's movement have insisted precisely that issues framed as private (the relationship between men and women in the home) are of public concern in need of general reflections (on gender inequality). In Eva Markvoort's case, the transgression of the private/public boundary becomes a way for her to find a public voice capable of articulating that her personal suffering has general implications that need to be confronted and changed (e.g. by more people signing up as organ donors).

EVA MARKVOORT AS CROWD-LEADER

A crowd 'is incapable of ever doing without a master', according to Le Bon (1895: 72). Rather than being rational or manipulative, the leader facilitates the formation of the crowd as 'the intensity of their faith gives great power of suggestion to their words' (Le Bon, 1895: 73). The aura of the leader is secured by his/her prestige, which may be *acquired* (via their name, fortune, or reputation) or *personal* (via personal characteristics; Le Bon, 1895: 81). Prestige motivates imitation as a form of social action: '[T]he thing possessing prestige is immediately imitated in consequence of contagion, and forces an entire generation to adopt certain modes of feeling and of giving expression to its thought' (Le Bon, 1895: 88). Eva Markvoort exemplifies someone who possesses personal prestige related to her individual characteristics, thus becoming an object of imitation (Tarde, [1895] 1903).

As we have demonstrated, in an act of sympathy, the blog commenters imitate her way of writing and describing reality (the focus on love), but imitation also occurs through bodily transformations as with the 'Reddy for a Cure' campaign, in which people dyed their hair red in remembrance of Eva (who was herself red-haired) and to raise awareness of CF (see Figure 1.2).[10] And when people describe Eva Markvoort, they focus on her ability to transmit energies and positive affect to her surroundings. The host of the 'Eva's Celebration of Love' event, CBC broadcaster Gloria Macarenko, describes her first meeting with Eva as follows:

> I was instantly impressed with Eva's spark; that spirit and that energy that you just instantly feel when you meet her . . . I will never forget the day in our CBC studios where she came bounding in with her fresh new lungs and she had this wild shock of red hair. You know she was the epitome for me of '*joie de vivre*'. *It just shone through her.*
>
> (Eva's Celebration of Love,
> part 1/3: 00.01.02)[11]

In other words Eva serves as a radiating figure, transmitting energy to and vitalising her surroundings—an instance of personal prestige that seems also to have had effect in an online context.

In his account of the various versions of 'the leader' in the theories of Freud, Tarde, and Le Bon, Urs Stäheli contrasts the logic of identification prevalent in Freud's thinking, which transforms the leader into a strong, law-creating ideal, motivating submission, with that of Tarde and Le Bon. In these two latter theories the leader is an affective and imitative force: not necessarily in control but, rather, a kind of medium. 'Being a medium of self-organisation, the figure of the strong and heroic leader is now translated into a magical and affective form of communication'

Figure 1.2   Screenshot from Facebook of Reddy for a Cure participants imitating Eva

(Stäheli, 2011: 77). In this way the crowd-leader (with connotations of control, manipulation, and dominance) becomes a crowd-facilitator (with the ability to move, intensify, and transmit the affective processes that motivate crowd formation). For example it was not Eva Markvoort's intention to create crowds when she started blogging. Her very first post stresses that she only wanted to connect with other people with CF.[12] The goal was thus to create what Catherine Squires calls a 'satellite public' (Squires, 2002: 463), where members (peer patients, in this case) could meet and share experiences without ever reaching the national public sphere. Nevertheless, as Eva Markvoort became the centre of massive attention, she began to explore the transformative potential of her capacity to attract attention by participating in campaigns and using the blog to raise CF awareness. That Eva Markvoort became an online crowd-facilitator through her diffuse ability to motivate affective transmission and imitation shows that the blog soon transgressed the identity logic of the satellite public by enabling the creation of open and affective gatherings around the blogging body.

One reason for Eva Markvoort's capability to affectively charge the people surrounding her is her personal prestige. Another is that she creates an understandable incarnation and image of a terrible but often apparently abstract disease: 'A crowd thinks in images', according to Le Bon

(1895: 15). Crowds are impressed not by statistics or rational abstractions, but by great events or images that clearly embody an event or problem: 'The epidemic of influenza, which caused the death but a few years ago of five thousand persons in Paris alone, made very little impression on the popular imagination. The reason was that this veritable hecatomb was not embodied in any visible image' (Le Bon, 1895: 37). It is not facts themselves that impress the crowd: 'It is necessary that by their condensation [the facts], if I may thus express myself, they should produce a startling image which fills and besets the mind' (Le Bon, 1895: 37). Le Bon's idea that crowds require condensing images and bodies for their mobilisation is confirmed by the many instances in which international mobilisation occurred only after the establishment of a strong image or icon (e.g. the girl fleeing naked from napalm bombs during the Vietnam War). This is also Eva Markvoort's role: she embodies a larger and, for many, abstract problem—CF and the lack of organ donors—by producing startling images that haunt the mind.

A third explanation of Eva Markvoort's crowd-leader potential is her specific social position. One might ask whether it is not also due to widespread cultural discourses that have taught us that true heroism includes the capacity to endure sickness and death with a positive spirit (e.g. see the sixteenth-century essays of Montaigne) that Eva Markvoort becomes such an affective transmitter. Is Eva Markvoort not re-enacting such cultural archetypes as the martyr who sacrifices him- or herself for a cause, or the endlessly good-hearted, self-effacing saint that we meet so often in religious writings, fairy tales, and film melodramas (e.g. Lars von Trier's Goldenheart trilogy)? Furthermore, Eva Markvoort's physical appearance makes her a more likely object of affective investment and sympathy than for instance people who do not fit cultural understandings of beauty— a fact pointing to the danger of cultural reproduction of stereotypes via media users' spontaneous attraction/repulsion to worthy objects of sympathy and online crowding. Eva Markvoort is, in other words, positioned in a social field that allows her to become a motivator of affect and an object of emphatic self-transgression—and therefore a potential crowd-leader.

This discursive line of thinking is not foreign to Le Bon. He maintains that messages of great intensity with the ability to be contagious and travel are somehow in agreement with the ideas (and discourses) of their time: 'At every period there exists a small number of individualities which react upon the remainder and are imitated by the unconscious mass. It is needful, however, that these individualities should not be in too pronounced disagreement with received ideas. Were they so, to imitate them would be too difficult and their influence would be nil' (Le Bon, 1895: 79). Here the irrational dimension of the crowd is somehow intertwined with established discourses and beliefs. In Eva Markvoort's case, these could be discourses on beauty, heroic sacrifice, endurance, and the tragedy of premature death.

CONCLUSION

Summing up this chapter, we have argued that it is possible to distinguish between three different types of crowds that prioritise the role of physical co-presence in different ways. These are the traditional *body-to-body crowd* based on physical co-presence (e.g. Canetti and Tarde); the *mediated crowd*, which has a strong offline dimension but uses media technologies as tools or communication environments (e.g. Baker); and the *online crowd*, which 'becomes one' by sharing relatively synchronised affective processes in online settings. Furthermore, by investigating the formal traces of mutual affect in the blog responses (e.g. redundancy, re-registering affect) and the clustering of energy and online presence in relation to certain events or videos (e.g. the video *Farewell*), we have shown that Eva Markvoort's blog seems to enable these collective affective processes. The online crowd is also supplemented by more complex assemblages of online and offline crowds at, for instance, the Eva's Celebration of Life memorial service. Finally, we have argued that Eva Markvoort functions as a crowd-facilitator, motivating both linguistic and bodily imitation (e.g. the Reddy for a Cure campaign), and that this was due to her own personal prestige, her image-producing embodiment of an abstract disease and problem, and her discursively challenging (in terms of language categorisation) and discursively channelled (in terms of cultural patterns of knowledge) production of affect.

Eva Markvoort has raised both awareness and important resources in relation to CF. Consideration of whether Eva Markvoort has gained a voice or is performing cultural reproduction could be pertinent here; but in light of the effects of the blog we argue in favour of characterising her as an individual who made a significant personal contribution enabling the normally disabled vulnerable ill body (normally socially dead) through the enterprising social initiatives undertaken during her illness. A critical reading would recognise Eva Markvoort as the perfect example of an entrepreneurial spirit or neoliberal logic impacting everybody, even those on the verge of dying, with the result that she lives her illness in a (very vital) way that helps to make the lives of relatives, friends, and bystanders easier as she does not despair. We nevertheless opt for the former reading to avoid neglecting Eva Markvoort's and her followers' own experience of empowerment through/ on the blog. It is beyond doubt that Eva Markvoort touched a significant number of people. At the time of writing, the blog consists of 564 entries, of which Eva Markvoort herself wrote the majority; relatives wrote the remaining entries after her death or during spells when it was impossible for her to blog. These entries have received more than 26,000 comments from around the world. The US, Canada, Poland, the UK, Australia, Finland, Brazil, Germany, Sweden, the Netherlands, and Russia are the countries with the largest number of visitors between 2010 and 2013.[13] The blog has also raised a significant sum for CF research ($1.4 million since her death according to a recent post[14]). The campaign '65for65Roses' is run by

Eva Markvoort's father, Bill Markvoort, and is a 1,200-kilometre bike ride to raise money for Cystic Fibrosis Canada. As of 30 March 2014, he had raised C$11,000. According to Canadian member of parliament Joyce Murray, the number of people signing up for organ donation in Canada clearly increased[15] thanks to Eva Markvoort—which implies that she succeeded in mobilising long-term investments, rather than short-term 'slacktivism' (Garde-Hansen and Gorton, 2013: 111).

NOTES

1. For other examples of this tendency, besides the blog of Markvoort analysed in this chapter, see www.facebook.com/StephensStory, http://theknockoneffect.bigcartel.com, www.cffatboy.com/, and http://www.jessicajoyrees.com/
2. http://65redroses.livejournal.com/42315.html#comments (accessed 10 November 2012).
3. http://65redroses.livejournal.com/42315.html#comments (accessed 10 November 2012).
4. http://65redroses.livejournal.com/42315.html#comments (accessed 10 November 2012).
5. http://65redroses.livejournal.com/2010/02/11/ (accessed 10 November 2012).
6. http://65redroses.livejournal.com/144422.html (accessed 10 November 2012).
7. http://65redroses.livejournal.com/142459.html#comments (accessed 10 November 2012).
8. http://65redroses.livejournal.com/142894.html (accessed 10 November 2012).
9. For user comments verifying the affective quality of the service: http://65redroses.livejournal.com/142685.html and http://65redroses.livejournal.com/144422.html (accessed 10 November 2012).
10. http://www.facebook.com/pages/Reddy-For-a-Cure/108071815888330?sk=photos (accessed 10 November 2012).
11. http://65redroses.livejournal.com/144422.html (accessed 10 November 2012).
12. http://65redroses.livejournal.com/2006/07/15/ (accessed 10 November 2012).
13. http://65redroses.livejournal.com/58813.html (accessed 10 November 2012).
14. http://65redroses.livejournal.com/150105.html (accessed 3 April 2012).
15. https://www.youtube.com/watch?v=GQML68gtsxI (accessed 3 April 2012).

REFERENCES

AHMED, S. 2010. *The Promise of Happiness*, Durham, Duke University Press.
BAKER, S.A. 2011. The Mediated Crowd: New Social Media and New Forms of Rioting. *Sociological Research Online*, 16. Available at: http://www.socresonline.org.uk/16/4/21.html [Accessed 2 October 2014].
BAYM, N. 2010. *Personal Connections in the Digital Age*, Cambridge, Polity.
BENHABIB, S. 1992. Models of Public Space: Hannah Arendt, the Liberal Tradition, and Jürgen Habermas. *In*: CALHOUN, C. (ed.) *Habermas and the Public Sphere*, Cambridge, MA, MIT Press.
BERLANT, L. 1997. *The Queen of America Goes to Washington City*, Durham, Duke University Press.
BLACKMAN, L. 2012. *Immaterial Bodies. Affect, Embodiment, Mediation*, London, Sage.

BORCH, C. 2006. The Exclusion of the Crowd. The Destiny of a Sociological Figure of the Irrational. *European Journal of Social Theory*, 9, 83–102.

BORCH, C. 2009. Body to Body: On the Political Anatomy of Crowds. *Sociological Theory*, 27, 271–290.

CANETTI, E. 1960. *Crowds and Power*, New York, Farrar, Straus and Giroux.

FISKE, J. 1987. *Television Culture*, London, Routledge.

GARDE-HANSEN, J. & GORTON, K. 2013. *Emotion Online. Theorizing Affect on the Internet*, Basingstoke, Palgrave.

HARDEY, M. 2002. The Story of My Illness: Personal Accounts of Illness on the Internet. *Health*, 6, 31–46.

HEILFERTY, C.M. 2009. Toward a Theory of Online Communication in Illness: Concept Analysis of Illness Blogs. *Journal of Advanced Nursing*, 2009, 1539–1547.

HEILFERTY, C.M. 2011. Ethical Considerations in the Study of Online Illness Narratives: A Qualitative Review. *Journal of Advanced Nursing*, 2011, 945–953.

HESS, A. 2009. Resistance up in Smoke: Analyzing the Limitations of Deliberation on YouTube. *Critical Studies in Media Communication*, 26, 411–434.

HOWARD, R.G. 2008. Electronic Hybridity: The Persistent Processes of the Vernacular Web. *Journal of American Folklore*, 121, 192–218.

KIMBY, C. 2007. *At skrive selvet. Brystkræftramte kvinders sygdomsrelaterede internetbrug*, Copenhagen, Copenhagen University.

KNUDSEN, B.T. & STAGE, C. 2012. Contagious Bodies: An Investigation of Affective and Discursive Strategies in Contemporary Online Activism. *Emotion, Space and Society*, 5, 148–155.

LACLAU, E. 2005. *On Populist Reason*, London, Verso.

LE BON, G. 1895. *The Crowd. A Study of the Popular Mind*, New York, Dover Publications, Inc.

MASSUMI, B. 2002. *Parables for the Virtual*, Durham, Duke University Press.

MCCOSKER, A. 2013. *Intensive Media. Aversive Affect and Visual Culture*. New York, Palgrave.

OLOFSSON, J.K. 2010. Mass Movements in Computer-Mediated Environments. *Information, Communication and Society*, 13, 765–784.

ORGAD, S. 2005. The Transformative Potential of Online Communication. *Feminist Media Studies*, 5, 141–161.

PITTS, V. 2004. Illness and Internet Empowerment: Writing and Reading Breast Cancer in Cyberspace. *Health*, 8, 33–59.

RUSS, C. 2007. Online Crowds—Extraordinary Mass Behavior on the Internet. *In*: TOCHTERMANN, K., HASS, W., KAPPE, F., SHARL, A., PELLEGRINI, T. & SCHAFFERT, A. (eds.) *Proceedings of I-MEDIA '07 and I-SEMANTICS '07*, 65–76. The Open Access Publication Server of the ZBW – Leibniz Information Centre for Economics. Available at: http://www.econstor.eu/bitstream/10419/44447/1/641113358.pdf (accessed 14 November 2014).

SAMPSON, T. 2012. *Virality. Contagion Theory in the Age of Networks*, Minneapolis, University of Minnesota Press.

SHARF, B.F. 1997. Communicating Breast Cancer On-Line: Support and Empowerment on the Internet. *Women and Health*, 26, 65–84.

SQUIRES, C. 2002. Rethinking the Black Public Sphere: An Alternative Vocabulary for Multiple Public Spheres. *Communication Theory*, 12, 446–468.

STAGE, C. 2014. The Entrepreneurial Illness Blogger. *In*: KNUDSEN, B.T., CHRISTENSEN, D.R. & BLENKER, P. (eds.) *Enterprising Initiatives in the Experience Economy. Transforming Social Worlds*, New York, Routledge.

STÄHELI, U. 2011. Seducing the Crowd: The Leader in Crowd Psychology. *New German Critique*, 38, 63–77.

TARDE, G. [1895] 1903. *The Laws of Imitation,* New York, Henry Holt and Company.
TARDE, G. 1901. The Public and the Crowd. *In: Gabriel Tarde. On Communication and Social Influence*, Chicago, University of Chicago Press.
THACKER, E. 2004. *Biomedia,* Minneapolis, University of Minnesota Press.
WALTER, T., HOURIZI, R., MONCUR, W. & PITSILLIDES, S. 2011. Does the Internet Change How We Die and Mourn? Overview and Analysis. *Omega: Journal of Death and Dying*, 64, 275–302.
WARNER, M. 2002. Publics and Counterpublics. *Public Culture,* 14, 49–90.

2   Global Assemblages of Suffering and Protest

This chapter follows instances of 'adding parts' to a global protest assemblage after the killing of Neda Agda Soltan in Teheran in 2009. We analyse at a global level how social actors have used Neda as a vulnerable body to articulate protests against the regime in Iran and thus become parts of and responsible for building the assemblage.

Over the past five years there have been a number of local-global uprisings related to political and religious oppression in the Middle East. A common factor in all these uprisings has been the sharing of iconic moments of individual suffering and vulnerability. The primary example used in this chapter is Neda Agda Soltan (1983–2009) who was killed in Teheran in 2009. Other similar cases include the young Egyptian man, Khaled Mohamed Saeed (1982–2010), who was beaten to death by Egyptian police in June 2010 in Alexandria. His death led to the mobilisation of protesters against the government of Hosni Mubarak—a process that culminated in the so-called Egyptian Revolution of 2011. The case of Mohamed Bouazizi (1984–2011), a street vendor who set himself on fire in Sidi Bouzid in December 2010 has similarities. He was protesting against a humiliating state system in Tunisia and his actions sparked public protests that led to President Ben Ali fleeing the country in early 2011. Malala Yousafzai's (1997–) story is also relevant to the theme of this chapter. She is the former Pakistani (now living in the UK) school pupil and education/women's rights campaigner who was shot in the head by Taliban gunmen in late 2012. Malala survived the attack and has become an icon of the struggle for women's rights, a speaker at the United Nations, receiver of numerous prizes, and in 2014 receiver of the Nobel Peace Prize. These stories and images of personal, bodily suffering all triggered the creation of media events, where affects were shared and used to mobilise both on a global scale and in the respective countries and regions.

The four young bodies all seemed to motivate affective responses and experiences of shared vulnerability; a sentiment expressed via protest slogans such as 'We are all Neda' or 'We are all Khaled Saeed'. As stated by Sara Ahmed (2004), affects often stick to objects and amplify via circulation. We add to this point by approaching affective media experiences as a catalyst both of material productivity and media circulation and as a force that glues various entities to each other, that makes the elements of a global protest assemblage hold together. In this chapter we take a closer look at the political potential of the victimised-vulnerable body as a soft power, capable of assembling or creating assemblages (DeLanda, 2006; Anderson et al., 2012; Frosh and Pinchevski, 2014: 603). This power to make people want to add to, build on, and keep alive the assemblages is derived from an ability to affect other bodies via user-generated spectacles of vulnerability. Here we analyse one of the first iconic events, which we approach as an important starting point for the social movements and protests against anti-democratic regimes and economic institutions.

On 20 June 2009 a young woman, Neda Agda Soltan (aged 26), was shot dead by a sniper as she participated in a street demonstration in Iran's capital, Teheran. Other civilians who witnessed the event captured this dramatic incident on their mobile phones. The protests were aimed at the Iranian government and President Mahmoud Ahmadinejad who was re-elected in 2009. His re-election was controversial, and the reformist 'green movement', led by Mir-Hossein Moussavi, accused the government of fraud and manipulation. The particular interest of our analysis is not the specific role of social media in the global mobilisation process that occurred after the killing of Neda. Rather, our interest revolves around how, with Neda as the iconic anchor or 'glue', images and objects were produced and entered into a global protest assemblage with bodies and technologies. In other words, the killing of Neda seemed to stimulate affective responses on a global scale. These were then involved in the production of a hyper-complex composition of bodies, things, images, technologies, relations, and affects.

INTRODUCING THE ASSEMBLAGE

The concept of 'assemblage' has been used in various disciplines: in archaeology it is used to describe artefacts that belong to the same group from a particular site; in ecology it refers to collections of species (e.g. mammals) in a certain time-space; in art it is used in relation to works of montage and collage; in geography for the continuous formation and deformation of sociospatial formations (Anderson et al., 2012: 174); and in consumer studies to describe brands as compositions of emotions, movements, technologies, signs, and products (Lury, 2009). The concept, as used in the Humanities and Social Sciences, often refers to Deleuze and Guattari's description of the term (in French *agencement*) in *A Thousand Plateaus: Capitalism and Schizophrenia* (1980) or later developments such as Latour's sociology of attachments (inspired by Gabriel Tarde) and Manual DeLanda's neo-assemblage theory.[1] Following Ben Anderson et al., the term has either been used as (1) a 'descriptor' of historical relations coming together, (2) an 'ethos' 'oriented to the "instability" of interactions' and potentials for "novelty and spatiotemporal difference"', or (3) a 'concept' for thinking relations 'between stability and transformation in the production of the social' (2012: 172).

In *A New Philosophy of Society* (2006) the philosopher Manuel DeLanda presents an elaborated account of the concept. Here he links it to a 'realist' social ontology that opposes idealist constructivism that describes language as capable of shaping the reality of what it articulates, and instead focuses on 'objective processes of assembly' (DeLanda, 2006: 3). DeLanda simply treats 'assembling' as a transcultural ontological process and describes how various social entities are related to each other in the formation of a wide range of social phenomena. In DeLanda's 'neo-assemblage theory'—that builds-on 'the relatively few pages dedicated to assemblage theory in the work of Deleuze' (DeLanda, 2006: 3)—'assemblages' are distinguished by not being 'totalities' or 'essences' characterised by relations of interiority between parts creating a common identity but rather by a 'whole' that cannot be reduced either to the mere sum of its parts (it is something more) or to a unity without parts (it is not that coherent). Calling something an 'assemblage' then means that you identify relations of exteriority among components/parts forming some sort of 'whole' with certain capacities, but that the parts of this whole are neither fully subsumed under a common identity (thereby no longer a part of something, but simply an essence of a totality) or fully independent (thereby not a part of anything; DeLanda, 2006: 10).

Assemblages are based on relations of exteriority between parts with certain relatively fixed properties, but potentially open capacities. 'These capacities do depend on a component's properties but cannot be reduced to them since they involve reference to the properties of other interacting entities' (DeLanda, 2006: 11). For example, a mobile phone as an object has fixed properties. Certain buttons can be pressed in certain ways that initiate certain processes, certain objects in the phone can perform the function of microphone and loudspeaker, and certain technologies in the phone can interact with other technologies in certain ways. But the capacities of the mobile phone are impossible to list. If the mobile phone is used by a decision-maker living in a large Western city the phone has the capacity to play a part in ending conflict, creating jobs, preventing famine, and so on. Meanwhile if the very same phone is placed in the hands of a grandmother living in a rural area it has a capacity to create intimate feelings between herself and her grandchildren living far away. The properties of the phone may be the same, but their capacities are actualised differently, depending into what kind of assemblage the phone is grouped.

Another important point is that these capacities are often beyond human control: When the phone is assembled with a grandmother, the telephone network, and a furious storm that destroys local telephone receivers or poles, then the capacities of the phone change. It may no longer be a link to the outside world and this changed capacity could create feelings of fear and isolation rather than intimacy. This means that any assemblage is accompanied by an unpredictable 'possibility space' (DeLanda, 2006: 29), as well as having 'an objective existence because they can causally affect the people that are their component parts, limiting them and enabling them, and because they can causally affect other assemblages at their own scale' (DeLanda, 2006: 38). This underlines that human agency is not cancelled out but, rather, is distributed or diffused (Anderson et al., 2012: 181) via the constraints and possibilities enabled by the assemblage and by properties of the singular part.

Assemblages are parts of bigger assemblages, or consist of smaller assemblages. A local market is an assemblage, which is also one part of the assemblage of regional markets, which again are parts of the assemblage of a national market (DeLanda, 2006: 18). Social groups are parts of networks, which are parts of organisations, which are part of cities, which are parts of nations, and so on. In that way assemblages can be described in terms of their extensity (numbers, not geographical extension) and their intensive features (the density of relations, centralisation of authority). Assemblages are objective phenomena in the world and are thus also spatial constructs. Their parts can be described in various ways according to DeLanda. They can play various roles in the assemblage on an axis from 'materiality' (bodies, things) to 'expressivity' (e.g. facial gesture), and from 'territorialisation' (the creation of any spatial boundaries of an assemblage via e.g. face-to-face communication) to 'deterritorialisation' (e.g. communication technologies that destabilise the spatial boundaries of an assemblage). Territorialisation is supported or strengthened by processes of 'coding', where tradition, social rules, or rational-legal authority give the assemblage a more enduring form, and opposed by processes of 'decoding' (e.g. when genes fail to control and determine behaviour or social rules are changed). 'The identity of any assemblage at any level of scale is always the product of a process (territorialisation and, in some cases, coding) and it is always precarious, since other processes (deterritorialisation and decoding) can destabilize it' (DeLanda, 2006: 28).

THE INTERNET AND THE ASSEMBLAGE

Manuel Castells has argued that in recent years a new type of social movement has appeared. It was anticipated by earlier protests in Spain, Iran, Iceland, and Tunisia but flourished particularly in 2011. This was the year of the revolution in Egypt, the Indignadas movement in Spain, and the Occupy Movement in the US. These local movements affected global change by offering 'hope of a possible change as a result of examples of successful uprisings in other parts of the world, each revolt inspiring the next one by networking images and messages in the Internet' (Castells, 2012: 220–221). All these examples of this new species of social movement shared characteristics: They relied on multiple online and offline forms of network, they all occupied public spaces, they managed to be both locally anchored to a specific place and globally visible to international publics via digital media, they were based in the present but experimented with imagining the future in new ways, they sparked indignation by publicising images of individual injustice and suffering in the face of ineffective or corrupt institutions, and they used non-violent protests and acts of civil disobedience to raise awareness of their causes (e.g. occupying public spaces; Castells, 2012: 221–231). The internet was not the cause of these new social movements, but provided the participants with useful tools and a networking infrastructure (Castells, 2012: 229) that facilitated 'mass self-communication' (Castells, 2012: 6–7).

Two events have been highlighted as pioneer examples of how political activism and online technologies can be intertwined. Harry Cleaver cites the Zapatista movement, which in 1994 used the internet to mobilise international support in its rebellion against the Mexican state (Cleaver, 1999). In 1999 anti-capitalistic protesters 'began employing the internet to foster affiliations and stage events' (Kahn and Kellner, 2004) during the so-called Battle of Seattle, where huge demonstrations against the World Trade Organization's Ministerial Conference took place. Another interesting example that preceded the Arab Spring uprisings is the protest against President Joseph Estrada in the Philippines in 2001, which used text messages to coordinate events. In the case of the protests in Iran, Elson et al. (2012) described how Twitter users sent tweets marked with the 'Iran Election' hashtag as identifier. These tweets were being sent at a rate of about 30 new tweets per minute in the days immediately following the election. (Elson et al., 2012: xi). This led author and blogger Andrew Sullivan to label the Iranian protests a 'Twitter Revolution' (Morozov, 2009). He wrote, 'You cannot stop people any longer. You cannot control them any longer. They can bypass your established media; they can broadcast to one another; they can organize as never before' and he concluded with his now famous phrase that 'The Revolution Will Be Twittered' (Sullivan, 2009). Neda's case exemplifies this shift to a situation where new media technologies turn the traditional media user into a globalising media produser.

This situation has two main consequences, which are relevant for understanding the case. First, cultural and technological media convergence clearly challenges the ability of the nation state to control—or in assemblage terms to 'code'—the stories that are told about internal events. Despite the lack of foreign journalists on the street of Teheran, local media produsers succeeded in spreading the event to the outside world. This verifies Brian McNair's point that 'the sovereign nation-state is faced with the erosion of many of its traditional powers, not least among them the power of control over information crossing its borders and circulating within its territory' (2006: 9). The second and related consequence is that the media users are empowered because of their ability to affect, communicate, and pass on information that they find important. Of course, one should not fall into the trap of technological determinism and claim that certain media technologies create positive social consequences (like individual emancipation), whereas others have negative ones. Older broadcast media also had the ability to disseminate individual and moving stories or visuals (e.g. the Chinese tank man image from 1989), and new media are likewise capable of supporting nation state agendas and censorship (e.g. China blocking Google) as state institutions attempt to 'control the flow' (Mirzoeff, 2005). Nick Couldry also points out that expressing oneself (for instance online) is not the same as being heard or having an effect on the world (Couldry, 2010). And traditional power structures that determine who can speak and with what weight are, of course, not always destabilised by the participatory culture. It does, however, seem to be overly pessimistic not to accept that the opportunities to produce and disseminate media material now available to citizens can have implications for the global distribution of knowledge about localised incidents. Previously, when broadcast media dominated mass communication the incidents cited earlier could easily have been hidden by states.

We argue that one of social media's socially transformative potentials is the provision of platforms that may be used to challenge established assemblages and motivate new ones. This can change the capacities of the material and affective parts under conditions of de- and territorialisation. The strength of this assemblage approach is that it avoids both an overtly optimistic technical determinism that views the internet and social media as inherently democratic and participatory, at the same time as tempering the pessimistic view that the internet simply disguises commercial and institutional power under a glittering surface of 'user participation'. By using the idea of assemblage when analysing the democratic potential of social media it is possible to maintain a differentiated understanding of the internet. Under certain circumstances the network of the internet is capable of connecting material and expressive parts in new and powerful ways—under others not (Fuchs, 2014: 84).

ASSEMBLAGES OF TRANSPOSITION

In this chapter we are particularly interested in material practices as forms of political action and assembling. Our analysis is inspired by the concepts of 'transposition' and 'thingification' developed by Scott Lash and Celia Lury (2007) in *The Global Culture Industry*. Lash and Lury argue that the contemporary global media culture creates a situation in which it is impossible to uphold the idea that mediation is basically about transmitting representations, because media products are also turned into objects and things/spaces are turned into media. In that way we experience 'the mediation of things' as well as 'the thingification of media' (Lash and Lury, 2007).

Thingification according to Lash and Lury refers specifically to *the way mediated products in contemporary consumer culture are turned into objects*. A Pixar animation is not only a film, but also a resource of material creativity (e.g. dolls, pencils, bags, games, etc.). In that way media materials are constantly (re-)materialised or 'thingified'. Although Lash and Lury are mainly describing phenomena linked to consumer culture, their thesis and awareness of blurred boundaries between mediation and materiality are also very helpful in relation to the case under discussion, because Neda herself moved between different ontological states. First, she was a body on the streets of Teheran. Second, she was an image that prompted outrage and was circulated all over the world via both online and broadcast media. And third, she was re-materialised via the creation of numerous objects, which can both be described as concrete materiality (a mask, a cup, a statue), but also as reworkings of images as the objects were modelled on prior mediations. In this way Neda became the focal point of a self-generating assemblage based on a constant and productive intertwinement of mediation and materialisation.

By incorporating the concept of thingification in our analysis we can focus on the way Neda—after becoming an image circulating all over the world—was turned into a range of new objects that themselves became part of the assemblage together with other actions, affects, institutions, and subjects engaged in or mobilised by Neda's death. These objects are often thingifications due to the fact that it was the circulating images of Neda that made it possible for people all over the world to create material forms that related to the event and her body, even though they did not witness the shooting first-hand.

Lash and Lury make a very helpful distinction between 'translation' and 'transposition' as different ways of describing the global movement of objects. If a certain narrative (e.g. Arthur Conan Doyle's stories about Sherlock Holmes) moves from being a book to being a television series and a film we are witnessing a process of translation since the varying forms are linked to each other because they reproduce a common 'aesthetic integrity' or 'discursive unity of sorts' (Lash and Lury, 2007: 25). The figures and cultural forms share the same origin (Conan Doyle's novel) and are characterised by a kind of narrative continuity during the serial and linear process of translative remediation (Bolter and Grusin, 2003). When faced with the Neda case we are instead dealing with a process of assemblage built through transposition 'in which it is the intensive features of the object, rather than any kind of aesthetic unity, that enable movement' (Lash and Lury, 2007: 25). Approaching Neda as such an assemblage that has been composed from input from different localities and ontological states (from body to picture to thing), it is evident that she travelled as a result of her intensity. In other words, she moves because her death elicits an immediate response and people react emotionally to the pictures, texts, and objects.

METHODOLOGY

An assemblage-perspective focuses on how connections between parts actualise certain specific, but uncountable, capacities of objects, and how these connections change over time to create new capacities. In a similar line of thinking Lash and Lury describe their method as based on the idea of 'following the object': '[I]n this sociology of objects, we track the object as it moves and transforms through a media environment' (2007: 31). In relation to Neda's case this would mean to follow how Neda moves from being a body and an image circulating online to being different kinds of things and to understand the cultural meaning of these things as they assemble. In other words our method will be to focus on tracing relations created between humans, media technologies, and things in the aftermath of a particular event, and to discuss the political impact of this historical composition process. In this sense we track down the affective impact of Neda by following the productive traces she leaves behind across a range of online and offline platforms.

In the analysis we focus primarily on the documentation of the killing, two user-generated attempts to protest against the Iranian regime ('Nedasites' and 'Nedaspeaks'), and two specific strategies of thingification: the portrait busts of Neda made by sculptor Paula Slater and the 'Neda-masks' used during the so-called Neda mask actions. It is impossible to delineate the borders and totality of the assemblage, and we have chosen our specific cases because they highlight first the transformation of the capacity of Neda's body, the number of global user-generated reactions to the killing, and different aspects of the thingification of Neda. By following some of the productive trajectories she motivated, we glimpse how Neda becomes the key figure of a global protest assemblage.

DETERRITORIALISING NEDA, DECODING IRAN

The killing of Neda is, of course, interesting for political reasons because it underlines the brutality of the Ahmadinejad government. Footage of Neda suffering quickly became an icon for the opposition's struggle against the regime and for international protests, as it seemed to incarnate the ruthlessness of the Iranian system. The short footage first shows Neda falling to the ground after being hit and the people rushing to help her. Next Neda is shown seemingly staring straight ahead as blood slowly starts spreading from her mouth and nose across her face. The images come across as extremely raw, unedited, and 'de-framed', which underline their intensifying potential and ability to transmit affect to viewers (Blaagaard, 2013; McCosker, 2013). On 23 June 2009—only three days after the shooting—US president Barack Obama explained that he had seen the video of the killing and that it was heartbreaking: 'I think that anybody who sees it knows that there's something fundamentally unjust about that' (Kennedy, 2009).

The movement of information from the streets of Teheran—via a camera phone, social media platforms, and broadcast media—to the White House was, in other words, extremely quick and efficient. The killing of Neda and the way it became a global event is significant when it comes to understanding the new potential of global media networks, the ongoing breakdown of the nation state's ability to control information and everyday citizens' mobile witnessing (Reading, 2011; Andén-Papadopoulos, 2013), and the documenting and spreading of information about local events to global audiences (McNair, 2006). Video footage of the killing of Neda made by local Iranians with a camera on a phone was posted onto social media platforms, thereafter spreading like a wildfire to millions of individual users of Twitter, Facebook, and YouTube, as well as to broadcast media all over the world (Mortensen, 2011).[2] The killing of Neda clearly shows that the participatory culture of new social media is a communicative force that is very difficult for state authorities to control. The Iranian regime had prohibited the foreign media from attending the demonstrations in order to suppress coverage, but despite these efforts the events became world news. This was all down to the fact that every owner of a camera phone can very easily record and disseminate information on a global scale with almost no delay (Tomlinson, 2007; Mortensen, 2011).

The assemblage perspective used in this analysis means it is possible to consider how adding Neda to the nation-assemblage of Iran might change or destabilise the assemblage. Also, it provides a framework to discuss the question of how the new relations enabled by the killing and sharing of documentation online transformed the capacities of Neda's body to affect and influence the world. Iran as nation-assemblage is and was heavily controlled by the regime. The exclusion of foreign journalists can be viewed as an attempt to stabilise the nation-assemblage via processes of *coding* (through legal frameworks). In doing this, the regime tries to avoid introducing new parts into the assemblage that could disturb its stability and immanent causality. As mentioned, the space of possibility of an assemblage is difficult to predict and control. The introduction of a new part consisting both of material components (a sniper, a weapon, a body being hit, people engaging in rescuing the body, technologies of documentation and dissemination, internet users sharing, mainstream media picking up the story) and expressive components (affects of indignation, compassion) dramatically deterritorialised or 'decoded' the initial assemblage by linking it to global online networks, international media, and publics, politicians, and citizens.

The case exemplifies the struggle between established institutions of power (e.g. the state of Iran) and ordinary internet users—a struggle which is sometimes won by the institutions, if they are able to keep old assemblages intact and stable, and sometimes by the users, if they are capable of entering new disturbing parts into old assemblages or creating new assemblages. We argue that Neda became an affective catalyst of assemblage practices as she disturbed a certain heavily coded assemblage. A very clear example of this is the (now closed) 'nedasites' initiative[3] where users critical of the Iranian regime were invited to take part in a DDoS (distributed denial-of-service) attack on websites affiliated with the regime. The platform made it possible to overheat attacked websites (e.g. gerdab.ir[4] which was set up to identify Iranian protesters and track them down) by producing an overload of communication requests that result in the site crashing. The iconic image of Neda's bloody face was placed in the main banner of 'nedasites', thus serving as a kind of affective legitimisation of the project. The logic behind the initiative seems to be that it attacks the system that attacked Neda—and because it attacked Neda, it deserves to be attacked. Nedasites thus exemplifies a user-generated attempt to decode the Iranian nation state by adding new external parts (huge amounts of communication requests) that decrease the regime's ability to act (its capacity to control and act online).

Another platform using Neda to stimulate user-generated protests against the Iranian regime is http://nedaspeaks.org/ (Figure 2.1), which is intended to serve as 'a global online march in support of human rights in Iran, in memory of Neda Agha-Soltan's death on the streets of Tehran'.[5] The US-based band The Airbone Toxic Event created the site, which invites people to upload images of themselves holding images with the text 'I am Neda' (at the time of writing approximately 1,000 images are available on the platform). These images somehow document the productive output of a 'becoming one' with Neda after an encounter with her suffering. Neda is not described as distinct *from* me, but *as* me. Furthermore, the band has produced a song narrating the killing of Neda, which can be bought on iTunes (a proportion of the profits go to Amnesty International) or watched on YouTube (where it has received more than 400,000 views). The site also has links to information about the human rights situation in Iran and the killing of Neda, and to a donation page at Amnesty International. The overall goal of the platform is to 'send a strong message to Iran's government (and the rest of the world) that its human rights abuses are not going unnoticed'.

Figure 2.1   Screenshot from main page of http://nedaspeaks.org

Compared to Nedasites, Nedaspeaks' intervention is less concrete because it relies on raising attention, awareness, and criticism in relation to Iran and is more vulnerable to accusations of motivating only low-intensity engagement. But as argued in the Introduction, impact and power is also a 'soft' way to mobilise affectively in order to change discourses and engage bodies. In this sense the platform, together with the range of other initiatives following the killing of Neda, can play a positive role in expanding, disseminating, and vitalising protests and knowledge about important political processes and problems. We will return to this discussion of impact at the end of the chapter.

WEAPONISING NEDA

In the case of both the abovementioned internet sites, and relating to the theories of biopower and biopolitics presented in the introduction, Neda's dead body is somehow being 'weaponized' (Bargu, 2011) by distant protesters as an affective soft-power tool designed to attract people to their cause. The cases reproduce and disseminate her status inside Iran as a 'bare life' in order to force receivers to relate and respond to the Iranian state's production of non-citizens (Darling, 2009). Iran in a classical act of state biopower tried to control how citizens moved around the streets and connected to each other during and after the election. Protesters' bodies were moved, attacked, imprisoned, and killed in the bid to maintain state control; to maintain the existing nation-assemblage. The protesters, however, performed biopolitical acts by claiming the collective right to protest. The documenting and disseminating of images and the rise of various productive communities (like Nedasites and Nedaspeaks) that keep Neda's body politically alive and powerful are also examples of counteractions of biopolitics (Hardt and Negri, 2009).

Users thus seemed to be able to circumvent the codings of the state by creating new connections between parts: Neda's dying body, witnessing bodies, mobile cameras, recorded sequences, friends outside Iran, YouTube and Facebook, CNN, and so on. The role of social media in relation to our case is thus one of deterritorialising a part (Neda as oppressed citizen) of one assemblage (Iran as heavily coded nation-assemblage) and enabling the creation of a new global/local assemblage based on protesting against the lack of human rights and democracy in Iran. So in this instance when the assemblage part is added to a new assemblage as a result of contemporary media dissemination, the part changes its status, meaning, and capacities. By being moved from one assemblage (Iran as nation) to another (global protest assemblage) the capacities of Neda's wounded/dead body change, because it is suddenly capable of travelling globally and mobilising politically and affectively. In the Iranian assemblage the body would have had very limited capacities to affect social processes, but when linked to mobile phones and social media, these capacities transform. As Neda enters the global protest assemblage she is also turned into an icon. She now has the ability to attract new affective investments fostering new contributions to the assemblage (e.g. by the sharing of images, production of objects, and debates about her death). In other words, she becomes a container of affective energy and political action due to the unjust action so clearly visualised in the images of her vulnerability and suffering.

The nation state of Iran attempted to regain control over the narratives and activities surrounding Neda's death. It strengthened internal control over the social visibility of Neda and tried to deconstruct the global soft power of Neda to assemble protest. Internally the regime prohibited the public mourning of Neda, it stopped the production of memorabilia related to Neda and supposedly vandalised her grave. Globally, Ahmadinejad argued in an interview broadcast on CNN that the regime had nothing to do with the killing and insinuated that the US could be involved.[6] An internal documentary claimed that the killing was in fact a performance and that local Iranians killed her.[7] Earlier, the regime had used the protest movement's erroneous use of images of another Iranian woman, looking similar to Neda and having a very similar name, to claim that Neda was actually still alive and living well outside Iran (Stage, 2012). Together these illustrate the attempts made to govern how Neda's body circulated internally in Iran and globally after her death by the state. These can be summarised as (1) the regime's attempt to contest Neda's status as victim and (2) the regime's attempt to track down an alternative perpetrator. The regime thus tried to both deconstruct and renegotiate the global, and relatively undisputed, victimisation of Neda.

These attempts at control nevertheless did not seem to be successful. After 20 June the image of Neda (in its various forms—and just like the portraits of Saeed, Malala, and Bouazizi), according to Aleida Assmann and Corinna Assmann, went from being a referential image to an iconic image symbolising a greater cause and struggle: 'What had started as an *image of* ends up as an *image for*' (Assmann and Assmann, 2010: 235). The HBO documentary *For Neda* (2010) offered further support for this view. This documentary has been viewed more than 500,000 times on YouTube, where both English and Farsi versions are available. The report described Neda as the incarnation of rebellion, curiosity, and bravery, and takes a stance that is opposed to the state of Iran. Before her death a lot of people inside and outside Iran already opposed the Iranian regime (not least the younger generations in Iran; Varzi, 2006; Khosravi, 2008), but the face of Neda made it possible to connect these otherwise separated 'parts' via the global mediation of Neda's vulnerability. The documentation of Neda's killing triggered outbursts of anger/outrage that motivated a range of political actions, which in their totality composed an assemblage around her.

ASSEMBLING NEDA AS MEMORABILIA AND MASK

Following Teresa Brennan's perspective, 'affects have an energetic dimension. This is why they can enhance or deplete. They enhance when they are projected outward, when one is relieved of them; in popular parlance, this is called "dumping"' (Brennan, 2004: 6). Neda's death can be understood in terms of the transmittance of affects between bodies. These bodies are then vitalised via 'dumping' affect through various productions/ activities expressing solidarity or affective commitment to the cause, and thereby—following the logic of Brennan—experiencing an increase in bodily energy.[8] This explains the almost autopoetic quality—or productive knock-on effect—of the Neda-assemblage as it consisted of productions dumping and expressing affect, that spread on a global scale, thereby contagiously attuning other bodies to participate in the further evolvement of the assemblage. Going to the streets to protest is, of course, a less likely reaction when feeling outrage after seeing the Neda video, if the receiver lives in a distant context. For that reason 'making objects' can also be understood as the distant receivers' attempt to make lasting contributions to the protest assemblage, not only sharing or liking but also producing and materially anchoring the affective experience motivated by Neda's mediated vulnerability.

Looking at the processes of composition following the death of Neda, the amount of material is enormous as she is integrated into public mourning rituals, demonstrations, image sharing practices online, and in new forms of material production as well (Stage, 2011; Gyori, 2013). The first type of materialisation we will analyse gives Neda an angelic or spiritual quality. American sculptor Paula Slater created two portrait busts called 'Neda "Angel of Iran"' (Figure 2.2) and 'Neda "Angel of Freedom"'. Slater's statues were made and exhibited in an American context, and provided clear examples of how Neda travelled online throughout the global media networks, which resulted in her being objectified and contextually interpreted. Both of the portraits are clearly modelled on heavily circulated images of Neda—one where she wears a scarf (Figure 2.3) and one where she does not—and as such the portraits are exactly thingifications relying on prior mediations.[9]

Slater explains her reason for making these busts in the following way:

> Neda has become known as The Angel of Iran, The Angel of Freedom. I was so saddened by the senseless murder of this lovely young woman that I wanted to turn the pain I felt into art. So I sculpted this life size bust of Neda and when it is cast in bronze I will donate it and hope it can help to memorialize this Angel of Iran. The Iranian government banned Neda's family from even having a memorial for her. However, you will not be forgotten Neda. It is my prayer that countries around the world will hold memorial services for this Angel of Freedom.[10]

Figure 2.2   The statue *Neda 'Angel of Iran'*
Artist: Paula Slater (www.paulaslater.com).
Courtesy of Paula Slater

Figure 2.3   One of the most disseminated images of
Neda

Following Brennan the sculptures become a type of affective dumping channelling the bodily pain motivated by experiencing the mediated vulnerability of Neda into external objects. In the quote Slater turns Neda into a sacred figure (*angel* is used four times) that is linked to signifiers such as 'freedom' and 'Iran'. The Neda busts, on one hand, refer not only to a very specific person who lost her life but also to a spiritual character—resembling a saint—whose death will be remembered in order to strengthen people's faith in certain ideas or values. In that way the thingification of Neda serves as a way of keeping her (ascribed) values alive or rather to create a portrait of a saintly figure to which people can connect and fight for larger ideas of freedom and justice. Thus, Neda becomes an example of a person who unwillingly made the ultimate sacrifice and therefore also a person who can be used to energise the struggle for the ideals related to her image. To make that point, Slater quotes Bryan Joseph Costales: 'When a tyrant dies, his rule ends. When a martyr dies, her rule begins'.

The quote linking Neda to martyrdom is interesting for several reasons. First, it shows that Slater actually reproduces a way of linking personal deaths, sanctified representations, and political causes, which has become a familiar process in Iran since the Islamic revolution. And second, this way of using Neda to protest against Ahmadinejad and the regime is quite different from the way she is used as an anti-regime icon in the Iranian context. Slater's Neda statues resemble 'martyr memorabilia', which according to anthropologist Roxanne Varzi (2006), was an important dimension of Aytollah Khomeini's rule in Iran during the 1980s. What is ironic in Slater's way of creating an anti-regime martyr is that in the Iranian context the protest against the rulers is also a protest against decades of martyr culture. As described by Shahram Khosravi in *Young and Defiant in Tehran* (2008) contemporary youth and student culture ('the third generation'), which played a prominent role in the 2009 election protests, is characterised by lesser religious activity, a critical attitude towards the parents' embrace of political Islam, and, as a part of this, the boundary between a less restricted private sphere and a very restricted public sphere (Khosravi, 2008: 137). In this perspective Neda does not so much become a martyr for the Iranian protesters as yet another proof of the injustices of decades of suppression. This produces a paradox in relation to Slater's thingification of Neda: In Iran Neda is supposedly used as an icon to fight the regime's martyr culture described by Varzi, while Slater keeps her tribute to Neda inside the logic of politico-religious sacrifice. This nevertheless underlines that the global protest assemblage created after Neda's death is based on relations of exteriority between various elements, not a strong identity. In various contexts Neda could be used as a part of the same protest, but with internal variations (e.g. fighting against martyr culture vs. producing a martyr) making any talk of a totality or essence nonsensical.

After her death a picture of Neda was turned into a mask, which was used during two so-called Neda Mask Actions in Paris (July 2009; Figure 2.4) and Washington (June 2010). The Iranian-French photojournalist Reza was the man behind the mask actions and before the second action in Washington he explained the basic idea in the following way:

> As you have seen in the Paris group photo, my main goal is to create a strong visual with the mask in each city, using the worldwide known monuments in those cities. Even though the photo shoot would be during the demonstration but the main conditions is that **NO other images, banners or words** should be held while this photo is taken but only the poem 'Ma hame yek Nedaeem, Ma hame yek sedaeem' in both Persian and English: We Are All One Neda, We Are All One Calling.
>
> (Reza, 2010, emphasis in original)

Before these photo shoots, the website http://wearealloneneda.wordpress. com/ had a picture of Neda that could be downloaded along with a five step manual describing how to construct the mask. In the mask actions Neda is not articulated as an elevated or sacred representative of larger ideas but rather approached as humanity incarnated. The killing of Neda is therefore represented as the abstract killing of 'the human being' understood as a singularity carrying rights and offered protection by the state.

Figure 2.4   Neda Mask Action in Paris, 25 July 2009

Photo: Reza Deghati. Courtesy of Reza Deghati

According to Judith Butler (2004; 2009) human beings are precarious creatures because their existence depends on the existence of others who do not take advantage of this vulnerability (e.g. the weakness and defencelessness of the human child). What we all have in common is therefore a fundamental existential vulnerability, and the Neda mask actions are exactly aimed at remembering this basic human vulnerability in a sociopolitical context (the Iranian regime) where it seems to be forgotten. In Iran—as in so many other places—the vulnerability of the human being is exploited for political control, rather than respected and protected. By borrowing the victim's face the protesters point at this vulnerability as a human condition and as an ethical principle, which must be taken into account during the formation of just political systems (Stage, 2011; Frosh and Pinchevski, 2014). Neda is clearly an exceptional human being in the sense that her destiny is particularly brutal. The point of the mask protesters nevertheless seems to be that Neda is also typical in the sense that she unveils the radical weakness and vulnerability of every human being—and particularly of those who face state formations that do not understand precariousness as an ethical invocation but, rather, as an invitation to control.

The affective potential of the two types of materiality mentioned earlier (statue and mask) is closely connected to the fact that they re-actualise the presence of a particular death where a young woman lost her life at the hands of a brutal political regime. The affective dimension is not only about giving the immediate response to the killing a material form but also about disseminating and creating affect when people encounter the objects. They act as 'containers of cultural energy' (Aby Warburg in Assmann and Assmann 2010: 233) or 'vibrant matter' (Bennett, 2010) with an ability to establish new relations of exteriority—and further acts of assembling—between objects and people. The thingifications of Neda are thus also acts of intensifying the affective potential of the event by sharing and multiplying spontaneous bodily reactions to the killing.

CONCLUSION: THE POWER OF MEDIATED VULNERABILITY

As shown in this chapter, Neda became a vital icon that motivated political action via the mediated experience of bodily vulnerability. Mediated vulnerability clearly acted as an affective force of political mobilisation and material production in relation to the documentation of Neda's death—a force that enabled new connections between parts with fixed properties that, as a consequence, changed the social capacities of these parts (e.g. Neda's body). Affect is important in understanding the mobilising potential of Neda's death—both on the streets of Iran, in social media, and through various forms of material production and transposition. Facing her vulnerability via the violent aggression towards her body simply seemed to motivate affective experiences of sameness or universality—expressed in statements such as 'I am Neda' and 'We are all Neda'.

The thingifications show that Neda is a figure with an extreme ability to travel around the world and assemble by means of a logic of transposition. This is underlined by the fact that the specific Neda objects do not tell the same narrative, but are characterised by a high degree of multiplicity as they create 'an intensive, associative series of events' (Lash and Lury, 2007: 25). During these transpositions of Neda the idea of a common origin is also lost in favour of 'the multiplication of origins' (Lash and Lury, 2007: 25). When Neda is spread all over the world and is turned into new objects, it is precisely because of her affective/intensive potential, and the objects created are therefore not related to each other because they have discursive unity but, rather, because they share and thingify the intensity of the experience of outrage related to Neda's death in different ways and contexts.

The name Neda in Farsi means 'voice' or 'call'. And Neda's voice was to some extent heard on a more structural level instead of just disappearing in the echo chambers of political online communication (e.g. Obama commented on the video, and Ahmadinejad was also forced to comment). The voice of Neda could nevertheless also be accused of being heard in a way that maintains a Western perception of Iran as a martyr culture and of Muslim women as victimised and passive. Such a reading would focus on how the support for Neda is in fact reproducing problematic orientalist discourses. How can we, in light of this, evaluate the overall political potentials of this process of affective mobilisation?

First we have to acknowledge the enormous reaction and numbers of activities that the mediation of Neda's killing motivated. In this sense the affective intensity of Neda as icon both offers a point of reference for an existing movement (the green protests in Iran) and a global catalyst for new protests (online/offline, material production). A lot of these activities could however be approached as forms of 'slacktivism'—defined by Evgeny Morozov as 'feel-good but useless Internet activism' (2009: 13)—thereby acknowledging the high number of activities but questioning their transformative political potentials. Through this perspective the number of internet actions could actually end up disguising the West's unwillingness to take proper action in relation to global problems (e.g. lack of human rights). Social media users performed the role of switchers (by using the rawness of the Neda video to enable new connections), and acted as agents of counter-power by renegotiating established power hierarchies as they connected otherwise separated networks (e.g. the streets of Teheran with global internet users; Castells, 2012). The mediation of Neda's vulnerability thus had enormous short-term effects in terms of creating media attention, dissemination, and global/local mobilisation against the regime.

The long-term effects of Neda's mediated vulnerability are still open to debate as Neda's importance for any positive change in Iran is impossible to determine accurately. At the time of writing, however, the seemingly more moderate Hassan Rouhani has replaced Ahmadinejad. Concerning human rights, freedom of speech, and a number of executions, Iran is still facing continuous and severe criticism from international organisations and the European Union. Rouhani was, however, the first Iranian president to have a telephone conversation with an American president since the fall of the shah in 1979 and he has limited parts of Iran's nuclear programme, a sign that Iran's foreign policy has changed in favour of a more dialogical approach. The post-election protest, however, did not create a political event in Iran that radically changed the system and opened up a new future. But it contributed to a regional process that culminated in historical riots in Tunisia, Egypt, and Libya. In each of these cases, such as Iran, the state was perceived as oppressive and the protesters were calling for equality, democracy, and more individual autonomy.

NOTES

1. Ben Anderson et al. argue that the difference between Latour's actor-network theory (ANT) and the assemblage theories of Deleuze and DeLanda is that 'relations' seem to be the primary social form of existence in ANT, while assemblage thinking focuses on the making and breaking of connections between existing entities with certain properties: 'assemblage thinking is more attentive to the autonomy of component parts' (2012: 181). Parts exist and have properties (and a degree of agency), but (some of) their capacities are only realised via relations to other parts of the assemblage.
2. A version of the video is available here: https://www.youtube.com/watch?v=bbdEf0QRsLM (accessed 23 April 2014).
3. https://sites.google.com/site/nedasites/ (accessed 23 April 2014).
4. https://sites.google.com/site/nedasites/news/afewwordstogerdabppl (accessed 23 April 2014).
5. http://nedaspeaks.org/learn (accessed 23 April 2014).
6. https://www.youtube.com/watch?v=rjiUSm9x2GU (accessed 23 April 2014).
7. https://www.youtube.com/watch?v=Shp7HE2YA_c&bpctr=1398257334 (accessed 23 April 2014).
8. This assumption is actually supported by a large empirical investigation made by Elson, Yeung, Roshan, Bohandy, and Nader have focused on the use of Twitter in Iran after the 2009 election and more specifically on the content from 2,675,670 tweets marked with the 'IranElection' hashtag and posted by 124,563 individuals from 17 June 2009 to 28 February 2010 (Elson et al., 2012). Here the authors argue that the level of swearing related to tweets using the hashtag (as a sign of frustration and anger) seems to rise systematically before larger protest events and therefore the level of swearing can actually be used to predict when protests will occur.
9. All images available online here: http://www.paulaslater.com/NedaPortrait Sculpture.htm (accessed 24 April 2014).
10. http://www.paulaslater.com/NedaPortraitSculpture.htm (accessed 24 April 2014).

REFERENCES

AHMED, S. 2004. *The Cultural Politics of Emotion*, Edinburgh, Edinburgh University Press.

ANDÉN-PAPADOPOULOS, K. 2013. Citizen Camera-witnessing: Embodied Political Dissent in the Age of 'Mediated Mass Self-communication'. *New Media and Society*. Advanced online publication.Available at: http://nms.sagepub.com/content/early/2013/05/30/1461444813489863.abstract [Accessed 2 October 2014].

ANDERSON, B., KEARNES, M., MCFARLANE, C. & SWANTON, D. 2012. On Assemblages and Geography. *Dialogues in Human Geography*, 2, 171–189.

ASSMANN, A. & ASSMANN, C. 2010. Neda—the Career of a Global Icon. *In:* ASSMANN, A. & CONRAD, S. (eds.) *Memory in a Global Age*. New York: Palgrave.

BARGU, B. 2011. Forging Life into a Weapon. *Social Text* (May). Available at: http://socialtextjournal.org/periscope_article/the_weaponization_of_life_-_banu_bargu/ [Accessed 2 October 2014].

BENNETT, J. 2010. *Vibrant Matter: A Political Ecology of Things*, Durham, Duke University Press.

BLAAGAARD, B. 2013. Post-human Viewing: A Discussion of the Ethics of Mobile Phone Imagery. *Visual Communication*, 12, 359–374.

BOLTER, J. D. & GRUSIN, R. 2003. *Remediation*, London, MIT Press.

BRENNAN, T. 2004. *The Transmission of Affect*, Ithaca, Cornell University Press.

BUTLER, J. 2004. *Precarious Life. The Powers of Mourning and Violence*, London, Verso.

BUTLER, J. 2009. *Frames of War. When is Life Grievable?*, London, Verso.

CASTELLS, M. 2012. *Networks of Outrage and Hope. Social Movements in the Internet Age,* Cambridge, Polity.

CLEAVER, H. 1999. Computer-Linked Social Movements and the Global Threat to Capitalism, Online article. Available at: http://www.antenna.nl/~waterman/cleaver2.html [Accessed 18 May 2010].

COULDRY, N. 2010. *Why Voice Matters,* London, Sage.

DARLING, J. 2009. Becoming Bare Life: Asylum, Hospitality, and the Politics of Encampment. *Environment and Planning D: Society and Space*, 27, 649–665.

DELANDA, M. 2006. *A New Philosophy of Society: Assemblage Theory and Social Complexity*, London, Continuum.

DELEUZE, G. & GUATTARI, F. L. 1987. *A Thousand Plateaus*, Minneapolis: University of Minnesota Press.

ELSON, S. B., YEUNG, D., ROSHAN, P., BOHANDY, S. R. & NADER, A. 2012. *Using Social Media to Gauge Iranian Public Opinion and Mood After the 2009 Election*, Santa Monica, RAND Corporation.

FROSH, P. & PINCHEVSKI, A. 2014. Media Witnessing and the Ripeness of Time. *Cultural Studies*, 28, 594–610.

FUCHS, C. 2014. *Social Media. A Critical Introduction,* London, Sage.

GYORI, B. 2013. Naming Neda: Digital Discourse and the Rhetorics of Association. *Journal of Broadcasting & Electronic Media*, 57, 482–503.

HARDT, M. & NEGRI, A. 2009. *Commonwealth*, Cambridge, Harvard University Press.

KAHN, R. & KELLNER, D. 2004. New Media and Internet Activism. *New Media & Society*, 6, 87–95.

KENNEDY, H. 2009. President Obama Calls Iranian Martyr Neda's Death 'Heartbreaking'. *Daily News*, June 23.

KHOSRAVI, S. 2008. *Young and Defiant in Tehran*, Philadelphia, University of Pennsylvania Press.

LASH, S. & LURY, C. 2007. *The Global Culture Industry*, Cambridge, Polity.

LURY, C. 2009. Brands as Assemblage. Assembling Culture. *Journal of Cultural Economy*, 2, 67–82.

MCCOSKER, A. 2013. De-framing Disaster: Affective Encounters with Raw and Autonomous Media. *Continuum: Journal of Media and Cultural Studies*, 27, 382–396.

MCNAIR, B. 2006. *Cultural Chaos. Journalism, News and Power in a Globalised World*, London, Routledge.

MIRZOEFF, N. 2005. *Watching Babylon. The War in Iraq and Global Visual Culture*, New York, Routledge.

MOROZOV, E. 2009. Iran: Downside to the 'Twitter Revolution'. *Dissent*, Fall, 10–14.

MORTENSEN, M. 2011. When Citizen Photojournalism Sets the News Agenda: Neda Agda Soltan as a Web 2.0 Icon of Post-election Unrest in Iran. *Global Media and Communication*, 7, 4–16.

READING, A. 2011. The London Bombings: Mobile Witnessing, Mortal Bodies and Globital Time. *Memory Studies*, 4, 298–311.

REZA 2010. Statement on http://weaarealloneneda.wordpress.com/2010/06/11/join-reza-for-neda-mask-action-in-washington-dc-on-june-12-2010/. (seen 6 January 2011).

STAGE, C. 2011. Thingifying Neda. *Culture Unbound*, 3, 419–438.

STAGE, C. 2012. Billedvåben: En strid om billeder med Neda Agda Soltans død og visuelle efterliv som eksempel. *Periskop*, 15, 141–154.

SULLIVAN, A. 2009. The Revolution Will Be Twittered. *The Atlantic* [Online]. Available at: http://www.theatlantic.com/daily-dish/archive/2009/06/the-revolution-will-be-twittered/200478/.

TOMLINSON, J. 2007. *The Culture of Speed. The Coming of Immediacy*, London, Sage.

VARZI, R. 2006. *Warring Souls: Youth, Media, and Martyrdom in Post-revolution Iran*, Durham, Duke University Press.

3 Charity, Seduction, and Productive Publics

In this chapter we look at a traditional field of mediated vulnerability—that of charity, donation, and philanthropy—and how globalisation and global media networks have affected these forms of giving. We claim a paradigm shift is taking place within charity in which donors change from being spectators to become 'productive publics' or 'parts of assemblages' that are seduced and challenged to act on injustice, distant vulnerability, and inequality.

We begin our discussion by looking at the Western perspective on charitable giving, drawing on Gibson-Graham et al.'s (2013) interpretation of what constitutes the West. Gibson-Graham et al. borrow a concept from Shahidul Alam to reframe the West as 'the minority world', that is those parts of the world where a fraction of humanity (one billion) earn more than 12,195 US dollars per year per capita (Gibson-Graham et al., 2013: 9). In this 'minority world' moral obligation towards others has increased as the connectivity of new global media has spread. Not only do we need to care for proximate others, but also for distant unfortunate others whose misfortune—hunger, poverty, diseases, victimhood of wars, genocides, political conflicts, political suppression, failed or uncaring states, lack of working opportunities, and natural disasters—we witness through the media. Ellis stated in 2000 that the twentieth century was the 'century of the witness' because the prototypical interpersonal relation in the mediated encounter meant that it was no longer possible to say that 'one does not know'. We argue that a major challenge in the twenty-first century for those living in the 'minority world' is to listen and then to try to do something concrete to address the issues faced by those less fortunate.

But there seems to be a paradox: Affect appears to be thriving as a political force in a range of social fields, but is retreating in the area of charity (see the ongoing discussion of 'compassion fatigue' or 'crisis of pity' in relation to distant suffering, and the rise of consumption-based charity). One might expect affective and emotional communication to engage citizens from the minority world in the sufferings of the majority world, but the increased competition between cause-related charity appeals seems to diminish the impact of such emotional forms of communication. We feel that this development is not a matter of affect simply disappearing, but rather an indicator that the traditional charity affect of pity has been transformed into other less visible (or tearless) affects that are motivated by more productive forms of charity work (anticipation, joy, sympathy, empowerment, relief). We detect a 'productive turn' in contemporary charity work, which changes the role of affect and mediated vulnerability in charitable exchanges.

More personalised efforts, such as becoming a 'foster parent' for a child through PLAN, the international development and aid organisation that operates in 50 countries and 58,000 communities worldwide, have existed for a long time. But, the difference today is that those doing the charitable giving do not just want to sit at home and respond to the odd typewritten letter supposedly from a child they have never met, they want to see, be given evidence of, or better still have first-hand experience of the impact of their giving. That is they want to help establish between the minority and majority worlds what Arvidsson and Peitersen (2013) have described as productive publics of affective closeness. One example of this new kind of giving is volunteer tourism, a type of tourism where people pay to participate in conservation or development projects. In 2013 this was one of the fastest growing niche tourism markets in the world (Guiney, 2012; Mostafanezhad, 2013). International volunteer abroad and Gap Year programmes exist within many established non-governmental organisations (NGOs). Other examples of this productive turn could be microloan programmes (e.g. Kiva.org) or charity events where the donor participates in an activity—running, doing math equations, cake baking, and so on—in order to raise funds for their chosen cause. This focus on productivity and impact is of course not in itself a guarantee that charity becomes more effective—on the contrary: It could also establish a space of charitable action with less attention on conflict or power differences. We do, however, understand the tendency as an attempt to avoid momentary investments and thus as an expression of an urge to 'invest' in more engaged ways than tapping in the long number on a credit/debit card, while wiping away tears triggered by distressing images and descriptions. Whether the urge to invest is effective or not, of course, depends on the transaction model established by each specific project.

This chapter contributes to a growing field of research that deals with charity, media, and emotional communication (Boltanski, 1999; Chouliaraki, 2006; 2013; Silverstone, 2007; Richey and Ponte, 2011). These texts look at the communication strategies of charity campaigns, and audiovisual material in general, to identify successful ways of increasing awareness and engagement. All offer important analytical concepts—such as proper distance, the benefactor in the spectacle, causumerism, post-humanitarian self-reflexivity—for the exploration of the mediated relationship between fortunate and unfortunate. But all also stay within a 'theatrical frame' that stresses the need for suffering to be displayed in order to mobilise the minority world to address the problems of the majority world. Some look very closely at how viewers are affected morally-emotionally by displays in flow media (Boltanski, 1999; Chouliaraki, 2006). Others explore the distance/ proximity distribution needed to produce recognition of the unfortunate other (Tomlinson, 1999; Silverstone, 2007). Some point to the increased customisation of the unfortunate other as a consequence of the suffering on display (Richey and Ponte, 2011; Chouliaraki, 2013). The two latter texts offer sensitive analyses of aid that comes with celebrity endorsement and both discuss the new 'coolness' of charity campaigns. Through their concept of brand aid that means both 'aid to brands' and 'brands that provide aid' (Richey and Ponte, 2011: 10), campaigns such as (RED) offer the possibility for people to shop and help at the same time (Andersen and Stage, 2010). Chouliaraki is not critical of the coolness of new charity appeals— even though they use celebrity endorsement to engage large audiences—but discusses the extent to which a relationship may be established between the donor and the donee in the cool campaigns. Such campaigns seem to be post-humanitarian and mobilise primarily through the critical and self-reflective mirroring of the donors' privileged position and conditions. Meanwhile, the unfortunate other has disappeared and is replaced by what Chouliaraki describes as the power of theatre, as a means to engage the cosmopolitan citizens. But Chouliaraki comments that: 'Without this agonistic engagement with otherness, I argue, there are no moral dilemmas to struggle with, no sides to take, no stakes to fight for, no hope to change the conditions of suffering' (Chouliaraki, 2013: 205). For Chouliaraki, the display of suffering is necessary in order to mobilise an audience in a normatively adequate way.

We agree with the scholars cited earlier that something new is taking place in charity, but we propose another model of the relationship between donor and donee, one in which spectacles of suffering oblige spectators, morally. Here mediated vulnerability is less visible, but 'the moral dilemma' of global inequality is not repressed. Vulnerability is at the heart of this type of charity too—without acknowledging that some people are more vulnerable than others, charity would not be an option at all—although it is not visually represented. And in this sense the vulnerability of distant sufferers is not forgotten, but implicitly acknowledged to a degree that new forms of engagement, beyond looking and paying, arise. To rephrasing Ellis, we know that we cannot say that we do not know and thus do not need to witness once again. Instead, we need to act.

Below we will investigate two examples of a productive response to the challenge posed by global inequality: One response results in the creation of a 'productive public' around charity issues, while another response leads to new assemblages that tighten ties between donors and donees. As a base for this discussion we refer to two case studies: one that analyses the actions and mobilisation campaigns of boarding school students affected by the donation event Danmarks Indsamlingen held on 1 February 2014 and televised on the largest Danish public broadcast channel, DR1, and one that looks at a project set up to collect music gear, which is sent off to one of the largest slum areas in the world—Kibera in Nairobi, Kenya—to support the evolvement of a local live-music scene. The idea for this project took root at a small Danish music festival in 2011.We have chosen these cases as two prototypical examples of the larger productive turn of charity we are investigating, and we pay special attention to the modes of production and participation, the empowering role of other forms of affect than pity (e.g. sympathy), and the material assemblages enabled. But first we outline the concepts of seduction, ethics, and productive publics, which are of great importance for our understanding of the cases, and for the transformation of the field of charity that encompasses these cases.

SEDUCTION AND ETHICS

Our suggestion is to look at how vulnerability mobilises bodies in relation to global challenges through *a relationship of seduction* that erodes any simple and unidirectional relationship of power between a fortunate and an unfortunate. In some sense the unfortunate has posed a permanent challenge to the citizens of the minority world: How to establish new economies and relationships that (1) do not keep on stimulating global inequality and misery and (2) acknowledge the resources and capacities of the majority world. We argue that seduction takes place in every charity relation: It is just the responses to the fundamental challenges that the unfortunate others pose to us that vary. Talking about this as seduction, of course, does not imply that the unfortunate strategically seduces the more fortunate but, rather, that *global inequality poses a challenge that seduces the fortunate to act and relate*. A relationship of seduction is, as a form of soft power, based on an invisible force prior to its visible impact on bodies and can thus only be detected through the actions and reactions of the seduced. It is an event that we can only determine after the fact, and it provides vulnerability with the empowering force of seduction, as Baudrillard states, '[i]t is through our vulnerability that we seduce never through our hegemony or hard-hitting signs' (1979: 113).[1] Framing vulnerability and charity as seduction means both to confer agency and capacities on the unfortunate vulnerable bodies that challenge us to respond and to stress that what seduces is in fact the change an invested response to the challenge could produce. The vulnerable unfortunate other thus seduces by incarnating a virtual better world and by inviting me to invest myself in this future scenario. A relationship of seduction is the affective counterpart of an ethical relationship of obligation, and in the forthcoming paragraphs, we determine the quality of a relationship of seduction adding elements from affect theories and investigate the relationship between affects and ethics, a particularly important issue in the field of charity. The difference in motivation between a moral or ethical obligation towards unfortunate others and the seductive prospect of being part of a new productive assemblage is huge. The latter offers the possibility of lasting involvement and exchanges across societies and cultures, whereas the former relies on the brief satisfaction gained from tapping in a card number and donation amount.

We thus see a shift that challenges the previously mentioned key texts' conception of emotional-affective involvement. First, if seduction is taken as the precondition of audiences and publics to act, then the symbolic equivalent changes. It is no longer (only) money and tears that are exchanged but also time, labour, and bodily effort. Seduction is exchanged through action, direct involvement, and cultural production. Second, digital media's participatory logics of produsage (Bruns, 2008), the creation of global productive publics, and new assemblages that take action succeed the theatre stage of broadcast media as the space for encounters between the donor and the donee. The way to react to the vulnerability of the unfortunate other seems to change from emotional investment in the spectacle of suffering to the affect involved in the direct action of producing new assemblages that increase the capacities of the bodies taking part in the assemblage.

We argue in the introduction that vulnerability is both a common corporeal condition and a feature that distinguishes some bodies from other bodies due to inequalities in socio-political-economic conditions, processes of recognition and non-recognition, inclusion and exclusion in specific contexts. Because victimhood is the non-contested status of a fate-induced condition, it seems to be a position that is only momentary and to be one that loses its legitimisation if it becomes a permanent condition. It is widely accepted that the privileged affects and feelings the charity field induce are sympathy and pity. According to Jeremy Rifkin (2009) these predispositions of human biology are accelerated and intensified by globalisation and pervasive new media that mean it is possible to extend the empathetic sensibility to our species as a whole. Here it is important to distinguish between pity that enables us to *feel* something *for* the unfortunate other, and sympathy or sympathetic imagination, which enables us to *feel like* the unfortunate other (Weissman, 2004: 110). However, in opting for a relation of seduction between the donor and the donee, the donor is less summoned as someone who must feel something but, rather, as someone challenged to a duel with injustice and inequality.

Sociologist Jean Baudrillard launched the concept of seduction as a spin-off from his book on symbolic exchange and death, in order to investigate non-institutionalised 'hidden' social logics of exchange without any display of production or economic accumulation. We find his concept of seduction valuable if one is to understand the social affective dynamics of charity. Seduction's primary characteristic is that it plays itself out invisibly and in secret, before or beyond any production or accumulation of for example signs of power and money and thus symbolic supremacy over traditional power. Seduction works through challenges and invitations to duel, and as such, it neither positions itself as natural nor contractual but as a challenge in which the duelers must invest. The seducer challenges you to equalise obvious inequalities and injustices. You always have to outbid the seducer by offering something that symbolically fits and outbids the original situation of the seducer.

Donors gather in productive publics, mobilise others, and become producers of donations. The nature of donations often implies the activation of the donors' bodies, labour, time, knowledge, and energies, rather than a financial transaction. To take part in donations and to create public awareness and productive publics around an issue and to take performative action, is what replaces the theatre of suffering and outlines a third way between 'a short-term self-oriented form of solidarity' and an 'other-oriented solidarity of deeply felt, ideological commitment' (Chouliaraki, 2013: 55). The change that has occurred in recent years does not appear to us to be self-conscious irony, but rather pragmatic and realistic: A bodily invested willingness to become part of the whole picture and to make a concrete visible and felt difference on the donor's own body as well as taking action on concrete issues. The charges of narcissism made against donors are not fully refuted through this third way of investing yourself, but the more labour, time, knowledge, and bodily and mental energy donors put into the charitable relationship, the less easy and appropriate an accusation of narcissism seems to be.

So can this bodily investment in charitable causes be ethical? By drawing on Spinoza's ethics (part III) and Protevi's (2009) work on political affect, it is possible to outline a 'bodies politic' for charity that supports our idea of seduction as a duel that challenges bodies to react. Spinoza ([1678] 1997) formulates his ethics after Descartes and before Kant. Being a radical materialist, considering matter and mind as one, Spinoza is opposed to Descartes' distinction between consciousness and matter: 'But the endeavor of the mind, or the mind's power of thought, is equal to, and simultaneous with, the endeavor of the body, or the body's power of action' (Spinoza, [1678] 1997: XXVIII). He likewise presents an alternative to the later Kant in taking emotions as a means to evaluate ethical actions. In formulating his ethics Spinoza wrote, 'We shall also endeavor to do whatever we conceive men to regard with pleasure, and contrariwise we shall shrink from doing that which we conceive men to shrink from' (Spinoza, [1678] 1997: XXIX). Here it becomes clear that an ethical action is one that enhances the capacities in the others' bodies (instead of obeying a universal law or recognising inherent properties and differences). Following this, Spinoza distinguishes between passions and emotions and he adds yet another quality, that of activity versus passivity: 'By "emotion" I mean the modifications of the body, whereby the active power of the said body is increased or diminished, aided or constrained, and also the ideas of such modifications. N.B. If we can be the adequate cause of any of these modifications, I then call the emotion an activity, otherwise I call it a passion, or state wherein the mind is passive'(Spinoza, [1678] 1997: III). Thus, following the idea that one does not have to distinguish between mind and body, an emotional action becomes ethical if it increases the active capacities of the other.

When considering charity as seduction, bodies become reversible (it is blurred who is increasing the energy in whose body) and mutually encouraging. Turning to Protevi and his thoughts on affects and the political, we can add some qualities to the ethical relationship between the donor and the donee in the charity relation. Following Spinoza, the ethical relation happens in the encounter and the result of such encounters can be measured in degrees of either power or empowerment in the involved bodies (Protevi, 2009: 50). Protevi uses the French distinction between *pouvoir* (power) as a transcendent power to guide bodies through chaos and *puissance*, meaning the empowerment of immanent self-organisation through chaotic times. Protevi adds the elements of activity and passivity that we remember Spinoza attributed to emotions (activity, joy) and passions (passivity, sadness). Taking the Nuremberg rallies as an example of a spectacle that fascinated publics at a specific historical time, Protevi distinguishes between the passive joy of the Nazi scenarios as the body politics created there were always dependent on the original scenery to operate: The beholder and the active participant are kind of doomed to repeat the same scene over and over again (what Freud would call a death drive) and the active joy that confers bodies with autonomous power and creative energy to imagine yet other scenes.

If one considers charity as a relationship of seduction that configures future, more equal and just worlds, and understands affects involved in this relationship within the framework of Spinozean ethics of empowering bodies through joyful encounters, an important translation is made from the affective and the ethical, to the political. The political thus is the unleashing of creativity and of immanent self-organisation in order to respond to—outbid and fundamentally change—an original scene of injustice and inequality.

PRODUCTIVE PUBLICS IN CHARITY CAUSES

What kinds of communities or publics become involved in global interdependency? Luc Boltanski (1999) opted in his book *Distant Suffering, Morality, Media and Politics* for a third way between abstract universalism and narrow communitarianism. This he called humanitarian cosmopolitanism, which could realise a politics of pity based on affective reactions. Chouliaraki (2013) analyses throughout her book *The Ironic Spectator, Solidarity in the Age of Post-Humanitarianism* how humanitarianism is succeeded by self-conscious irony and consumerism. For Chouliarki, this results in a reduction in the likelihood of a politics of pity and instead favours the emergence of a narcissistic consumerist perspective. Ulrich Beck, meanwhile, takes a perspective that mixes solidarity and risk-management, which he describes as *realistic cosmopolitanism*. In some ways this is close to Silverstone's concept of 'proper distance' (Silverstone, 2007)—affirming the other as both different and the same (Beck, 2006: 58) so that the traps of abstract universalism (the other as the same) and postmodern particularism (the other as different without any sameness) may be avoided. Beck talks of relations of responsibility with respect to world risk, and states that the rich and powerful nations are endangered by global interdependencies. 'Not only the danger represented by Iraq and North Korea, but also the condition of Africa, for example, weighs on the conscience of the world. But we could relieve our conscience if the world community accepted this challenge. The solution to these problems does not lie in navel-gazing but in the cosmopolitan opening of Europe' (Beck, 2006: 177). In this contemporary thematising of the relationship between fortunate and unfortunate, between a politics of pity, a risk-managing realistic cosmopolitanism, and a post-humanitarian view, we find Arvidsson and Peitersen's concept of *productive publics* helpful when trying to understand what could constitute a realistic cosmopolitan community around a cause.

A productive public is, first of all, productive meaning that it is part of participatory cultures involved in destabilising the relationships between consumption and production as well as between usage and production. Second, it is a public, not a crowd and not a community. A community is a tight-knit group of people kept together through face-to-face interaction, often on common territory; a public is a 'mediated association among strangers that is directed towards the pursuit of a "common thing". Publics are thus weaker forms of association than communities, in the sense that they can involve a larger range of actors in weaker ways' (Arvidsson and Peitersen, 2013: 54–55). Productive publics seem to realise the complete fusion of market and culture as these publics often emerge around a brand, but they are less easy to control because they represent an emergent 'third' modality of value creation, for example ethical capital beyond the direct control of markets (Arvidsson and Peitersen, 2013: 55).

The ethical economy, according to Arvidsson and Peitersen, is often performed by a productive public around a common ethos that realises the good life in the Aristotelian sense, practices affective closeness and trust amongst strangers, is open and inclusive, and has generalised measures recognised by the participants in the productive public in question. Ethical capital is able to support shared conventions about the nature of reality (it puts forward an argument about a topic) and is able to support the charisma whereby an organisation or a public can attract 'free labour' and other 'gifts' from its members, as well as from the public at large (Arvidsson and Peitersen, 2013: 102). Charitable causes thus make productive publics with ethical capital if they are charismatic or seductive and provide the members with a common purpose and direction.

'WHEN MUM IS MISSING'

Mediated charity peaks in Denmark in the yearly donation event called Danmarks Indsamlingen (DI), which is broadcast on the public service channel DR1. This annual event has been running since 2007, but the phenomenon of donation shows began as early as 1957 with a series of three shows titled

Entertainment for Millions, The Hungarian Fundraising Campaign, which were hosted by a well-known Danish show-biz celebrity. These early Friday or Saturday night events mobilised audiences through the combination of three strategies: celebrity endorsement (artists perform for free, celebrity hosts add glamour to the show); diverse entertainment features; and the visible display of donations from companies, organisations, NGOs, and private individuals. In media scholarship *Entertainment for Millions* is widely recognised as the event that marked the birth of Danish television culture. These events are (and were) both live and extremely ritualised, as well as being created with the intention of capturing the attention of large audiences (Dayan and Katz, 1992: 8). Using Dayan and Katz's (1992) genre distinctions to label various media events—'contest', 'conquest', and 'coronation' which relate to Weber's three types of authority: rationality, charisma, and tradition—we can say that Danish television culture started out with the contest as a main script. This contest was both between donors and donor countries, as Denmark competed against the other Scandinavian countries to see which country could raise the largest amount of money.

The national campaign and donation show on Danish Television in 2014 had the theme 'When Mum is Missing' and collected 87,414,404 DKK for various global projects (Figure 3.1). It is interesting to observe that contemporary broadcast charity events still have the same elements as those held in the 1950s, only the announcers and guests tend to be more outspoken. The contest is not only a genre characteristic but also a highly visible feature in the content of contemporary donation shows: There are lotteries, celebrities compete against each other to attract the most donors, and there are

Figure 3.1   Screenshot from www.dr.dk of the 2014 show with boarding school students in front

sporting competitions between amateurs and professionals (a recent example involved professional football celebrities competing against African lay football players in a dribbling competition that used a special 'local' soft ball, which clearly gave an advantage to the donee players). There are also competitions between specific volunteering groups who have committed themselves to raise money: primary schools, boarding schools, Boy Scout organisations, workplaces, and so on. The mixture of commercial interests and humanitarian aid that started out as a daring one-off experiment in 1957, when commercial placements were banned on public TV and radio, has now become the rule with a constant stream of private companies' names appearing during the whole event.

Social media are also increasingly supplementing flow media campaigns in order to mobilise younger generations, for example by letting them produce audiovisual material on social media platforms like YouTube. In 2014, all pupils at Danish boarding schools were invited to self-organise and compete to see who could raise the most money for the causes being promoted by the annual broadcast charity donation show. The pupils invested time and energy in their promotions, which included various kinds of video presentations, and thus took a first step into a type of self-organised charity work that takes charity off-stage and places it centrally in the lives of the pupils.

During the 2014 DR1 show more than 1,200 YouTube clips were produced. Some of the videos were official statements and functioned as marketing for the show itself, for example the visit of Denmark's Crown Princess Mary to Myanmar. This set the scene for the 2014 theme 'When Mum Is Missing'. Other clips included footage of a couple collecting the prize of two minutes' free 'shopping' in a supermarket. Then there were the boarding school students' video productions designed to encourage the audiences to donate and participate. Regardless of the official status, the aim of all the clips is to get people to mobilise around charity. Or, in other words, it is the attempt of the already seduced to seduce others to relate to and act on the cause.

The top 20 most viewed clips on YouTube that relate to this event provide insight into mobilisation strategies around charity issues, both from the perspective of the official media and contributors such as the boarding school students who were involved in raising money for 'When Mum Is Missing'. The two main strategies used by the official media are first to encourage consumption impulses: either ethical consumption by supporting the companies having specific corporate social responsibility strategies around DI, for example the jewellery brand Pandora and Coop, the largest retail association in Denmark that accounts for 42 per cent of all retail sales, or participation in lotteries and other contests associated with the event through the display of prizes. Second, the event uses celebrity endorsement whose humanitarian performances Chouliaraki investigates through the concepts of persona (the construction of an authentic public self) and personification (strategies of witnessing more or less emotional; Chouliaraki, 2013: 90).

The celebrity endorsement in DI is of a different kind that, to a higher degree, responds to the seduction and the challenge that charity poses to the fortunate. The celebrities—in this case, national TV and radio hosts, actors, and sports celebrities—are asked to produce/do something out of their comfort zone: play the guitar and sing a song (off-key), play a well-known television series signature tune on flute (without any skills in that kind of musical performance). Others must take up direct bodily challenges such as eating very hot chilli or strangely composed food live on screen. We find it interesting that the celebrities are asked to sacrifice their well-being momentarily—and thus in some sense, briefly, replace the distant sufferers as the mediated object of pity and vulnerability. The affective mobilisation strategy works by creating scenarios where the celebrities' bodies are momentarily vulnerable and put at risk. The donors' responses to the seduction of the unfortunate bodies are a symbolic exchange that also involves the donors' bodies.

So, returning to the boarding school students, how did they seduce and produce charisma around the campaign 'When Mum Is Missing'? Their primary response was to produce and upload a video on YouTube in order to mobilise others. Their secondary response was to self-organise to raise money in their local communities by mobilising various stakeholders to the cause: getting sponsors, engaging local companies and shops in order to collect prizes for lotteries; having celebrities give concerts/performances for free; asking local sports clubs, parents, and students at other educational establishments to do fundraising; and so on. A productive public, such as a local boarding school that is engaged in raising money for the campaign 'When Mum Is Missing', thus seems to be a highly charismatic and authentic public for local stakeholders to rely on. Also, through sharing their experiences of creating productive local publics, the boarding schools were able to form a mediated community.

When we look at the content of the clips produced by these schools, we can divide their affective mobilisation strategies into two. Many clips evoke the *sympathetic imagination* (the *feeling like*) by mirroring the vulnerability any child or young person would feel if his or her mum were missing. This happens either through staged narrative scenes with sad youngsters who have lost their mother, with depictions of what one would miss if mum were not there (someone who helps clean up and wash clothes, is there when you want to talk about intimate issues, helps organise the social calendar, etc.; Figure 3.2). These scenarios all focus on the donor and on how he or she would feel if his or her mum were missing. This is supposed to create an affective experience of sameness with the vulnerable bodies in order to elicit a donor response.

The second strategy used in many clips is one of *contagion*. This took various forms, for example one group of students made a meta-video that demonstrated how to make a YouTube clip that motivated people to give to charity, whereas other groups made a direct request for donations: 'Do like us, support Danmarks Indsamlingen, send an SMS now'. There were also

Figure 3.2   Screenshot from YouTube video by pupils from Bøvling Boarding School

less narrative forms that relied on generating enthusiasm and energy. For example, Oure boarding school's video showed a group of students performing an African-style dance. The clip came across as kind of messy and amateurish, which gave the video its authentic appeal. Vesterdal boarding school made a black-and-white audiovisual message with quickly changing clips of young people gathered in an assembly hall doing gymnastics and hugging. A short textual message that read 'More ready than ever is Vesterdal boarding school to support DI' cut through the images. The clip played out to a soundtrack of movie music that had been played in front of an excited live audience. For the 2012/2013 event, Skals boarding school used a war metaphor to represent the students' way of taking up the challenge and responding to the seduction of the unfortunate others (Figure 3.3). For this clip the students dressed in camouflage uniforms and were filmed crawling through mud, wading through water, and jumping over fire as they fought their way towards the collecting box, gathering a whole army of collectors along the way. The soundtrack to this clip built up to a dramatic crescendo; the drums and strings played faster as the choir got louder and louder.

All the previously mentioned strategies—both online and offline—count as productions of productive publics working around a common charity cause. When we look at the boarding school students' efforts it is quite substantial in terms of the self-organisation, creativity, and energy put into the projects. Their responses to the seduction of the unfortunate others, however, hardly refer directly to vulnerability as a mobilising tool, and in this case the students efforts do not result in a closer relationship between donors and donees. This kind of relationship is, however, evident in our second case.

Figure 3.3   Screenshot from YouTube video by pupils from Skals Boarding School

MUSIC OPPORTUNITIES IN KIBERA

We now look at a project that was set up to send a mixture of new, used, and discarded musical instruments to Kibera, one of the largest slum areas outside Nairobi in Kenya. In this case the donors are more involved both in the mobilising and the implementing processes, which makes the donation appear more as volunteering for a worthy cause than simply donating to it. In this case the project organisers set out to mobilise and engage citizens through a focus on the global distribution of vulnerability, rather than harnessing images and texts related to specific vulnerable unfortunate bodies as mobilisers. Here we use the concepts of seduction and assemblage to characterise how charity establishes new constellations of humans, technologies, materiality, and nature that change both donors and donees.

As mentioned in the previous chapter the parts of an assemblage have independent properties and the assemblage, as a whole, is more than its constituent parts (DeLanda, 2006; Anderson et al., 2012). The concept originates in Gilles Deleuze's outline of what he calls the smallest unit capable of agency (Deleuze and Parnet, 1996: 65), namely the 'agencement', translated as assemblage. One meaning of assemblage is to be positioned in the middle of an emergent world, a world that develops through the arrangement and linkage of various heterogeneous elements (Deleuze and Parnet, 1996: 66). In the beginning 'assemblage' was not a concept or an enunciation but a relationship. What the 'assembler or the assemblage' does is to create a (new) world in which the relationships are not ones of identification or separation (proximity or distance) but of pure difference held together by sympathy between the constituent elements.

The crucial feature that Deleuze draws from Spinoza's ethics is the felt presence of future possibilities. The well-known Spinozean ethical-affective law is formulated as the following: 'The affects signal becoming: sometimes they [the affects] weaken us to the extent they diminish our ability to act and decompose our relations (sadness), sometimes they strengthen us to the extent they empower us and make us become a more far-reaching, inclusive and superior individual' (Deleuze and Parnet, 1996: 74).[2] The important thing here is that the affects point to the virtual in the actual as a moment of becoming that could happen, but does not have to happen. The affects thus are bearers of possible new futures. Two other characteristics of assemblages are especially important, one being that new assemblages only succeed if the social machine at stake is able to incorporate them (an assemblage is never only technological) and the other being that the relations in an assemblage are not strong ties, relations of kinship, and descent but weaker relations of connections, alliances, and acquaintances tied together by contagion and epidemics (Deleuze and Parnet, 1996: 84). The relationship between a vulnerable unfortunate body and a morally obliged fortunate subject is thus replaced by a relationship of seduction between the donor and the donee and by a more reversible relationship in which new bodies develop and new capacities see the light of day as a result of new assemblages between the allied.

Let us thus imagine the charity process in two steps:

1. Seduction: to mobilise donors' bodies to engage and invest in the charity relation. The seducer obliges the seduced to put down a higher stake, to invest even deeper. The tool of seduction is enterprising behaviour, vitality, and future change for the better within reach. The unfortunate other is no longer depicted as a vulnerable dying or suffering body, a victim of inequality, even though that may still be the case, but as possibilities of new assemblages disclosing worlds yet to come. The relationship between the donee and the donor is not a relationship of identification or of possession but one of sympathy meaning a body-to-body-relation that increases the vitality capacities in anybody (Deleuze and Parnet, 1996: 67).
2. Empowerment: to increase the active power in the other's body and to unleash the creative active emotion of joy in the other's body, in order for him or her to imagine and build other worlds. The empowering of the others' bodies is unleashing my own opportunities. I, for my part, also feel empowered because I enjoy having impact directly and visibly on the world as my deed realises a utopia in the here and now. The utopian moment in the here and now that the charity relation realises is the hope for change, opportunities, and new exchanges between donors and donees.

'I feel frustrated because I am always asked to support this and that and play at this and that and then we were a team who talked about the fact that it would be funnier to do something that we could actually follow, be a part of while building on the relations and network we already had' (Festival TV: 00:00–00:40). Danish musician Poul Krebs here implicitly expresses the desire to go beyond the Live Aid concert format. Live Aid, which took place on 13 July 1985 in London and Philadelphia, is still considered the most successful fundraising event in history. The strap line for the all-day stadium concerts, which were the brainchild of Irish singer/songwriter Bob Geldof, was 'The Day the Music Changed the World'. In total, 58 acts played 16 hours of music to live audiences totalling 170,000 and a worldwide television audience of more than 2 billion. The event raised an unprecedented, and not yet surpassed, 150 million UK pounds, which went to help victims of the Ethiopian famine in 1984–1985.

The case in question relates to an idea that was born at the much smaller Danish music event—SMUKFEST—in 2011. Some of the concertgoers and musicians felt that it would be a good idea to send unwanted musical instruments, amplifiers, microphones, soundboards, sound test kits, and so on to Kibera, one of the worlds' largest slum areas located on the outskirts of Nairobi in Kenya. The hope was that these donations could help nurture emerging musical talents in the area, where there were many humans and few material resources This case serves as a good example of the productive shift in charity, where donors move away from charitable models that rely on monetary donations to help regulate unequal resource distribution, to a situation in which the empowerment develops through a mutually energising encounter.

The donors in this case are composed of a heterogeneous group of public institutions, NGOs, and small to medium enterprises (SMEs): Danish Center for Culture and Development, a self-governing institution under the Danish Ministry of Foreign Affairs that manages culture and development programmes in the Middle East, Asia, West Africa, and East Africa; Sustainable Energy, a member-based NGO with activities in Denmark and developing countries that is working towards a sustainable world; The Boarding School of Oure Sport & Performance; Wasabi Film, a Danish film production company that makes trailers for The Skanderborg Musical festival; and Globetown, a network-based NGO that includes musician Poul Krebs among its founders. Krebs is also the principal organiser of the gear project to Kibera; Acoustics, a guitar shop selling both new and used guitars; and 4Sound, a web-based musical instruments shop. Finally, the festival audience at the Skanderborg Music festival in 2011 could contribute by donating the deposit from their returnable empty cans and bottles. The Kibera project could be seen as part of the corporate social responsibility of this small Danish music festival, and the Globetown and Culture Connect NGOs.

The donee is Kibera—a slum area outside Nairobi with a population of 1.5 million people. Already a wide variety of projects is operating in this area. For instance the Kibera public space project 'ARCHETICTUREAU'[3] the project 'Young-gifted-and-black' (YGB) that works with talented citizens in Kibera to help them in their art forms and to develop ways to participate in sustainable development in Kibera, and 'Culture Connect', which is a NGO that specialises in music and in Kibera aims to arrange encounters between the up-and-coming talent and established Kenyan instrumentalists, sound engineers, and producers, in order to promote sharing and learning.

CAPACITIES OF ASSEMBLAGES

We divide the analysis of the Kibera charity project as an assemblage into three parts: The first part looks at how the social actors themselves *frame* the project, the second part investigates the project as a *charity process* rather than a charity project, and the third part takes care of the *long-term impact* and capacities of the gear project.

The gear project started out as the managing director of Culture Connect's dream. He wrote, 'My dream is to establish 10 rehearsal rooms, a sound studio living up to international standards, an instrument repair shop, and to offer integrated music education for young musicians' (Musikeren, 2011: 23). Obviously the gear project is a response to the lack of instruments and music opportunities in Kibera, and the attraction and seduction for the donors is to broaden the global professional network of musicians. The gear project makes a donation in the form of used music related materials and it is debatable from the outset whether this can actually be considered charity. Abbi Nyianza, a famous Kenyan singer on the Afro-fusion scene who has just opened a studio and a production house, INDIGO CREATIONS, in the Nairobi suburbs, frames the project as charity with an important impact: 'It's charity, so we are doing it for Kenyan children, so that they may dream bigger dreams, find the belief that they can do this, they can grow, they can become whatever they want to become' (Abbi Nyinza in Festival TV: 1:11). Danish musician Poul Krebs frames it differently: 'It's not charity, but cooperation and cultural exchanges . . . we say: we would like to play with you. That requires instruments, so let's set about that as the first thing' (Musikeren, 2011: 23). Instead of donating money directly, the gear project stems from the will to enlarge the interests of a professional group that importantly is not a governmental institution but a small NGO providing self-organised charity. From the perspective of the donee youngsters, the project provides an opportunity to be a pattern breaker and do something else than gather old iron. From the perspective of the donors, the prospect of new global musical exchanges and projects of cooperation appear to be the main motivator.

Musician Thomas Menzer describes his motivations and expectations in terms of affects, both in content and form (what DeLanda calls the expressive role of assemblages): 'I am very busy with this festival [Good

Governance festival in December 2012]. But I am pretty sure that it will hit me like a hammer when I am staying there at the new place and we have people in the rehearsal room, in the studio and on stage. It's . . . we come closer . . . [his face lights up in a big smile] It's good. It's really good [he chuckles]' (Festival TV: 7:56–8:14). The affective reward that he achieves by the imaginary prospect of a possible future is expressed by his body language (big smile and his chuckling) and by the way he pauses and stops the flow of speech when he has to communicate the feeling of vitality that this project obviously gives him.

The second feature of the assemblage focuses on processes (history, labour, materiality, and performance) instead of just describing a network of relations. The gear project started out in 2011 and the first fruits of this initiative were put on show at the Good Governance Festival in Kibera in December 2012. The initiator of Globetown, musician Poul Krebs insists that this project is different to donation concerts where musicians just stand up and play for good causes. 'We are going down there and we continue the cooperation, we follow that container nothing like just playing and then moving on' (Festival TV: 0:26). The possibility of a longer lasting, and thus more sustainable, impact appears to lie in the fact that the charity gift is material and may be used to create new assemblages: 'It is moving; this long journey, from the first idea to establishing a music venue, we wanted to create a process and we knew the receivers and we knew the gear' (Kulturnyt P1, 11 March 2014).

Manuel DeLanda (2006: 12) refers to processes of territorialisation and deterritorialisation that either stabilise or destabilise the identity of an assemblage. Processes of territorialisation could either happen spatially to define and sharpen spatial boundaries of actual territories, or could refer to non-spatial processes that increase the internal homogeneity of an assemblage. Processes of deterritorialisation, on the contrary, are processes that destabilise spatial boundaries or increase internal heterogeneity in assemblages (DeLanda, 2006: 13). The gear project that ships used musical instruments, amplifiers, microphones, soundboards, and sound test equipment from an environment of abundance to an environment of shortage presents an assemblage of these contrasting cultural and social contexts. Menzer states that '[n]othing less than a revolution for the Kenyan and the East-African music scene, there is nothing close to it' (Musikeren, 2011: 23) and '[d]own there [in Kibera] there is nothing, we talk year 0' (Festival TV: 2:27). Having the ability to foster new assemblages, the music gear project, on one hand, exemplifies not only how components in the assemblage, the material music gear, stay the same while moving from one social context to another but also how they transform in the destination context. The music gear that in a Danish context appears slightly used, a bit old-fashioned, vintage, and not up-to-date gains a new significance when it is introduced into Kibera. The gear project recycles well-functioning instruments and thus takes care of abundance in rich Western societies while in the destination they become new magic totems once attached to a musician: 'It is astonishing to see how the musicians feel overwhelmed when they just can turn up the sound and it still sounds fantastic. As one said: We have to stop looking at the instruments and listening to what we are doing' (Festival TV: 6:20).

The old instruments are re-vitalised for the local musicians because of the lack of instruments in their environment; the gear is re-enchanted in the new context; and it is re-energised through its links with celebrities, as we noted in the introduction. The prestige possessed by the musicians Wafande, Pharfar (a well-known Danish rapper who plays drums) and by Juliani re-vitalised the instruments when they played at the Good Governance Festival held in Kibera in December 2012, and thus, it became part of the assemblage, transforming the music gear into immaterial music, the very expression of sympathy in the new assemblage. (See Figure 3.4.) The music gear has a long history and seems to 'contaminate' the new contexts with the positivity of its old successes.

The Kibera music project seems to deterritorialise otherwise stable assemblages: the live-music scene in Denmark and the live-music scene in Kenya. The new assemblage that the music gear project creates is really heterogeneous and hybrid. The ethnic amalgams, mobility, and flows around the project are salient. Ethnic Danish musicians based in Denmark (Pharfar, Poul Krebs) relate with ethnic Danish musicians based in Kenya (Thomas Menzer and Mzungu Kicha aka Espen Sørensen), ethnic Kenyan and Tanzanian musicians living in Denmark (Wafande, Abbi Nyinza), and, of course,

Figure 3.4 Screenshot from a YouTube video showing Wafande, Pharphar, and local musicians at the Good Governance Festival in Kibera 2012

Kenyan-based celebrities (Juliani) and celebrities to be (Vicmass, a local talent from Kibera who attended a workshop in 2012 in Kibera).

In the Kenyan context, the music gear has properties and a history that are important in order to understand its value: It has a history in Danish music scenes, rehearsal rooms, and studios, and as such, it represents a long history of music culture, it is recognisable by Danish musicians, and it serves as mediator of the Danish–Kenyan music assemblage that this charity project tries to create. The charity assemblage thus has the capacity to deterritorialise national assemblages and create trans-local assemblages (McFarlane, 2009)—even though at first sight it may seem like yet another bilateral cooperation. As one of the main attractors in this project is literally to realise a version of the virtual potential in the other, to literally witness the emergence of a music scene because of the materiality in the form of music gear inserted into the environment, the driver is the affect of vitality that this induces: To empower the other and support the ability to self-organise if the material ground is seeded. Of course, this is also an opportunity to exert influence on the future music scene in Kenya. Because this project first and foremost supports live music, it poses a challenge to digitally produced music, for example rap and hip-hop, but it builds on the strong talent of percussionists in Kenya and traditional ways of producing rhythms. This charity project thus has the capacity to support a development that connects with the musical cultural heritage in sustainable ways.

CONCLUSION

To sum up this chapter, we have argued that the field of charity has changed with a switch to projects that demand bodily investment; emphasise (creative) labour, in for example productive publics; and encourage long-term relationships from donors—even if the end result is a monetary donation. In this sense, the tendency can be seen as a reaction against the dangers of short-term charity. Global inequality, and the vulnerabilities it distributes unevenly across bodies, is present in the cases as a permanent challenge to how one can respond by acts of production. We have introduced the concept of seduction in order to understand the relationship between the donor and the donee. This concept can be seen at play in our case studies: in the first instance in the creation of productive publics around a certain charity issue. Here citizens are engaged in *producing* their responses and seducing new donors to get involved. In the second case, seduction plays a part in the creation of new material-expressive assemblages and constellations of sympathy that open the way for alternative futures.

The cases we have investigated have relatively concrete positive effects. The boarding school students collected 976,219 DKK (130,000 euros), and Skals Boarding School won the competition for the fifth time in a row with its collection of 200,000 DKK. The YouTube clips are also often incorporated in the schools' knowledge creation activities and provide the stakeholders with practice of high-level project management. Although the Kibera project is small, it nonetheless offers new opportunities for a materially poor region in East Africa. The actual impact of the gear project includes the running of workshops with Pharfar, Juliani, and Vicmass and a new annual music festival titled the Good Governance Festival. The festival, which has both musical and political aspects, connects the Danish and the Kenyan music scenes, and in the run-up to the general election in Kenya in March 2013 it became a commemoration of the events that surrounded the presidential election in 2007, which included violent outbursts that left 1,200 people dead and led to the prosecution of prominent Kenyan political figures by the International Criminal Court. Thus, the Good Governance Festivals' specialty is that it has a Danish touch strengthening the bilateral relations between the two musical and political cultures. At the time of this writing, 40 live concerts have taken place as part of the Kibera project, and 350 musicians have used the instruments in order to play gigs and earn money. The project has also helped to build a new music venue with a capacity of 300 to 500, which runs weekly gigs on a Thursday night. Previously, Nairobi only had one smaller venue that could hold up to 100 attendees. Through the project the discarded Danish music gear has been transformed into a common, shared resource that needs care and maintenance. In- and out-lists are used to access the gear, and as of March 2014 it was still intact (Kulturnyt P1, 11 March 2014). Another long-term effect of the project is that Danish musician Poul Krebs now co-operates with a Kenyan female poet, actress, singer, guitarist, and composer Lydiah Dola. Poul has helped Lydiah launch herself on the Kenyan music scene with newly written songs about the Kenyan day of independence. They have also begun to compose songs together. Other trans-local results have occurred: Mzungu Kicha aka Espen Sørensen's song 'Jitolee' has been a hit in East Africa as well as the hit 'Better than Them', performed by late Danish/Jamaican singer/writer Natasja together with Jamaican star Beenie Man and produced by Danish rapper Pharfar, who apparently has gained a musical reputation in Kenya. The music gear assembles musicians from the whole of East Africa and Denmark, and it assembles territories that are both spatially and symbolically very distant from one another (a rich society of abundance and a suburban slum). The charity project initiates a process of mobility from one context to another that gives emergence to new assemblages of landscapes, musicians, sounds, and sights. The instruments not only become part of new assemblages; they also make musicians and these musicians have a space for cultural expression that can attract larger audiences.

The productive turn in charity clearly stresses an active attitude in contrast to a more passive beholder attitude; however, the accusations of narcissism that are levelled at all forms of charity are not refuted once and for all by the productive turn. But it is nonetheless plausible to argue that the self-organised projects that the fortunate take part in over a longer period stand a stronger chance of becoming a part of a more longitudinal mind-set and behaviour change in the people involved than do models that prioritise financial giving. It could be argued that in the new model the voice of the unfortunate other is heard and seen less than in former spectacles of suffering, and that is a plausible risk. But it is also hoped that the seductive virtuality that the unfortunate presents is a strong enough voice to let those from the majority world be heard.

NOTES

1. Our English translation of 'C'est par notre fragility que nous séduisons, jamais par des pouvoirs ou des signes forts'.
2. Our English translation of 'Les affects sont des devenirs: tantôt ils [les affects] nous affaiblissent pour autant qu'ils diminuent notre puissance d'agir, et décomposent nos rapports (tristesse), tantôt nous rendent plus fort en tant qu'ils augmentent notre puissance et nous font entrer dans un individu plus vaste ou supérieur (joie)'.
3. http://architectureau.com/articles/kibera-public-space-project/ (accessed 19 June 2014).

REFERENCES

ANDERSON, B., KEARNES, M., McFARLANE, C. & SWANTON, D. 2012. On Assemblages and Geography. *Dialogues in Human Geography*, 2, 171–189.

ANDERSON, S. E. & STAGE, C. 2010. Comsumption That Matters. *MedieKultur, Journal of Media and Communication Research*, 49, 151–170.

ARVIDSSON, A. & PEITERSEN, N. 2013, *The Ethical Economy: Rebuilding Value after the Crisis*, New York, Columbia University Press.

BAUDRILLARD, J. 1979, *De la Seduction*, Paris, Denoël/Gonthier.

BECK, U. 2006, *Cosmopolitan Vision*, Cambridge, Polity Press.

BOLTANSKI, L 1999, *Distant Suffering, Morality, Media and Politics*, Cambridge, Cambridge University Press.

BRUNS, A. 2008. The Future Is User-Led: The Path towards Widespread Produsage. *Fibreculture* [Online], 11. http://eleven.fibreculturejournal.org/fcj-066-the-future-is-user-led-the-path-towards-widespread-produsage/ [Accessed 20 June 2011].

CHOULIARAKI, L. 2006. *The Spectatorship of Suffering*, London, Sage.

CHOULIARAKI, L. 2013. *The Ironic Spectator, Solidarity in the Age of Post-Humanitarianism*, Cambridge, UK; Malden, MA, Polity Press.

DAYAN, D. and KATZ, E. 1992, *Media Events: The Live Broadcasting of History*, Cambridge, MA, Harvard University Press.

DELANDA, M. 2006. *A New Philosophy of Society, Assemblage Theory and Social Complexity*, London, Continuum.

DELEUZE, G. & PARNET, C. 1996. *Dialogues*, Paris, Champs Essais.

ELLIS, J. 2000. *Seeing Things: Television in the Age of Uncertainty*, London, I.B. Tauris.

GIBSON-GRAHAM, J.K., CAMERON, J, & HEALY, S. 2013. *Take Back the Economy, An Ethical Guide for Transforming our Communities*, Minneapolis, University of Minnesota Press.

GUINEY, T. 2012. 'Orphanage Tourism' in Cambodia. When Residential Care Centres Become Tourist Attractions. *Pacific News*, 38 (July/August), 9–14.
MOSTAFANEZHAD, M. 2013. The Politics of Aesthetics in Volunteer Tourism. *Annals of Tourism Research*, 43, 150–169.
McFARLANE, C. 2009. Translocal Assemblages: Space, Power and Social Movements, *Geoforum*, 40(4), 561–567.
PROTEVI, J. 2009. *Political Affect, Connecting the Social and the Somatic*, Minneapolis, University of Minnesota Press.
RICHEY, L.A. & PONTE, S. 2011. *Brand Aid, Shopping Well to Save the World*, Minneapolis, University of Minnesota Press.
RIFKIN, J. 2009. *The Empathic Civilization. The Race to Global Consciousness in a World in Crisis*, Cambridge, Polity.
SILVERSTONE, R. 2007. *Media and Morality, On the Rise of the Mediapolis*, Cambridge, Polity Press.
SPINOZA, B. de [1678] 1997. *Ethics Part III. On the Origin and Nature of Emotions*, The Project Gutenberg Etext of the Ethics. Available at: http://www.gutenberg.org/dirs/etext97/3spne10.txt [Accessed 1 May 2010].
TOMLINSON, J. 1999. *Globalization and Culture*, Cambridge, Polity.
WEISSMAN, G. 2004. *Fantasies of Witnessing, Postwar Efforts to Experience the Holocaust*, Ithaca, Cornell University Press.

Magazines

Musikeren. Fagbladet for Professionelle Musikere. 2011, Nr. 9 (September), 20–24.

Websites

FestivalTV: Smukfest. 2014. www.smukfest.dk/content.asp?id1=227&id2=640&id3=0&id4=0
Culture Connect: www.cultureconnect.co/Home.html
Globetown: www.globetown.dk/

TV

DI 2014, When Mum Is Missing, 1 February, on DR1, 20:00–24:00.

Radio

Kulturnyt P1, 28 November 2013.
Kulturnyt P1, 11 March 2014.

4 Green Activist Bodies and the Sublime

In this chapter we investigate and discuss activists' embodied responses to what they perceive as the capitalist exploitation of nature. Vulnerability is here turned into a self-inflicted condition used to attract attention and highlight the need for immediate action and affective engagement in sustainability issues. Our focus is on mediated vulnerability as a strategically produced activist—soft power and biopolitical—tactic in contrast to the bodily vulnerabilities discussed in the previous chapters, that are beyond the control of the inflicted person (illness, political violence, global inequality).

Among the most well-known activist examples of mediated vulnerability are FEMEN (originally set up in the Ukraine), which fights the patriarchal oppression of women with naked 'sextremist' performances; the Russian group Pussy Riot famous for their criticism of the alliance between the church and Vladimir Putin (e.g. in their activist event in the Cathedral of Christ the Savior in Moscow in 2012); and the Russian activist Petr Pavlensky, who has staged radical body-events involving constraint (e.g. wrapping himself in barbed wire in front of government buildings in Russia, lip-sewing to support Pussy Riot, nailing his scrotum to Red Square) to highlight the apathy and the limited forms of citizenship in contemporary Russia. What unites these activist performances—besides their regional proximity—is their staging of civil disobedience, or biopolitical protest, at iconic sites that symbolise state authority, and their use of bodily vulnerability (shown by manipulation of their own bodies or by placing their bodies in confrontation with the authorities) in media spectacles.

In the movement's manifesto FEMEN declares, 'In the beginning was the body, the sensation the woman has of her own body, the joy of its lightness and freedom. Then came injustice, so harsh that it is felt with the body; injustice deprives the body of its mobility, paralyses its movements, and soon you are hostage to that injustice. Then you push your body into battle against injustice, mobilizing each cell for the war against the world of patriarchy and humiliation' (FEMEN and Ackerman, 2014: vii). The quote exemplifies how the body in these kinds of activism is often conceptualised as a trans-human commonality, as an ideal of freedom, as an object of political control and biopower, and as a biopolitical weapon of resistance and counter-mobilisation. In this way the body is something all humans have, something to protect, something being hijacked, and something that can be used to avoid or counter further hijacking.

The potential for resistance is certainly related to the ability to attune audiences through mediated vulnerability and to stimulate viral dissemination of pictures and narratives. In these types of activism bodily vulnerability is used to engage publics affectively in forms of victimhood somehow implicitly affirmed or narrated, or even re-enacted, through the activist performance. This kind of manufactured vulnerability (Doherty, 2000) simply presents, relives, or incarnates existing or predicted processes of suffering and victimisation (e.g. of women, citizens, animals, nature). The activist body becomes a 'flesh tool' that can be used to connect bodies that may not be in tune with global publics to localised and victimised bodies in need of empathy and political action. In this way, as outlined earlier, the body is used as a soft power or biopolitical medium that immaterially relates non-victimised bodies to proclaimed less fortunate bodies (of all kinds) via mediated images and spectacles of vulnerability.

The staged character and strategic use of vulnerability and the contexts of its appearance often make such events more contested and conflictual than does the material in the previous chapters. It is easier to reject or criticise when challenged to engage by activists whose vulnerability is exposed through self-inflicted acts. Furthermore, body activists often attack existing authorities in ways that produce more affective ambivalences due to the various political discourses already present in the context (e.g. sustainability discourses vs. liberalist discourses or left wing discourses vs. conservative/religious discourses). In this way the power of vulnerability is not necessarily to unite but, rather, to attune—that is to force viewers to relate to a certain issue in their own way (Knudsen and Stage, 2012).

We analyse two cases—one from the US and one from Australia—in which climate activists manufacture and stage their bodily vulnerability as a political weapon in the fight to elicit adequate political responses. Our interest in these cases is threefold: first, to understand how the particular strategy discussed deploys human vulnerability; second, to investigate how the biopolitical strategy circulates in the media context of the activist performance; and, third, to discuss the potential for a strategy of vulnerability to put environmental issues on the agenda and to mobilise citizens around environmental challenges. These performances differ from the abovementioned examples from Ukraine and Russia by using human vulnerability to mediate nature's suffering, and they also highlight the interdependency between these vulnerabilities: Humans are also part of nature, and if nature dies, so do humans. In this way the green body activists in this chapter take a more posthuman approach to the body than FEMEN, Pussy Riot, or Pavlensky, because it is not the human body that is important in itself but, rather, its position as 'a piece of nature' that will eventually suffer if non-human nature is exploited and polluted. The strategies are very similar (creating mediatised, biopolitical spectacles), but the aims are different (human rights/equality vs. acknowledgement of post-human responsibilities). The human body is thus not used to affirm the rights of humans facing oppressive states in our cases but, rather, the rights of nature facing oppressive, rationalist humanity. In this sense the vulnerability of the human body is to some extent used against humanity itself (cf. the criticism of the effects of human intervention in nature), as well as to deconstruct the rationalist idea of humans as 'something other than nature'.

We argue that the activists' manufactured vulnerability seems to consist of both a staging on the activists' bodies of a virtual disaster that could occur sometime in the future, and the mediation of nature suffering now. Finally it is discussed whether contemporary activism should be evaluated according to its ability to build institutions or its facility to create 'breaking visual events' that disseminate and circulate on various platforms and are able to evoke political enthusiasm and create new belongings through excessive visual repertoire. Linked to the outlined normative questions, the chapter also considers whether in some circumstances the activists run the risk of reproducing inadequate cultural patterns through depoliticising sustainability discourses.

METHODOLOGY

Our empirical material consists of two cases in which the environmental activists stage their bodies as part of a mediatised and affective tactic. Our cases are (1) Julia Butterfly Hill's famous two-year tree-sit that began in 1997 with the aim of halting Pacific Lumber's felling of ancient redwoods in Northern California, in the US, and (2) the Weld Angel project, a 2007 artist-activist performance protesting the logging of old-growth forests in Weld Valley, Tasmania, Australia. Both cases are analysed as expressions of 'vulnerable power', as described in the Introduction, and they are compared because—despite their common logic of bodily investment—they are quite different in terms of their use of media technologies, aesthetic-symbolic tools, and established contextual resources.

Our material is collected via a 'snowballing' strategy that began with a web search for YouTube clips. We searched channels and videos on You-Tube related to the two acclaimed protest events in order to get access to both the audiovisual dimension of the protests and to other types of responses (e.g. mainstream news media sequences and comments below the video). We also searched more widely online to find responses in forums, articles, or clips from mainstream media related to the cases and potential official sanctions (in terms of verdicts, agreements, etc.). During the process we focused on identifying patterns at both the level of the activists' performance and the wider culturally affective responses to these performances.

In processing this material we investigate the specific body-tactics used by the protesters by analysing their visual, audiovisual, and written self-presentations—taking a special interest in affective and bodily communication strategies—and on how these tactics are received in a wider cultural context: Do they attune other bodies in relation to the environmental cause, do they create attraction or repulsion at the level of discourse, and do they mobilise media attention and how? In other words, we analyse both on the level of content (how did the activists and respondents signify the events) and on an aesthetic-affective level by trying to tease out the various affective potentials of the body-events (how is the body involved in the performance, how is vulnerability staged and communicated). In this way, we attempt to track the cultural life of these activist bodies and to discuss on what levels (e.g. pragmatic, discursive, affective, or relational) the body-events are or are not effective.

THE ANTHROPOCENE AND ECOLOGICAL POST-HUMANISM

We understand the activist performances in this chapter as post-humanist responses to the era of 'the anthropocene'. The term *anthropocene* was coined by the chemist Paul J. Crutzen and biologist Eugene F. Stormer in 2000 and refers to a new era (following the 'Holocene') beginning in 'the latter part of the eighteenth century', when 'the global effects of human activities have become clearly noticeable' (Crutzen and Stoermer, 2000: 17). The anthropocene describes the époque when 'mankind's activities gradually grew into a significant geological, morphological force' because of the increasing size of the human population (a tenfold increase over three centuries) and processes of urbanisation and industrialisation. The anthropocene is defined by major environmental changes: The earth's fossil fuels will be exhausted in a few generations, 30 to 50 per cent of the land surface has been transformed by humans, 'greenhouse' gases and species extinction are increasing to mention just a few examples (Crutzen and Stoermer, 2000: 17). In other words, humankind has disturbed natural biological and climate processes to such a degree that it has started to produce its own, often dangerous and unsustainable, nature.

The activist performances investigated in this chapter are without doubt focused on the natural and human vulnerabilities created as a result of 'the anthropocene'. They acknowledge the fact that humans are destroying nature's own processes—and that the need to react is urgent, an urgency expressed through the investigation of grand spectacles of human endurance, will to change, danger, and sublimity. In this sense the activists seem to argue for a movement from a humanist to a post-humanist approach to nature and climate changes (Braidotti, 2013). According to Rosi Braidotti 'the post-human' is a concept that encompasses attempts to counter the arrogance of a human-centred perspective in which nature is often treated as a form of dumb matter that should be mastered to increase the well-being of humankind. The alternative 'proposes an enlarged sense of inter-connection between self and others, including the non-human or "earth" others, by removing the obstacle of self-centred individualism' (Braidotti, 2013: 49–50). Taking a post-human approach to the anthropocene would mean less of a focus on fulfilling human needs as a primary goal, and more emphasis on integrating humanity into the rest of the living world in a sustainable way that upholds and respects other forms of life and vitality. In this way, 'the post-human' also represents an ethical and normative turn with a focus on ascribing higher value to neglected agencies such as women, minorities, and nature.

Humanism, according to Braidotti, has fostered a range of relevant ideals—social justice, respect for human decency and diversity, positivity of difference, openness—which are also part of a post-human ethics. Subjectivity thus is still important as it shapes human actions, and Braidotti believes that a 'new generation of "knowing subjects"' is needed (Braidotti, 2013: 11). The post-humanist perspective argues in favour of 'a more complex and relational subject framed by embodiment, sexuality, affectivity, empathy and desire as core qualities' (Braidotti, 2013: 26). This new knowing subject could be a more ecologically reflexive subject who takes the interconnections between humans and non-humans as its point of departure. We follow in the footsteps of the embodied relational post-human subjectivity that Braidotti vouches for, but we disagree with her perception of the collective force of vulnerability as a 'reactive bond' (Braidotti, 2013: 50). We argue that activist stagings of vulnerability can promote this new post-human ethics, with its increased reflexivity and focus on interconnectedness. The use of staged vulnerability is designed both to show the human body's interdependence on its surroundings and to touch, fascinate, and puzzle the viewer and thus involve them in non-conscious ways.

CREATIVE ACTIVISM AND GLOBAL MEDIATION

Looking at recent academic work on protest movements and events, for instance the Occupy movement, the authors tend to stress how bodies, and their capacity to create events or new spaces of appearance (Porta, 2008; Butler, 2011), can become political tools by claiming (momentary) control over public spaces: 'The bodies on the street redeploy the space of appearance in order to contest and negate the existing forms of political legitimacy' in Judith Butler's words (Butler, 2011, 6). This is also the case in our empirical material, where activists seem to combine the traditional direct action strategy of civil disobedience by taking control over spaces without legal authority to do so, with the symbolic strategy of 'creative activism' focused on staging events aimed at creating media circulation and public response (Harrebye, 2011).

Silas Harrebye argues that civil society can be understood as a mediating space between the private sphere and the political system, and defines an activist as 'a non-profit-oriented, active citizen engaging socially in the civic sphere to change society for the better by communicating conflicts and/or solutions where no one else can or no one else does it. As such, civil society must be seen as having a critical mediating role between the privately atomized citizen and the public regulatory system—both due to its particular normative, organizational, and public possibilities and as a mediating platform for creative activists' (Harrebye, 2011: 411). This move from the private to the civil sphere—focused on creating social change—can be made in various ways and by using different kinds of strategies. Harrebye thus distinguishes between (1) the radical activist who uses violence and wants revolution, (2) the confrontational activist who uses non-violent civil disobedience to create transparency and openness, (3) the creative activist who makes innovative public spectacles to stimulate public reflection, (4) the professional activist who lobbies inside the political system to reform, (5) the occasional activist who participates in large scale demonstrations where the number of bodies present counts, and (6) the everyday maker who focuses on local and mundane solutions to challenges (Harrebye, 2011: 421). The activist performances explored in this chapter combine the strategy of civil disobedience (illegally occupying smaller areas in non-violent ways) with the strategy of creative activism, which is 'a civic, project-organized, active citizenship where critical perspectives on societal issues or a political system are communicated in imaginative ways through a strategic political happening' (Harrebye, 2011: 417).

Another reason for creating spectacles of vulnerability—besides making a specific political message about sustainability—is undoubtedly to set up pictures and narratives for the media (Hjarvard, 2008; Lester, 2010). Even though our activists protest via direct action at the scene of the crime, it is really the media exposure that attracts attention and the possibility of mobilising a broader public. How the media processes evolve—which stories are told in what way—is nevertheless not easy to predict. The interpretation of vulnerability depends greatly on its specific 'scene of enactment' (Anderson, 2010: 1), the narratives that the protesters tell, and the way in which audiences in various contextual settings understand and are affected by the performances. Also the varying historical contexts of the two cases under consideration mean that the activists have different possibilities and strategies in terms of motivating media attention.

Butterfly Hill's 1997 performance preceded the spread of user-generated social media platforms and subsequently was mostly designed to attract the attention of the mainstream news media and address their criteria for newsworthiness. Hill decided that an attempt to break the record for the longest tree sit would be newsworthy. The Weld Angel (2007), performed by Alana Beltran, could take advantage of the emerging participatory culture of social and DIY media (Jenkins, 2006; Kaplan and Haenlein, 2010; Knobel and

Lankshear, 2010; Gauntlett, 2011). In this instance the aim was to attract the mainstream media by first creating material that could be disseminated online via services such as YouTube. Despite these differences, the success of both actions depended on their ability to get media audiences switched on to their message in a short time, which meant the actions had to have an affective resonance or produce affective empowering encounters that transcended the action in question. Circulation of details of the activism in various media was essential if the activists were to lengthen the effect of their political activism. The question was whether people would act or react politically when looking at, partaking in, or commenting on these events.

SUBLIME BODY-EVENTS

The political activist strategy of performing events is a strategy of body-event-making. We define body-events as events that (1) circulate body imagery with high intensity and energy in the media, (2) transmit affects in various manners by producing encounters between bodies (e.g. to empower citizens to disseminate and create events), and (3) stage virtuality by making sensible the new, unseen, 'not yet', and possible via bodies. The protesters in our cases are moving politics outside of parliaments and away from the streets into the woods, staging moments of interruptions—in more or less successful ways—that aim to reconfigure the life we live together. Their strategy is sensuous-aesthetic. According to Panagia politics begins with the advenience of an appearance (2009: 153), a statement that intermingles political and sensual-aesthetical spheres in hitherto unseen ways. In this sense the green body activists try to awaken and 'sensitise' the receiver and thus focus on 'learning to be affected as an ethical practice' (Gibson-Graham and Roelvink, 2009: 325). This is done by using a form of inter-bodily communication that transmits a sense of urgency, a will to radical change, and an invitation to care both for the human body in peril and the nature, whose suffering the body translates into affective attunements. Para-doxically, the activists seem to start with the human body and not nature as a non-human actor in order to integrate it into a 'new body-world', where it is decentred by nature and technologies (Gibson-Graham and Roelvink, 2009: 322).

What our analysis adds to the existing literature is a more developed focus on the role of affective transmission and virtuality in the activist body-strategy's attempt to visualise something that is both here and not here yet. Other theorists have already argued that affect/emotion is an important part of activist protest events, but they primarily focus on how the protest event can boost emotional energy and solidarity among the activists themselves (Porta, 2008; Protevi, 2011). We would argue that the use of bodily vulnerability is also an attempt to deploy affective processes that engage both the media and external receivers via body-to-body transmissions, or minimal/

non-conscious communications (Despret, 2004; Blackman, 2012), of enthusiasm and urgency (Knudsen and Stage, 2012).

The overall protest message in our cases seems to be that (1) a major environmental disaster is waiting in the near future, (2) it will turn nature/the earth into a generalised victim, (3) the protester anticipates and represents this future victimhood in the present by means of manufacturing bodily vulnerability (e.g. by climbing to the top of a tree), and (4) the victimisation process can only be halted by external forces (e.g. the political/capitalist system) acting in ways that prevent the future disaster from evolving. 'Do *you* (aka the political/capitalist system) really want to turn us all into victims?' seems to be the question asked by the protesters via bodily self-investment, thereby turning the present body into a transmitter of urgency that makes the present political system accountable for both the existing suffering of nature, the continued misery of the protesting body, and for the prevention of future disasters.

The body is thereby used to create a 'heterochronic' or time splitting performance, where the body becomes a screen that shows a virtual disastrous version of the future (cf. that humans could all become victims). Or from Gilles Deleuze's perspective, the bodies create an actualisation of a virtual future, that is virtual because it is real but not yet there, and therefore, it can be stopped from being fully actualised via acting in certain sustainable ways in the present (Deleuze, 2001). The disaster virtually exists in the present as something 'engaged in a process of actualization' (Deleuze, 2001: 31). The protesting body—thus acting like a bio-medium or screen (Bolter and Grusin, 2003; Thacker, 2004)—offers a glimpse of this actualisation by *making sensible the victim we are all about to become*. Manufactured vulnerability is in other words used as a prophetic tool that invites the 'hard' political system to start acting in a caring way towards the 'soft' body and the nature surrounding it.

A key affect that we will pursue here, which is particular to the political mobilisation wished for by the body-event protesters, is enthusiasm. Jean-François Lyotard describes enthusiasm as an important political affect following Kant's contest of the faculties. Lyotard (1986) introduces the concept anew in his book *L'enthusiasme. La critique kantienne de l'histoire*. Here he points to the Kantian idea of enthusiasm that makes it possible to move beyond the obstacles of the given. In this way enthusiasm is sublime—and a force of mobilisation—as it helps the mind transcend hindrances of the given (Kant, 1790: 198). In *Kritik der Urteilskraft* (*Critique of the Power of Judgment*, 1790) regarded as the foundations for modern aesthetics, Kant distinguishes between two kinds of sensory aesthetic sceneries: displays of beauty and displays of the sublime. Displays of beauty evoke pleasure in the mind of the viewer because there is harmony between the sensory input and the human cognitive apparatus while sceneries of a sublime character evoke pain due to the fact that the sensory input exceeds the cognitive apparatus. However, the feeling of the sublime is, according to Kant, a paradoxical feeling of joy (*jouissance* in French) and pain due to the fact that the imagination cannot find an adequate expression of the experienced phenomenon in the concepts and language at hand. The sensory input exceeds imagination and language and produces both repulsion (fear) and admiration. The sublime can be of an either 'mathematical' or 'dynamic' kind, where the first is motivated by the inability to grasp a quantitative size or structure (e.g. the Egyptian Pyramids or St. Peter's Basilica in Rome), and the latter by the fear (experienced from a safe position) of mutable objects like an active volcano, hurricanes, the endless ocean, waterfalls, or rivers. The sublime is an affective experience as it creates 'negative Lust'/'negative desire' (Kant, 1790: 165) motivated by a tension between the formlessness of the spectacle and the cognitive categories struggling to structure this chaos. In this brief moment—between the imagination being puzzled by sensory input that it cannot grasp and the rescue of language to express the overwhelming sensory perceptions—the sentiment of the sublime reigns. Kant combines the aesthetic feeling of the sublime with the feeling that spectators of the French Revolution had, which according to Kant was enthusiasm. We use here the reading of Kant's *Philosophy of History* (1788) that Jean-François Lyotard presents in *L'enthousiasme, La Critique Kantienne de l'Histoire* from 1986. Enthusiasm is according to Lyotard a more aesthetic feeling than an ethical one and it is an affect of painful joy (Lyotard, 1986: 63) that energizes because it expresses a desire for the future. Pain is involved—and joins the aesthetic sublime—in that the desire is not represented: 'The enthusiasm does not see anything, or rather it sees nothing and considers it to be impossible to represent' (Lyotard, 1986: 63)[1]. Enthusiasm is thus a political pathos (that Kant called delusional), which can hit you at historically and politically important moments of violent ruptures such as revolutions as they start out by being formless. Enthusiasm and the feeling of the sublime are evoked in our cases by spectacles of vulnerability that point to the possibility of transgressing the given hindrances through intensified involvement in the cause.

JULIA BUTTERFLY HILL: THE ENDURING MEDIA-BODY

Julia Butterfly Hill (born 1974) began the longest tree sit ever on 20 December 1997. Hill's tree-sit took place in a 55 metres high tree that was around 1,000 years old and located in Northern California, US. The tree was later named Luna, as part of the attempt to prevent Pacific Lumber from cutting it down. Initially Hill only planned to sit in the tree for a couple of weeks, but she eventually stayed on the two small platforms for 738 days—until 18 December 1999 (Figure 4.1). That Hill managed to live in the tree for so long appealed to the mathematical sublime: Living on a platform for such a long time in order to demonstrate dedication to a cause is incomprehensible to many people. During the action fellow activists provided Julia with

Figure 4.1   Julia Butterfly Hill in Luna
Photo: Shaun Walker. Courtesy of Shaun Walker.

supplies. Pacific Lumber, meanwhile, tried to stop the activists delivering supplies so that Hill would be forced to leave the tree. But Hill stayed on her platforms. She only left the tree when the activist organisation Earth First came to an agreement with Pacific Lumber regarding the preservation of Luna and all the other trees in a specified 61-metre buffer zone. Earth First paid Pacific Lumber 50,000 US dollars with the understanding that the lumber company would not carry out logging activities in the specified area of forest. In return, Pacific Lumber agreed to donate the money to research at the Humboldt State University. So, the performance had a very tangible local effect as a piece of woodland was preserved and the university received additional research funding.[2]

From Hill's perspective, however, her protest had a much wider effect because she demonstrated to the environmental movement that this kind of 'political sensation' involving vulnerability and personal endurance could make a difference. After the tree sit, Hill wrote books about the experience and she became the subject of many news stories, features, and documentaries in media around the world. Hill had become a veritable 'green celebrity'. Perhaps she can even be described as a defining figure of the 'affective ecology' of the redwoods area in Northern California (Davidson et al., 2011)—or at least of the specific situational ethos of victory linked to the area, where Luna is situated.

It is striking that when analysing Hill's framing of the performance, it seems to need no elaborated justifications. The age of the trees and forest are simple self-evident reasons for not cutting them down according to Hill. Hill seems to focus very much on respecting and honouring the ancient character of the trees.[3] Age in that way becomes a key reason for preserving the tree, and there is an almost religious tone to Hill's justification of her cause as nature is invested with a metaphysical quality of 'wisdom', 'beauty', and 'power', escaping the discussion and sometimes contested choice between preservation and modernisation of natural and cultural heritage resources. In this sense Hill's approach to nature is saturated by Braidotti's post-human ethics where non-human vitality gains significance.

Of our two cases Hill's is the one that most explicitly formulates the role of her body in the activist performance by remediating its capability. She simply describes herself as a microphone sitting on a giant radio tower: 'I tell people that I am living on the world's most amazing radio tower that receives and transmits all of the messages of the universe and I have just been blessed to be the microphone'.[4] It is significant that Hill intertwines her own body (I/me), media technologies (radio tower/microphone), and nature (the tree she is sitting in). Following her line of thinking there seems to be a strong material connection or relationality between her body and the nature/tree thereby turning her body into a mediator for the three. Hill in other words articulates an idea of immanence making body, nature, and technology undividable. She sees herself not as a singular human being living out an individual agenda, but as an actor in a network with other (also non-human) actors, which in their relation to her define her subjectivity, actions, and ethical responsibilities. Thus, she puts herself at nature's disposal.

This assemblage between human and non-human actors is very clearly stated and visualised in a short interview sequence made during the tree sit, in which Hill describes how she feels the pain of the trees being felled around her, while visualising the actual cutting of the tree via her bodily movements:

> The hardest part of all, if I had to pick one point, would be when they were cutting all the trees down. I start to cry every single time I talk about it, because it was like sitting there watching your family killed in front of you. And you listening for hours [Hill makes the sound of a chainsaw cutting wood while wrenching her body . . .] and you feel like it is going right through your body. And then they stop the chainsaws

and they pound this wedge in. "Clink", "clink", "clink". And you can feel it. "Auw", "auw", "auw" [Hill throws her body back as if she is being hit]. And then they give the final "clink". And then she goes [Hill makes the sound of a falling tree] and it screams. And you have to sit there and listen to it scream as it is dying. Every single time a tree went down, part of my self died. Part of myself was ripped out. And it was the hardest thing I think I have ever gone through in my life.[5]

Hill uses her body as a vulnerable media/nature-body, which mediates the suffering nature and the long history it represents to her social context. Her bodily materialisation of the suffering nature, the messages about the future danger humankind is facing because of environmental changes, and the commitment necessary to turn this disaster around through her own endurance and self-inflicted vulnerability are all used to raise awareness of Hill's cause. In this way mediation and materialisation are radically conflated in the body of Butterfly Hill and the human body becomes part of the same lifecycle as the tree. Her strategy is at one and the same time to select and individualise one of many trees and to 'become the trees', thereby performing an interconnection between her body and Luna, making Luna human and her own body non-human and vice versa.

Hill's creative activist performance seems primarily to be positively framed by citizens and the mainstream media. The majority of comments on the most viewed YouTube videos are positive and praise her performance. Users write comments like these, verifying Hill's ability to transmit affects and motivate enthusiasm: 'Thank you for sharing, what an inspiration!', 'we love you you are a true inspiration, and thank you', and 'I am getting goosebumps. Ugh i thought I was passionate!'. And her example also motivates experiences of future disasters that could occur as a result of the activities of the anthropocene, and also of a posthuman connectivity between nature and humanity: 'I don't understand how one can not worry about the environment. It is what sustains us, human life. Without it, what is there? Do you not care what the future holds? We are destroying our planet at a increasingly rapid rate. The changes are happening now. Its not even a matter of future generations anymore, but just future years. What will this hurricane season bring? How much more damage will Deepwater Horizon do? What will we have once we've used up all the resources this planet has to offer?'. But her performance also raises criticism and discussion: 'What a hypocrite. Your clothing, make up, shampoo & conditioner, your ear rings, nail polish, the fence behind you in the video, the transportation aspects involved to make this video possible, the camera being used AND all the damn computers around the world making it possible for you to voice your bull shit!', 'Damn hippies' and 'i'm curious about what this accomplished in the long run, besides saving one tree. They are still clear cutting, so it didn't stop that'.[6] This clearly shows how the use of mediated vulnerability is affectively mobilising, more than affectively unifying, when used strategically as an activist strategy.

From what we can detect the mainstream media coverage of the tree-sit is primarily positive towards Hill. An example is a NBC portrait from 1999, in which Hill's performance is perceived as a question of personal courage, love, and belief rather than as being excessive and over the top.[7] The journalist that visits Hill in the tree simply frames Hill's performance as a singular person's heroic attempt to save something valuable for the entire of humankind. And instead of mocking the performance for being radical, the portrait critically engages with Pacific Lumber as a company having received many public warnings for cutting the woods too aggressively. Hill thus succeeded in performing the role of a romantic environmentalist with just ideals fighting greed, which underlines Harrebye's point about creative activism as an effective way of raising fundamental critique without facing charges of 'extremism'.

The key to understanding this public reception is, first, the temporal dimension of the performance itself and the scene of enactment. As Hill tried to raise awareness of the cutting of the redwoods she quickly realised that the media needed a 'hook' or a new angle to the story and decided that breaking the record of the longest tree-sit could be a way of attracting media attention: 'So I thought, if I stay and break that record—Americans love record breaking and numbers—maybe that will get the media to talk about what is happening out here'.[8] Hill was well aware that the longitude and endurance of the performance would simply make a good media story. She thus forced the media to notice her by putting herself in a precarious situation and showing extreme dedication over a long time.

THE WELD ANGEL: AN ICONIC BODY FOR THE FUTURE

During March 2007 anti-forestry installations and sit-ins were conducted to defend the ancient forests of the Weld Valley in Tasmania, Australia. Weld Valley is part of the Southern Tasmanian Forests, which is home to the tallest hardwood forests on Earth with some trees nearly reaching 100 metres. The temperate wilderness areas and the flora, for example eucalyptus trees, make the area important to biodiversity. Tasmania is also a centre of a big logging industry mainly run by Forestry Tasmania, a state government–led initiative, which produces large quantities of woodchips for export. Weld Valley is placed in the far south of Tasmania and is one of the oldest and most spectacular forest areas on earth. Many civil society groups took part in this environmental battle both on a local level—Forest and Free Speech (treedom-fighters), Wildcare Incorporated, Huon Valley Environmental Centre—and on a more global level, led by activists such as the Eco-Warriors.[9]

The protest in Weld Valley consisted of two road blockades and a bridge sit. One activist was hanging in a sling off the bridge over the Weld River, and seven kilometres from him Allana Beltran, wearing a long white curtain wrapped around her waist, white body paint on her face, and wings of white cockatoo feathers she had dug up from the shorelines and the forest floor attached to her back, was attached to a giant tripod blocking the entrance to the Tahune forest airwalk tourism venture (Figure 4.2). She had become the 'Weld Angel', the 'Angel of the Forest', and her haunting image was about to enter Tasmanian folklore. 'I did it because I thought it would look beautiful', she said in a matter-of-fact manner, 'and if I was going to be arrested as a visual artist, I wanted to make a visual statement'. Beltran sat in her forest aerie for nine and a half hours listening through headphones to Tibetan monk music, as the police ordered her down through megaphones. 'I was praying for the forests and for people to realise what they are doing. I was ready to sacrifice myself to this cause. I was ready to stand up for these ancient forests' (*Tasmanian Times*, 27 February 2008).

The figure of the angel evokes strong narratives in the eyes and minds of the beholders: It stands for a live incarnation of the forest as the vulnerable and sacred other, and it is symbolic of all humankind as victims of a careless non-sustainable politics. Weld Angel offers a spectacular sight: Physically vulnerable on the unsteady tripod but culturally robust, the bio-semiotic expression of the angel, the bodily incarnation of a strong sign (the descending movement), and the significant elevation of the body (the ascendant movement) has a strong visual force because it at one and the same time elevates bodily matter into an ideal icon and descends heavenly creatures into our messy affaires.

Figure 4.2   The Weld Angel
Courtesy of Allana Beltran.

The bare form and sight of Weld Angel evokes the sublime: For a short moment one is disoriented: What is this? How did it get up there? Is it suspended or floating in space? On a purely aesthetic level, the angel is suspended in something that looks like an easel so elevating the body into a piece of art. The strong and dramatic image of the angel has affected many viewers on YouTube. All comment on the huge impact her installation has had on the debate about forest protection in Tasmania. 'I was moved to tears by this video! Amazing!'. 'I fell in love with your angel when I went to a Styx forest protest in 2008. She is so beautiful and so powerful'. The inherent question in this forest performance seems to be, Do you really want to sacrifice an angel—and the nature she symbolises? Weld Angel stages the forest as sacred and humans and their technologies and capital as the ones committing sacrilege if the forests are violated. The strong visual image of the impersonated angel and the 'anglified' body makes it a strong image for future activists.

The big impact of the Weld Angel is due to the fact that it became an icon of the ecological war against forest logging in Tasmania in general. This can be seen in protection campaigns such as Pure Tasmania in which the description of the wild nature of Tasmania's southern forests is accompanied by the highly manufactured image of Allana Beltran's angel. Local artists likewise recirculate the icon as merchandise in various settings, and strong local environmental groups (Huon Valley Environmental Centre) as well as global NGO movements (Eco-warriors) make the action emblematic in their environmental activism. Allana Beltran is also one of the *Eco-Warriors* participating in eco-activism 2.0 that presents itself as a global revolutionary movement with the remit to save the world through environmental actions in the twenty-first century. On its website, the Eco-Warriors have pictures of 'the revolution' from around the world; they are very active on social media, Facebook, Twitter, and Flickr; and their target audience is young as is evidenced by claims such as the following: '13 years old is the age of the youngest Eco-Warrior—Felix Finkbeiner from Germany is the founder of Plant for the Planet, a group that planted 3.5 million trees worldwide'.[10]

The fact that Weld Angel has had a long afterlife through circulation and dissemination in various media is proof of its status as a visual event and its ability to put environmental issues on the agenda of local media usually unwilling to circulate environment movement-sponsored messages (Lester, 2010). It also demonstrates its ability to generate enthusiasm and emotional intensity around local environmental issues by creating visual events that add to the narratives of the area.

Another aspect of the strong afterlife of Weld Angel is Allana Beltran's personal investment. She was arrested just after the event and placed on a 12-month good-behaviour bond that prohibited her from re-entering the Weld Valley. The Tasmanian Police and Forestry Tasmania also sued her for close to 10,000 AU dollars. The Huon Valley Environment Centre immediately created a defence fund in order to raise the money. Later the police dropped its claim, but Forestry Tasmania vowed to continue with the legal action, although the amount was reduced to AU$2,000. Beltran's personal sacrifice as a measure of her engagement is clearly a key focus of this activism. Immediately after the lawsuit, Beltran's partner, Ben Morrow, was treated for bowel cancer. Beltran supported him through chemotherapy while dealing with the media on her doorstep and their daily requests for interviews and her participation in debates with forestry spin doctors. Ben Morrow died in July 2009. He was only 34 years old. Beltran, like Hill, whose tree sit is described earlier, made a significant personal investment in the environmental cause, but the two cases differ when it comes to the role of the sublime as a catalyst of affective enthusiasm. Hill performs a strategy of hope on a micro-geographical level via appeals to the mathematical sublime (the age of the tree, its height, the numbers of days Hill lives in the tree) and as such she becomes an exponent for an affective ecology (Davidson et al., 2011). Meanwhile, the visual body-event-strategy used by Weld Angel to add a virtual, but real, image to the narratives of Weld Valley is best described as having a dynamic sublime quality pointing to the not yet there-ness of the image.

VULNERABLE IMPACTS

In the remainder of this chapter, we discuss and try to draw conclusions about the problems and potentials of the investigated mobilisation strategy. Working with creative activist cases related to civil disobedience that use radical bodily self-investment raises the question of whether this type of activism is in fact related to traditional, and radically antagonistic, logics of terror in which the ultimate personal sacrifice is used to force the public to acknowledge the existence of a certain group or project. This is not the case, as we see it. Traditional terrorism leaves images of destruction (Juergensmeyer, 2000), whereas the non-violent, or agonistic (Mouffe, 2000), character of civil disobedience in our cases does not create civilian losses or transmissions of physical suffering to other bodies. The only potential sufferers are the disobedient activists themselves as they incarnate the radical will to political change. The activists operate by creating biopolitical interruptions or 'pauses' in the flow of the political system by incarnating a prophetic change, a virtual image in the present.

One potential problem of this visual activist strategy is not its momentary character but its potential disconnectedness with any concrete context. We always have to reflect on the justness or the negotiable character of any political activist strategy in order not to fall into the ideological trap of building non-negotiable certainties (e.g. the ideals of conservation that all environmental groups seem to praise). Many scholars warn against the depoliticisation of the sustainability discourse or 'the rights of Nature' (Swyngedouw, 2011). The strong imagery could make people oblivious of the rightness of the cause and thus the 'why' of activism.

In this chapter we have argued against a traditional humanist idea of the body having certain ethical qualities in itself as a proper framework for understanding our cases. As we see it the (post-human) body becomes a certain kind of culturally effective body via mediations and interactions with objects and technologies (tripods, machines, trees, the internet). In that way the bodies are not only prophetic but also prosthetic in the sense that their effects as 'soft bodies' depend on their intertwinement with extra-bodily post-human dimensions (e.g. objects, media, discourses) and in their scenic interconnections and chiasmatic exchanges between human and non-human in the cases.

The pragmatic potential of this strategy is its ability to create short-term delays (e.g. stopping machines) and to attract media attention as a result of the often-spectacular quality of self-sacrifice. In the two cases, vulnerability is staged as encounters between hard power (police, machines, etc.) and vulnerable power in the form of post-human bodies. The power of the cases has to do with the scale and intensity of actual danger and scale and intensity of sacrifice in the cases. The risk and the sacrifice are obvious in Hill's case as the bodily danger and the time-consuming endurance of her endeavour are quite astonishing. Beltran also demonstrates significant sacrifice and her stubbornness in continuing fighting while her partner was dying of cancer adds credibility to her own and the cause's legitimacy. We thus argue that the mobilisation of audiences through affective touched-ness also depends on the scale of danger faced by the activists and the level of sacrifice experienced. Our material activists, who face real dangers and who make large personal sacrifices for bigger causes (thus expressing the enthusiastic and sublime will to go beyond the given) during their body-events, seem to be good triggers of affective transmission and mobilisation in relation to other bodies.

The most interesting potential of the protest strategy is nevertheless its ability to create 'temporal potentiality' by displaying or actualising a virtual disastrous version of the present and the future in the present. By endangering the body the two cases turn the activist's body into a 'first human victim', pointing at a virtual future misfortune for humankind. The power of the vulnerable protest body in relation to environmental activism is thus its capacity to create body-events that use the flesh as a screen or medium to open the present to future dangers and hopes through civil action—and thus implicitly to new practices in the present that prevent the actualisation of forthcoming disasters. In the process of staging what *could happen* the protesting vulnerable body also mediates nature in different ways. One performs metaphorical identifications with nature thereby mediating it through cultural representations of powerful icons (the angel) while one performs metonymically herself as nature or becoming its direct voice.

CONCLUSION

The evaluation of the overall effect of the strategy depends on how you define or frame the notion of effect. The strategy creates clearly identifiable effects by delaying certain processes, motivating media coverage, and giving a voice to repressed non-human agencies. In the right circumstances it can also be effective in invoking enthusiasm and creating affective belonging to places through a visual aesthetic repertoire and thereby help energise the environmental movement's struggle to prevent the dangers produced through the activities of humans in the anthropocene. This type of effect is of course more difficult to identify and measure. The lack of long-term institutionalisation in relation to our cases could mean two things: (1) that the projects have only short-term effects or (2) that the logic of contemporary activism is not based on building institutions but on individuals moving from project to project and maintaining awareness of environmental problems via these ad hoc processes. Following Leah Lievrouw, contemporary political engagement of new social movements, like the environmentalist movement, can only be understood when based on 'a "permanent campaign" in which members participate or contribute on an as-needed basis, instead of being organised into disciplined, goal-directed drives' (Lievrouw, 2011: 155).

Donatella Della Porta in a similar way suggests that protest events can have lasting effects on social movements at *cognitive* (e.g. internal/external knowledge creation/sharing/development), *affective* (e.g. creating emotional ties and mobilising feelings of justice/injustice), and *relational* (e.g. creating new communities/identities and fostering social capital) levels (Porta, 2008: 30). In other words, political actions can have lasting effects on social discourses and the formation of post-human subjectivities and practices without building institutions or organisations. This means that contemporary activism should not only be evaluated according to its ability to build or build on institutions, but according to its ability to create 'breaking visual events', that disseminate and circulate on various media platforms and that are able to create cognitive, relational, and affective changes (e.g. enthusiasm) through their excessive visual repertoire. Whether or not the strategy is effective also depends on its capacity to mobilise the spectator according to the logic of the singular project. In our material this seems to happen, as the prosthetic and dedicated bodies—creating enthusiasm and new ecological belonging via endurance and aesthetic experiences of sublime uncertainness—become important facilitators and icons for future sustainable actions. In that way the protest body actually succeeds in opening the future and mobilising action in the present and as such contributes positive energy to the broader environmental movement.

NOTES

1. Our translation of 'L'enthousiasme quant à lui ne voit rien, ou plutôt voit le rien et le rapporte à l'imprésentable'.
2. Pacific Lumber acknowledged that it was concerns regarding Hill's safety that finally made them agree not to cut Luna. http://www.youtube.com/watch?feature=endscreen&NR=1&v=RF2NlAJzBps (accessed 27 May 2014).
3. http://www.youtube.com/watch?v=FyLiOnmBZLw (accessed 27 May 2014).

4. (00.03.03): http://www.youtube.com/watch?v=UXc_1V6-u4I&feature=relmfu (accessed 27 May 2014).
5. (00.05.10): http://www.youtube.com/watch?v=FyLiOnmBZLw (accessed 27 May 2014).
6. See all comments at https://www.youtube.com/watch?v=C-sLTVsNv0U, http://www.youtube.com/watch?v=72Z2wmgLiTc (accessed 27 May 2014).
7. http://www.youtube.com/watch?v=uFRdy7o3DPE (accessed 27 May 2014).
8. (00.08.40): http://www.youtube.com/watch?v=DT0LkvYNnfY&feature=relmfu (accessed 27 May 2014).
9. On an island roughly the size of the Netherlands and Belgium combined there is an average of 15,000 hectares of native forest being logged each year, according to the Wilderness Society, although the Tasmanian government insists the figure has fallen to 11,000. Trees such as the *Eucalyptus regnans* can grow as high as 97 metres and reach 400 years old.
10. http://www.nextecowarriors.com/contact/ (accessed 27 May 2014).

REFERENCES

ANDERSON, P. 2010. *So Much Wasted. Hunger, Performance, and the Morbidity of Resistance*, Durham, Duke University Press.

BLACKMAN, L. 2012. *Immaterial Bodies. Affect, Embodiment, Mediation*, London, Sage.

BOLTER, J.D. & GRUSIN, R. 2003. *Remediation*, London, MIT Press.

BRAIDOTTI, R. 2013. *The Posthuman*, Cambridge, Polity.

BUTLER, J. 2011. Bodies in Alliance and the Politics of the Street. *transversal*, 10, 1–14.

CRUTZEN, P. & STOERMER, E. 2000. The 'Anthropocene'. *Global Change News Letter*, 41, 17–18.

DAVIDSON, T.K., PARK, O. & SHIELDS, R. (eds.) 2011. *Ecologies of Affect. Placing Nostalgia, Desire, and Hope*, Ontario: Wilfrid Laurier University Press.

DELEUZE, G. 2001. *Pure Immanence. Essays on A Life*, New York, Zone Books.

DESPRET, V. 2004. The Body We Care For: Figures of Anthropo-zoo-genesis. *Body & Society*, 10, 111–134.

DOHERTY, B. 2000. Manufactured Vulnerability. *In:* SEEL, B., PATERSON, M. & DOHERTY, B. (eds.) *Direct Action in British Environmentalism*, New York, Routledge.

FEMEN & ACKERMAN, G. 2014. *FEMEN*, Cambridge, Polity.

GAUNTLETT, D. 2011. *Making Is Connecting*, Cambridge, Polity.

GIBSON-GRAHAM, J.K. & ROELVINK, G. 2009. An Economic Ethics for the Anthropocene. *Antipode*, 41, 320–346.

HARREBYE, S. 2011. Global Civil Society and International Summits: New Labels for Different Types of Activism at the COP15. *Journal of Civil Society*, 7, 407–426.

HJARVARD, S. 2008. The Mediatization of Religion. A Teory of the Media as Agents of Religious Change. *In:* HJARVARD, S. (ed.) *The Mediatization of Religion*. Bristol: Intellect.

JENKINS, H. 2006. *Convergence Culture*, New York, New York University Press.

JUERGENSMEYER, M. 2000. Theater of Horror. *Terror in the Mind of God. The Global Rise of Religious Violence*, Ewing, University of California Press.

KANT, I. 1790. *Kritik der Urteilskraft*, Frankfurt am Main, Suhrkamp.

KAPLAN, A. & HAENLEIN, M. 2010. Users of the World, Unite! The Challenges and Opportunities of Social Media. *Business Horizons*, 53, 59–68.

KNOBEL, M. & LANKSHEAR, C. 2010. DIY Media: A Contextual Background and Some Contemporary Themes. *In:* MICHELLE, K. & LANKSHEAR, C. (eds.) *DIY Media. Creating. Sharing and Learning with New Technologies*, New York, Peter Lang.

KNUDSEN, B.T. & STAGE, C. 2012. Contagious Bodies: An Investigation of Affective and Discursive Strategies in Contemporary Online Activism. *Emotion, Space and Society*, 5, 148–155.

LESTER, L. 2010. *Media and Environment*, Cambridge, Polity.

LIEVROUW, L. 2011. *Alternative and Activist New Media*, Cambridge, Polity.

LYOTARD, J.-F. 1986. *L'enthousiasme. La critique kantienne de l'historie*, Paris, Éditions Galilée.

MOUFFE, C. 2000. *The Democratic Paradox,* London.

PANAGIA, D. 2009. *The Political Life of Sensation*, Durham, Duke University Press.

PORTA, D.D. 2008. Eventful Protest, Global Conflicts. *Distinktion: Scandinavian Journal of Social Theory*, 9, 27–56.

PROTEVI, J. 2011. Semantic, Pragmatic, and Affective Enactment at OWS. *Theory & Event*, 14, 1–4.

SWYNGEDOUW, E. 2011. Whose Environment? The End of Nature, Climate Change and the Process of Post-politization. *Ambiente & Sociedade*, XIV(2), 69–87.

THACKER, E. 2004. *Biomedia*, Minneapolis, University of Minnesota Press.

5   War Commemoration and
Affective Media Rhythms

In this chapter we focus on rhythmic constructions of bodily vulnerability and war commemoration on YouTube and the apparent opposition to these unifying rhythms found in the related comments. We highlight the political democratic potentials of digital commemoration through an investigation of various forms of affective dissensus and arrhythmia.

The analysis presents a case study of 28 YouTube tribute videos to fallen Danish soldiers in Afghanistan and Iraq. It focuses on the strategic attempt to turn the bereaved soldier-body into a collective object of grief, both on a content level and on a rhythmic level, by inviting the viewer to submit to a common affective pulse. The videos' attempts to semantically and rhythmically construct the soldiers as common objects of grief are repeatedly disputed and opposed by the people commenting on them, as is evident from the examples that follow. These comments seem to oppose the unifying rhythms offered by the videos and, instead, appear to favour an 'arrhythmic' space of affective dissensus (Lefebvre, 1992). It could, therefore, be argued that the tribute videos on YouTube establish a more democratic situation as a 'globital memory field' (Reading, 2011) characterised by public commemorative disagreement. The chapter thus examines how the video tributes are culturally reproductive in their attempt to produce national attachments and how they tend to elicit agonistic responses in the form of affective outbursts, contestation, and criticism in the related commentary.

Contrary to the chapters on illness blogs, political violence in Iran, and green activism bodily vulnerability is not visualised directly in this material (we see no hurt or suffering soldiers or civilians). Instead, the videos constantly communicate that the soldiers put themselves in danger—and make themselves vulnerable—for the benefit of a greater cause and that this sacrifice ought to motivate respect, compassion, and recognition. In this sense the vulnerable body and the hard body of the heroic soldier seem to intertwine in complex ways as the receiver is invited to simultaneously acknowledge the victimhood of the deceased and the heroic contribution of the soldier's body vulnerable in the combat zone. This conflation of victimhood, vulnerability, and heroism is nevertheless not accepted without dispute in the comments, whereas other vulnerabilities and victims (e.g.

civilians) are presented as more just objects of affective investments. In this way vulnerability and victimhood, and the positive attachment connected to these concepts, become objects of discursive struggles where affect is both part of the content of the struggle (who should feel what for whom?) and of the intensity of the struggle itself (the aggressive and heated interaction).

Between 2003 and 2007 Danish troops took part in the war in Iraq and six soldiers were killed. Alongside the military involvement in Iraq, Danish troops have also participated in the war in Afghanistan from 2002 to 2013. In this conflict, which was initiated by the US government in 2001 as a response to the attack on the World Trade Center, Danish soldiers have primarily been involved in combat against Taliban soldiers, as well as in some rebuilding activities in Helmand province in southern Afghanistan. About 750 Danish soldiers have been participating in the war in Afghanistan and 43 have been killed. In this chapter we consider the use of social media platforms to commemorate and create video tributes to some of these fallen Danish soldiers. This material, until now unexplored, makes it possible to analyse both the cultural negotiation of war activities (e.g. how they should be remembered) and the new types of commemorative and affective practices made possible by social media platforms. The YouTube practice of private commemoration in public space creates new intersubjective relations around grief (Wahlberg, 2009). It could even be described as the virtual version of spontaneous social and ritual practices such as the laying of flowers, the lighting of candles, or the writing of inscriptions that are often associated with accidents and murders. In all these instances the memorial becomes a *commemorative emergence* due to the fact that it is continuously reinvested with new affects and meanings.

METHODOLOGY

For this study we looked at 28 YouTube videos, which memorialise the death of Danish soldiers (see the Appendix to this chapter). The videos are amateurish in style and not produced by professionals. In other words they are examples of the already mentioned DIY-culture based on citizens' ability to produce and disseminate media materials/objects, which were formerly closely linked to professional practices (e.g. movies, music videos, music recording, animation, etc.). The videos have been found through an extensive search on YouTube and are included in the study because they explicitly commemorate fallen Danish soldiers in Iraq or Afghanistan. The information concerning the videos (e.g. number of views) was registered on 28 April 2011 with exception of two videos (marked *), which were registered on 31 May 2011 (see the Appendix at the end of the chapter for a complete list of the videos).

Our investigation of these 28 videos proceeds on two different analytical levels; one focuses on the videos and responses as communicative and affectively strategic articulations and the second level deals with the media arena or environment itself (Meyrowitz, 1997; Ashplant et al., 2004). With respect to articulation we do both a content oriented and a rhythmic analysis of how the videos attempt to transmit the need to grieve to their audience. We also look at how the 'grievability' of the fallen soldiers is clearly contested in the comments. Our second point of interest—the social role of the media arena/environment itself—focuses on how the media space of YouTube allows for a new type of commemorative practice, which, unlike the official monuments of the nation state, is marked by affective dissonance (grief, anger, indignation, distress) and explicit difference of opinion concerning the status and legitimacy of the war. Following this outline our research tries to address (1) how the (affective and discursive) relation between bodies is established and responded to in the videos and comments and (2) what type of commemorative practice the specific media space of YouTube enables.

DEFINING RHYTHM

The public mourning of dead soldiers usually takes the form of commemorative monuments or ceremonies performed by official representatives of the army. When the memorials are turned into what we call 'commemorative emergences'—works in process—their status as commemorations may change considerably. Looking at the video tributes the traditional official monument is replaced by an interactive commemorative space in which the memorial is constantly in a state of becoming, as citizens transform it interactively. The communicative situation established by the videos links various human bodies: The body of the deceased soldier, the body of the tribute-produser that has been touched in order to produce the tribute, the viewers' and the commenters' bodies. The implicit aim of the tribute videos is to communicate and produce a communal grief, which extends the personal grief of the produser. Judith Butler treats the construction and distribution of grievable bodies in her book *Frames of War* from 2009. She introduces the concept of 'precariousness' referring to bodily vulnerability as a shared human condition. In war, some lives are mourned and others not—all depending on the context. Some lives simply cannot be grieved, as they have never counted as lives at all (Butler, 2009: 38). Who is recognised as someone to be mourned is politically and socially determined, discursively spread, and dependent on structures of recognisability. The structures of recognisability are interpretive schemes that distribute bodies and create the distinction between bodies one might fear losing (e.g. one's countrymen and -women) and indifferent bodies (e.g. the enemy). In order to feel grief the bodies we mourn have to be inscribed in a circuit of social affect: 'Our affect is never merely our own: affect is, from the start, communicated from elsewhere. It disposes us to perceive the world in a certain way, to let certain dimensions of the world in and resist others' (Butler, 2009: 50).

Awareness of 'rhythm' is essential when studying the affective dimensions of the videos. As audiovisual constructs that use music, rhythm is, of course, closely linked to the acoustic choices made by the video producers. But rhythm is not only to be found in music. Rather, it is a force of repetition (always open to difference) that can attune or position decentralised bodies in various ways. Henri Lefebvre, together with Catherine Régulier, proposes a distinction between 'mechanical repetition' and 'rhythm' as the latter is a form of repetition, which constantly introduces smaller differences, modulations, and intensification/deintensification (e.g. the heartbeat, which is a constant, but not mechanical rhythm; Lefebvre and Régulier, 1992b: 79). Meanwhile, Lefebvre, who focused primarily on the rhythms of urban spaces, believes that rhythm on a social level may be analysed and understood as a composite of rhythms that connect bodies, spaces, and temporalities in various ways.[1]

In the vast literature on rhythms two key understandings prevail: The first one, held by Lefebvre among others, focuses on the complex intertwinement of rhythms as a way of approaching an analysis of the social as such, whereas the second investigates rhythm as a converting/transformative expressive force, bridge, or passage between two milieus or assemblages. From Lefebvre's perspective rhythm is closely linked to the 'tissue of the lived, of the everyday' (Lefebvre, 1992: 21). When wanting to understand how a certain space-time (e.g. a social media platform) works as a temporally unfolded experience of presence one must, according to Lefebvre, take into account the different rhythms that constitute the everydayness of a specific site. This analysis of rhythms shifts the focus from 'the present' (as fixed objects, content, structures) to 'presences' by investigating the dynamic temporality and becoming of a certain social situation: 'The act of rhythmanalysis transforms *everything* into presences, including the *present*, grasped and perceived as such', says Lefebvre (1992: 23). Looking at the videos from a rhythm perspective, instead of a strictly content oriented perspective, would mean that you try to grasp how these constructs invite the receiver into certain temporal patterns of repetition that attune the body affectively by increasing or decreasing energy/attention or by stimulating certain affective responses.

Lefebvre defines rhythm as that which 'connects space, time and energies that unfold here and there' (1992: 18). A body using energy to move, for instance, constitutes a certain (fast, slow, normal, not normal) rhythm in this particular space-time. To investigate the complexity of social rhythms surrounding us, Lefebvre, in his last book *Rhythmanalysis* (1992), and in shorter articles (Lefebvre and Régulier, 1992a; Lefebvre and Régulier, 1992b), makes a range of distinctions between different types of rhythms. Among the most important are the following: (1) *biological rhythms* (e.g. the heartbeat, sleep cycles) versus *social/educated/rational rhythms* (e.g. clock time, work/leisure periods, the rhythm of a sermon). Here the difference is between rhythms defined by the human body and socially constructed rhythms defined by conventions—and in some sense our case material is focused on prolonging the social rhythms of the deceased soldiers after the destruction of their biological rhythms (Stage, 2014). (2) *Cyclical rhythms* (e.g. day/night, the seasons, the year) versus *linear rhythms* (e.g. a series of hammer blows, walking at a certain pace, a metronome). Here the cyclical rhythms are 'the rhythms of beginning again' (Lefebvre, 1992: 90), while the linear rhythms are often more mechanical and metric. This means that cyclical rhythms are open to new becomings (today being different from yesterday), while linear rhythms reproduce 'the same phenomenon, almost identical, if not identical, at roughly similar intervals' (Lefebvre, 1992: 90). (3) *Rhythms of the self* (e.g. private evening rhythms of watching TV, reading and sleeping, the rhythms of mornings, of eating) versus *rhythms of the other* (e.g. public rhythms of political and religious ceremonies in public space, rhythms of the supermarket, of the workplace; Lefebvre and Régulier, 1992a: 95). The relations between these rhythms are of political concern as they refer to the possibility of having individual or private rhythms, while at the same time co-existing with or even having the opportunity to affect the more socially conventional public rhythms. According to Lefebvre it can be a political action to change the rhythm of a place or a society by for example blocking flows, creating slow movements, or by spreading excited rhythms of mobilisation to citizens, because new rhythms always, more or less momentarily, change the 'tissue' of the social.

It is clear that biological, social, cyclical, linear, self-oriented, and other-oriented rhythms often intertwine or enter into a composite of rhythms making the distinctions between them blurry. Besides the qualitative differences between rhythms, Lefebvre therefore also describes different ways that rhythms can intertwine or relate to each other (Lefebvre, 1992: 67–69). (1) *Polyrhythmia* refers to the coexistence of various rhythms and seems to be a constitutive condition of social life. In cities different social rhythms can overlap and intertwine with biological rhythms of human bodies. (2) In certain circumstances polyrhythmia can be turned into *isorhythmia*, which occurs when various rhythms find a common rhythm. Lefebvre refers to the symphonic orchestra because the different rhythms of living bodies are here subsumed under the rhythm of the composition (Lefebvre, 1992: 68), and in some sense, music seems to be a key tool for the creation of these experiences of bodily sameness in time. (3) *Eurhythmia* occurs when different rhythms stay heterogeneous, but in a harmonious way. For example the body has a heartbeat and a rhythm of hunger and sleep, and it often follows rhythms of work and leisure. When in a healthy state the body is thus polyrhythmic and eurhythmic at the same time because the overlapping of rhythms is not destructive. (4) *Arrhythmia* is the disruption of eurhythmia and refers to moments of disruption, irregular rhythms and—in its most fatal form the final desynchronization of body and world through death.

Arrhythmia is most often shocking and disturbing, but irregular rhythms 'can also produce a lacuna, a hole in time, to be filled in by an invention, a creation' (Lefebvre, 1992: 44).

In some sense Lefebvre's description of arrhythmia as a bridge between states, between regular rhythms and creation, comes close to Deleuze and Guattari's conceptualisation of rhythm itself in their famous essay about the refrain, stating that it is 'difference that is rhythmic, not the repetition, which nevertheless produces it' (1987: 314). Deleuze and Guattari thus focus on rhythm as a form or repetition that orders, territorialises and stabilises—stating that '[r]hythm is the milieus' answer to chaos' (1987: 313). This is exemplified by the small child who is frightened and so begins singing a song to create some sort of stability, the housewife singing to herself while fighting chaos in the home, and the bird singing to mark its territory against enemies. At the same time they also acknowledge that rhythm is a form of anti-dogmatic repetition that maintains or produces difference, passage, or movement: 'What rhythm and chaos have in common is the in-between' (Deleuze and Guattari, 1987: 313). To illustrate this point Deleuze and Guattari once again mention the bird that can both territorialise its nest with its song, and, by slightly changing the intensity of its singing, transform the home into a scene of courtship by using rhythm to seduce and attract. Rhythm in this way creates a passage between 'heterogeneous space-times' (Deleuze and Guattari, 1987: 311)—like when sounds of war signal the transformation of a piece of land from a zone of agriculture (stimulating ploughing) to a battlefield (stimulating killing). In this sense rhythm is repetitive coordination that territorialises (by creating certain space-times) and motivates passages and movement. What Deleuze and Guattari add to Lefebvre is an increased focus on rhythm as a transformative and performative force of coordination/territorialisation that can change or bridge different milieus (nest vs. scene of courtship, farmland vs. battle field)—and in some sense can create a movement between them. In relation to the videos this observation is relevant to understand how rhythm is used performatively to enable a passage from YouTube as a space of everyday entertainment to YouTube as a commemorative space. It is also relevant for our analysis of the relationship between the rhythm of the videos and the comments below that somehow disrupt the rhythm by introducing an element of dissensus, which itself may be contested and somewhat tamed. In other words, Deleuze and Guattari can help show how rhythm is used as a tool for creating spatial passages and as a form of social organisation that is always working in a zone between chaos and order.

The videos to a large degree reproduce established schemes of culturally grievable or indifferent bodies. The comments below the videos, however, seem to trace another kind of affect that is obviously polyphonic and infected with difference and the negation of common cultural schemes. Here affect in its totality of heterogeneous forms marks the introduction of difference, dissensus, and democracy, because it indirectly deconstructs the consensual model for commemorating war and distributing grief. In order to better conceptualise these affective and non-conscious processes of transformation one could turn to linguist Julia Kristeva's (1974) doctoral thesis *La révolution du langage poétique*. According to Kristeva, affect is not produced as a result of discursive schemes, but as a pre-linguistic force that disrupts discourse. She distinguishes between symbolic and semiotic processes in language, subjects, and societies. If the *symbolic* (phéno-text)—roughly speaking—is the already established discursive layers of meaning in language, subjects, and societies, the *semiotic* (géno-text) is primarily energetic processes and destructive/productive drives that precede the distinction between subject and object, for example the entrance to the symbolic order. When a subject of enunciation obeys the rules of communication and the addressee is addressed following the grammatical and social rules and codes of communication, phéno-textual structures rule. If the géno-textual processes prevail (they are always present but more or less repressed), bodily drives, repetitions, rimes, intonations, and mimetic gestures become more obvious, thereby denoting charge and transport of energy. The géno-textual responses in this sense create a state of arrhythmia according to Lefebvre, a re-introduction of chaos according to Deleuze—or simply a different kind of prelinguistic and bodily embedded rhythm according to Kristeva.

AFFECTIVE MEDIA RHYTHMS AND DISCOURSE

In our analysis we avoid earlier almost technologically deterministic positions regarding mediation and rhythm—for example that broadcast media rhythms lead to national synchronisation (Scannell, 1988; Silverstone, 1994) or that new media rhythms threaten healthy biological rhythms (Crary, 2013)—in favour of a more open approach that understands social media platforms as polyrhythmic spaces, where for example the rhythms of communities, the everyday, bodies, music, and textualities intertwine in complex ways, the actual affective dynamics of which only become apparent through the analysis of case studies (Apperley, 2010). We thus investigate YouTube as a social media platform, which, among other things due to the many users co-creating this content community (Kaplan and Haenlein, 2010), is saturated by various more or less harmoniously coexisting rhythms (e.g. the everyday biological and social rhythms of users), the rhythm of the content on display [e.g. expressed in music], the arrhythmia of commenting).

We argue that social (media) spaces are saturated with rhythms positioning bodies in certain ways that trigger affective responses. Julian Henriques, drawing on Lefebvre, describes the relation between rhythmic repetition and affect as two-sided in his analysis of the affective transmissions in Kingston dancehalls: 'Repetition can *cause* affective attachment', for instance when DJs use certain techniques of repetitive intensification to capture the crowd and create a 'common vibe', but 'affect can also *cause* repetition' through for instance traumatic experiences with an affective force that binds subjects to repeat certain behaviours, or when the hunt for certain affects makes the subject repeat patterns of activity (2010: 77; see also chapter 5 in Blackman [2012] on knots, affect and rhythm). Henriques uses the terms 'vibration' and 'propagation' to explain the affective force of rhythm in the sense that specific rhythms create certain vibrations that attune bodies affectively by touching them via a 'pattern of intensity' that propagates in complex situations made up of spaces, technologies, bodies, music, routines, and so on (2010: 58). In this sense he argues that 'the propagation of vibrations could offer a materialist model of affect' and that 'affect is expressed rhythmically—through relationships, reciprocations, resonances, syncopations and harmonies. Affect is transmitted in the way wave dynamics are propagated through a particular medium' (Henriques, 2010: 58). To investigate the affective force of rhythmic vibrations he suggests three key strategies: *counting* frequency (the pace and cycles of repetition in e.g. dance moves or sound), *measuring* amplitude/intensity (e.g. high/low force), and *listening* to the timbre of the event (e.g. a warm, cold, ecstatic, lazy quality) (Henriques, 2010: 60). These strategies are clearly chosen to try to grasp the non-representational vibratory quality of a music event—by for example avoiding cultural connotations, the content of the song, production history, gender positioning, and so on in relation to the event in favour of a presence approach (see Lefebvre) that focuses on the material affective transmissions established during the event.

Henriques's analysis of the dancehall sessions seems to suggest that their rhythmic vibration creates moments of sameness (everybody feeling 'vibesy') or coordination as 'vibes connect musical beats with heartbeats' (Henriques, 2010: 64). Rhythms, in other words, seem to be good at creating common vibes, isorhythmia, affective sameness, 'entrainment, or group movement with the same pulse' (Protevi, 2009), or crowds where the many become one (Le Bon, 1895) by moving into 'a specific state of communal excitement' or 'a single creature of dancing', which Elias Canetti terms 'the rhythmic crowd' (1960: 31–33). Music is very directly approached as an affective tool by one of the DJs in Henriques's study who underlines how rhythms can be deployed to connect to bodies in non-representational ways that use the permeability of human bodies to bypass cognitive categorisation and interpretation (you feel and are absorbed in rhythms before you consciously understand or interpret them as rhythms).

Relating this to our videos John Protevi has shown how music has historically been used to attune warriors in certain ways (e.g. to intervene in practices of frenzied violence or 'berserking') and thus how 'music is regulatory rather than merely expressive' because 'music is a powerful way of searching the machinic phylum for bio-social assemblage formation to draw out practices forming bodies politic that can contribute to group functionality' (Protevi, 2009; see also Canetti, 1960: 33). In the current study, however, the videos are not primarily focused on attuning soldiers, but rather on local audiences, so the rhythms are not only non-representational vibrations but also biopower technologies that can be used to bodily embed certain discourses, values, or dispositions to act through designs that try 'to govern imitation at a distance, through rhythms' (Borch, 2005: 94).

Following these politicised uses of rhythm, and referring back to the affect/discourse-discussion in our introduction, we would thus argue in favour of looking at the affective-discursive messiness and intertwinements in our material instead of simply affirming rhythm as either a pre-discursive or strictly discursive force (Wetherell, 2012: 52). We thus approach (musical) rhythm as a partly non-discursive force that constantly intermingles with discourse in ways that makes it difficult to uphold a strict distinction between the discursive and affective. This of course becomes particularly important in uses of rhythm as found in the YouTube videos under study. Here the material is explicitly political and clearly promotes narratives about the legitimacy of specific historical processes of warfare. The vulnerable soldier-bodies are used as objects of communal grief, while the associated musical rhythms become a non-conscious trigger of collective affects and group entrainment. In this way rhythms and interpretative schemes of recognisability intertwine in the videos' attempts to produce responses of affective sameness (grief and sympathy) towards imperilled Danish soldiers.

COMMEMORATING WAR

The twentieth century saw an increase in individualisation in war related memory practices and representations (Blair and Michel, 2007). We have also seen a shift from war remembrance, which confirms and fortifies the nation state to remembrance practices that stress the importance of individual psychological responses 'to the death and suffering that war engenders on a vast scale' (Ashplant et al., 2004: 7). War remembrance is thus increasingly seen from the viewpoint of the still living and continues to become ever more individualised (cf. every man his memorial).

The web culture of commemoration characterised by easy access, openness, and interactivity underlines this increasing individualisation of grief—but it also turns commemorative arenas into more heterogeneous 'globital memory fields' saturated by conflicted ideas of what should be remembered and how it should be remembered in digital spaces (Reading, 2011). The virtual memorials (i.e. the tribute videos) on YouTube are examples of vernacular memory in the making as individual users constantly inscribe them with interpretations of the past.

The tribute video is historically first and foremost an American invention related to amateur documentations of important events in life, and second, it is inspired by funeral videos. The latter is a memorial video tribute produced by the funeral home to be shown at the service (Wahlberg, 2009). Wahlberg ascribes the often sentimental and kitschy nature of the tribute videos to the commercial influence on amateur culture. In a Danish cultural context in which funeral home videos do not exist, the video tributes seem to herald a new memory practice that has developed through copying the memory practices of more experienced warring nations. The astonishing similarity between the 28 videos we analysed could stem from the fact that they are imitating the same source, although one of our most important findings is that the video tributes are not memorials referring to the singularity of the deceased person or expressing the singularity of the bereaved, as is often the case in American tribute videos (Andén-Papadopoulos, 2009).

We see YouTube as the arena or sociopolitical space in which individual produsers articulate their specific war memories. And the grievers likewise hope to find communal consolation (Wahlberg, 2009) or a transnational realm of pity, compassion, and sympathy; in other words a *community of affect* beyond political differences. Several scholars have criticised this tendency to depoliticise specific wars in order to commemorate 'those lost in war' (Grider, 2007). Marita Sturken furthermore concentrates on consumerist tendencies in attitudes towards difficult and traumatic pasts and especially on kitsch as a key feature in evoking the idea of a universal emotion shared by humankind (Sturken, 2007). This linking of consumerism and kitsch leads to innocence and comfort preventing a politicised view of the situation to emerge, according to Sturken (2007). This criticism is relevant, but we see a third way between a naive praise of a realm of affect beyond political differences and a severe criticism of this endeavour for being consumerist kitsch, a way that allows a range of political positions in relation to war commemoration and in this sense re-politicises the whole act of commemorating.

RHYTHMIC TRANSMISSIONS OF THE GRIEVABLE BODY

Overall, the YouTube videos can be described as their producers' attempts to create a social rhythm in relation to bodies that have lost their biological rhythm, due to the most radical form of arrhythmia: the body dying. In other words, the videos give a prolonged temporal and experiential-affective presence to bodies that would otherwise not have an existence or be part of the social tissue. But this existence is narrated in specific ways, and using certain rhythmic strategies, that inscribe the bereaved in the social in an inclusive way positioning them as collectively grievable bodies. Turning to the content level of the 28 videos it is possible to see various similarities. First of all, the death of the soldiers is continuously related to greater political or historical dimensions and thus different from the American tribute videos that insist on the recognition of the fallen soldiers 'as persons, as unique individuals' (Andén-Papadopoulos, 2009: 24). The Danish videos do create individualisation, however, by showing the pictures of each and every fallen soldier over and over again, but each soldier's death is continuously legitimised inside the framework of a very salient discourse of heroism.

An example of a video that connects the individual loss to a greater cause in order to establish the dead soldiers as an object of affective inclusion is *In memory of the danish soldiers who died fighting for peace* (20 October 2008). The video lasts 7 minutes 19 seconds and is a mash-up of different photos of soldiers in action, monuments, and burial ceremonies in Denmark (e.g. coffins wrapped in the Danish flag), private and official photos of 22 of the dead soldiers, graphics with textual statements, and finally a few recordings of planes dropping bombs and soldiers in combat. The producer of the video is—as is the case for a lot of our material—rather difficult to personify as the video is uploaded on a YouTube channel called DeDanskeSoldater (TheDanishSoldiers). The channel's name suggests a professional or institutional bond between the producer and the dead soldiers—an interpretation which is supported by the video itself as it ends with the text: 'We are still fighting' (7.10). This shows that even though the video may have a rather amateurish and 'vernacular' style, it does not necessarily mean that it is non-institutional or not promoting official or professional discourses on the war.

The visuals are accompanied by very dramatic and expressive background music (classical, choral, and pipe music), which clearly frames the actions performed by the soldiers as epic and more than normal. In this sense the rhythm of the music creates a passage between various states of media use on YouTube (e.g. entertainment, learning) and YouTube as a commemorative space used to honour Danish soldiers. In this way, the rhythm 'territorialises' YouTube so that it becomes an arena for commemorative encounters. Taking Lefebvre's perspective, various rhythms coexist in relation to the video. The viewer of course meets the video while being embedded in a range of social rhythms (of e.g. work, relaxation) and biological rhythms (of e.g. heartbeat, sleeping/being awake). But the video in itself also intertwines different rhythms. For instance most still images in the mash up are shown at five- to six-second intervals giving the video a certain linear rhythm or frequency, but there are also irregularities, for example at the beginning and end (e.g. the recorded war sequence). This visual rhythm is supplemented with an auditory rhythm, which starts out with a slow frequency, low amplitude, and sad or melancholic timbre. The frequency and amplitude slowly increase to create a new quality of epic grandeur, while the timbre (realised in the sound of the solitary and lingering flute) produces the most direct communication of vulnerability in the material because it seems to present both the fragility of being a soldier at war and the sadness connected to the 'post-vulnerable' state of death. Here vulnerability is transmitted via rhythmic vibrations, rather than semiotic content. Like in the Jamaican dancehall investigated by Henriques, the receiver is being modulated into a common rhythm, pulse, or state of entrainment because of the vibrations created by the music (or, following Lefebvre, into a state of 'isorhythmia'). We are invited to feel the state of loneliness and sadness related to war and its causalities—but also its perceived grandness or meaningfulness. The modulation tries to connect to and mobilise the body and to intensify its affective

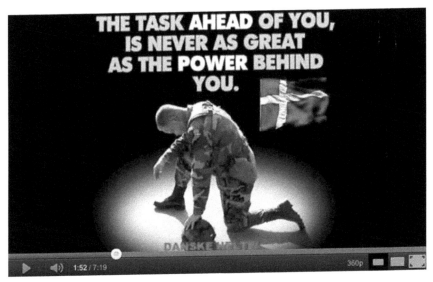

Figure 5.1   Screenshot from *In memory of . . .*

attachment to the soldiers and the cause via the increasing amplitude (the music being louder, more intense, or sonically dominant) and frequency.

The music creates connotations of Hollywood cinema or epic battle movies such as *Braveheart*, which underlines how discourse and power constantly sneak back into the equation. The first dramatic culmination of the music coincides with the first images of the Danish soldiers who have died in war. These photos are followed by a poster with the statement 'The task ahead of you, / is never as great / as the power / behind you' (1.52) placed above a kneeling soldier, a Danish flag, and the text 'Danske helte', which means 'Danish heroes' (Figure 5.1). The losses are also directly addressed later in the video via three textual sequences: 'Our brothers did not die in vain / Danish soldiers are still keeping the peace in Kosovo. / And every day Danish soldiers in Afghanistan engage the taliban in combat' (5.18). The video's multimodal assemblage of visuals, text, and rhythm thereby integrates the singular loss into a narrative of heroism, necessary sacrifices, and national coherence. A heroic narrative, which is underlined by more or less conscious references to established war icons (e.g. Joe Rosenthal's 'Raising the Flag on Iwo Jima' from 1945; Figure 5.2).

This heroic interpretation of the bereavements is—following Butler— also a way of allowing for the dead body of the soldier to become an object of affective response and inclusion at the level of the receiver. The video is not so much about communicating factual information (we do not see the names of the dead soldiers or when/where/how they died) but about creating an affective connection to 'the Danish soldier' as such. This connection both *supports* and is *supported by* a national discourse of heroism because

Figure 5.2   Screenshot from *In memory of . . .*

the soldiers not only are affirmed as national heroes via the aspired affective response but also become objects of affect because they are acknowledged as heroes. The video is thus an example of a strategic use of affective communication that serves a certain political understanding of warfare by attempting to create a specific relation between the singular soldier, a greater political cause, and the affective response of the receiver. Rhythmically the video is then best approached as strategic attempts to use the non-representational, vibratory, or 'soft' power of rhythm and music for purposes heavily embedded in political discourses of the wars in Iraq and Afghanistan as 'just wars'. In this sense the video tries to instil a collective and national rhythm through music. Rhythm becomes, following Protevi, a regulatory tool for group functionality by being used to draw citizens into a state of affective entrainment where discourses can be felt and thus perhaps accepted. As we will now show this attempt to create political 'isorhythmia' in relation to the war is opposed by the comments, which instead create arrhythmia—or affective rhythms, according to Kristeva.

As mentioned, the videos invite the receiver to engage in a collective (national) rhythm, but this invitation is received in many different ways in the comments, which thereby create a state of dissensual arrhythmia. Arrhythmia is then a user-generated force of disturbance that makes it impossible to establish a common rhythm (and affect) in relation to the wars in Iraq and Afghanistan. On a content level, three strategies of creating commonality in the video tributes can be identified—a communitarian patriotism, an appeal to the locals that they should honour those who secure peace, and the idea of war as a way of creating a better world. Comments that fall into these categories do not, however, go undisputed. It is for instance crucial for some respondents to establish a link between nationality and religion, whereas others try to deconstruct this introduction of religious ideas: 'May God be with our brave soldiers in the struggle for freedom' (FSKpatriot, 8 months ago)[2]; 'God bless the Danish troops, God bless our contry, may God keep us in awe of the tru values which seem to be forgotten' (dolphlalala, 3 months ago)[3]; 'God is dead' (HOLDTHAPHONE, 2 months ago).[4] Attempts to link war, religion, and national identity can be quickly critiqued.

An argument about the soldiers as securing the 'home' against the enemy is likewise criticised. This is done by focusing on the damage done by the soldiers in foreign contexts. Here the soldiers are not defending local security but, rather, are creating local (but distant) instability. And instead of being the ones that sacrifice and deserve respect, the soldiers are described as the brute power destroying other families: '[D]oes a child that becomes a part of Taliban because nato killed his father not have a family? Or fathers that become Talibans because their children or someone close to them were killed'? (GrimmjowProduction, 1 year ago)[5], and 'And what about the innocent civilian victims? Should they not also be commemorated??' (HOLDTHAPHONE, 3 months ago).[6] Here the idea of the soldiers as self-sacrificing is opposed in favour of the civilians who died at the hands of these soldiers. In that way the 'grievable body' is no longer, or not only, the soldier, but also the local people who have died because of the war.

The third idealistic argument about creating a better world has many adherents: 'Since we are forced to do this, its better to believe that we are fighting for a better tomorrow than over money"'(TehWipeout 1 year ago); 'fighting for the greater good' (24402989123456, 1 year ago); 'ill fight for what I see as right', 'when I become 19–20 I want to fight for a freecountry where children and women can do what they want' (Stefan 123234, 1 year ago).[7] But this argument is also not undisputed, and according to some, the presence of Danish soldiers in Afghanistan mainly serves the economic and political interests of superpowers: 'This war is all about money and not sacred idealism' (humanityfirstnow, 1 year ago); 'You are going there as cannon fodder for the good of a global elite, get over it' (humanityfirstnow, 1 year ago); 'You are simply a bunch of hired killers' (humanityfirstnow, 1 year ago); 'You are not defending your country in Afghanistan you are invaders' (humanityfirstnow, 1 year ago); 'That however doesn't change anything with the fact that Denmark has ABSOLUTELY nothing to do in Afghanistan watching a USoil pipeline' (jakslevius 1 year ago).[8]

Following Butler it first of all becomes clear that the different participants in the discussion reproduce different interpretative schemes in relation to the war and that these different schemes also allow for the production of grievability in different ways. For some, not least the produsers of the videos, the grievable body is the body of the Danish soldiers, while others point at the civilians as the more just objects of grief. Furthermore, it is obvious that affect is contagious in a highly complex and fragmenting way (Knudsen and Stage, 2012) in the sense that the feeling of grief in a video can produce counter-affects (like consideration of the harm done to civilians) and that these counter-affects produce ever more affects (like anger over the lack of grief in relation to the soldiers). Such affects are clearly contagious but not necessarily harmonising because social actors make sense of events by using different interpretative frameworks.

But looking at the totality of outburst and affective responses to the videos, affect also plays a different role. Affect is not only channelled by discourse but can also—inspired by the aforementioned affect theory of Kristeva—be analysed as (opposing) political energies of arrhythmia (Lefebvre) that disturb discourses or a certain organisation of the social. In this sense the comments present affective responses that oppose or refuse to enter into the 'heroic rhythms' of the videos. This arrhythmic tendency can be traced in the formal characteristics of the language used in the comments. One formal feature is the amateurish character of this online communication: the misspellings, the lack of factual knowledge (e.g. in mistaking Danes for Dutch), and the talking about the war in Iraq instead of Afghanistan. This amateurism does not, however, disturb the communication significantly. Another feature is the number of *markers of authenticity* such as misspellings, morphological errors, and so on that do not follow the rules of written language, as well as mixed versions of various languages that bear witness to the variety of linguistic contexts meeting online. Examples from the comments to 'Danish soldiers fighting in Helmand' (2 April 2008) include 'From a german soldiar' (FschJgBtl261, sidbadw, 1 year ago) and 'mutch respect to the Danish army. very good soldiers. From a swiss army soldier' (cardgohst, 1 year ago). These authenticity markers express the genuine glocal character (Robertson, 1995) of online communication that works despite and because of differences in language competencies.

The last of the formal features we want to stress is the expressive and conative functions of language pointed out by Roman Jakobson. The former is related to the addresser adding information about the speaker's internal state and the latter to engaging the addressee directly by vocatives and imperatives (e.g. the use of capital letters, punctuation (especially exclamation marks and signs of omission), expressive signs (e.g. :) or :(and onomatopoeia). These formal choices are expressions of the emotional state of the addresser in the communication situation. An example from the comments to 'Danish soldiers fighting in Helmand' (2 April 2008) is 'those are British soldiers duhhhhhh unless the Danish stole are enfields??' (MRAK47itification, 2 months ago). Another from a response to 'Til ære for de danske soldater der faldet i krig' (24 Marc 2008): 'pff!!! God xD you crazy' (martinboanders, 2 months ago) (Figure 5.3).[9]

All these formal features indirectly point at the type of memory practice that YouTube enables. It is less conventional, it is messy and filled with flaws, it is bottom-up, it is clearly marked by the affective state of the participants, it is in a state of becoming (i.e. always open for new inscriptions), martinboanders For 3 år siden som svar til Brian Blangstrup Dahl

@kvaser68 pff!!! gud xD du crazy!!! hvis den såkaldte gud fandtes, hvorfor er der så sådan nogle total onde mennesker i verden som rige røvhuller, soldater og taliban?? giver jo ingen mening

Figure 5.3   Screenshot of géno-textual excerpt

and it is 'dissensual' by definition. By focusing on the inscriptions of highly differential affective responses on the YouTube interface, affects are regarded as conflicting political energies that reveal what democracy is all about: upholding the possibility of disagreement and dissent. In that way the affective clashes and disruptions of conventional rules of communication—or following Kristeva: the géno-textual disturbance of the phéno-text—point at the opportunity for change and the many possible ways of intervening in this political debate. In opposition to many official monuments, the videos thus reveal that the commemoration of war is a contested and always politicised phenomenon. And, as we see it, there is something democratically promising about using this composite of affective and discursive clashes to commemorate war.

DEMOCRATIC ARRHYTHMIA?

An important discussion is whether or not these discursive struggles over who should be recognised as vulnerable bodies in need of sympathy and respect during war—and thus as the true victims of war—create genuinely political spaces of agonistic disagreement, or rather antagonistic spaces of hate and verbal attacks (Mouffe, 2000). The official state legitimisation of war is in many ways reproduced by the DIY videos, but by making it possible for the viewers to express and leave arrhythmic traces of disagreement (via the comment function) the media space created around the videos becomes polyphonic and politically fragmented. In this way the political, contested, and selective character of war commemorations is revealed and inscribed into the commemorative object itself.

This type of media memorial, where dissent can be articulated as part of the continued rewriting of the media text, is by far more representative of for example the Danish population's views on for instance the war in Afghanistan. Approximately half the population supported Danish troops' involvement in the war in 2008 and 2009, but by 2010 this had dropped to one-third of the population. Also by 2010, 69 per cent of the population were under the impression that the war in Afghanistan could not be won.[10] From this perspective the media space of YouTube allows for a commemorative practice that permits action (instead of passivity) in relation to a war memorial and it gives voice to an existing plurality of opinions and affects regarding the ongoing war activities or, in rhythmanalytical terms, the 'rhythms of the other', which in this regard would be state institutions creating public monuments often in the midst of urban activities, are being challenged by the diverse and fragmenting 'rhythms of the self' of online produsers. Following Lefebvre and Régulier, arrhythmia, and the affective dissonance that it presents, can be a democratic response, if arrhythmia is the result of an attempt to expand the possibility of individual differences in society and thus to affect 'the tissue of the social' by avoiding the 'dressage' of imposed political rhythms (Lefebvre and Régulier, 1992a: 100).

The transformation of the commemorative space into a political arena without a common ground of communal grief disintegrates the arguments put forward by Grider (2007) who suggests that the virtual character of the internet escapes the materiality of war and death thereby depoliticises the losses. It also confronts Sturken (2007) who points to the use of kitsch in order to invoke universal emotion shared by humankind, which she sees as a way to preserve a depoliticised innocence in relation to warfare. Because of the foregrounding of dissent as a part of commemoration itself we approach the online memorial as an interesting successor of the official monument and we understand the polemical reactions from produsers to the video tributes' official framings as a democratic response and an attempt to re-politicise the de-politicised articulations. The polemical reactions are not present in the rare cases where the tributes are personal (e.g. 'Dan Gyde—Begravelsen' ['Dan Gyde—The funeral']; 17 December 2008). Political contestation appears only when official framings of the war are uncritically adapted by the videos.

The democratic potential of YouTube depends on whether you think it should optimally offer a 'space of rationality', where reason will prevail, or a 'space of articulation' or 'arrhythmia', where voices and 'rhythms of the self' (sometimes irrational or playful) can be expressed—but not always heard (Couldry, 2010). Following the French thinker Jacques Rancière, we argue that the online memorials analysed in this chapter confront what one could call the 'consensual' model of democracy (Ranciére, 1999). The consensus model is prominent in many traditional monuments that assume a sort of national unity or basic agreement about the warfare of a certain nation. For democracy—or non-consensual democracy—to take place, according to Rancière, singular individuals have to appear to not represent anyone but themselves in order to conduct dispute as an alternative to a consensual model of democracy in which the community's and the individual's strivings are the same. And as such the online memorials are democratic monuments as they reveal the lack of communal consensus in relation to the war and create a hyper-complex arrangement of singular voices speaking in their own way. Scrolling down the YouTube page is, in this way, enabling a direct experience of the messy and unfinished chaos of democratic and affective energies.

Whether one accepts that the often brute and hostile interaction about the tribute videos on YouTube can be approached as political deliberation depends on the definition of this concept. According to Aaron Hess effective deliberation is 'conducted through the use of reasonable argument (Goodnight, 1999) toward reaching common ground (Barber, 2003; Sunstein, 2007) as opposed to divisive arguments derived through fallacies' (Hess, 2010: 109). Following this Habermasian ideal Hess is sceptical towards the democratic and political potential of YouTube, as this platform often seems to motivate a rather extreme, demonising, and overtly playful type of interaction (Hess, 2009; 2010). Political deliberation could also be threatened by copyright issues on YouTube limiting free speech and criticism, by the financial interests of the media platform, (Burgess and Green, 2009; Hess, 2009), or by the fact that it—just like many other types of online communication—is often very difficult to verify who has produced a video or comment (Smith and McDonald, 2011). These problems all point to the fact that it is important not to end up in a deterministic understanding of new technologies that equates social media with democracy or that overlooks the institutional and economic forces that also affect these technologies.

These concerns are also highly relevant in our case, which is certainly characterised by incidents of flaming, ambiguous authorship, and rather incomprehensible intertwinements of institutional and non-institutional voices. Following McDonald and Smith's nuanced acknowledgement of both the potential pitfalls of online communication and the necessity of 'exploring new models of deliberation as they occur in the new media landscape' (2011: 306), we nevertheless maintain that this type of communication is a democratic improvement compared to the previous dominant practices of war commemoration focused on national unity and coherence. This is the case for two reasons: First, the increasing ability for ordinary citizens to share their view on war (commemoration) is in itself a positive democratic change. It is simply easier for many people to participate in commemorative practices in different and oppositional ways. Second, the bare manifestation of disagreement in relation to war memorials has a democratising effect—whether or not this disagreement is playful or irrational—because the commemoration of war has previously been dominated by hegemonic official voices. Our point is, however, not that YouTube delivers an optimal platform for political deliberation as such or that one should approve of all kinds of online communication as long as it is oppositional, but rather that YouTube's ability to make dispute visible has a democratic potential in relation to social phenomena, which have often been 'depoliticised' or deprived of controversial character.

CONCLUSION

In the article we have analysed our empirical material on two different levels focusing on the level of articulation (the content of the videos and comments) and the level of the media arena as a space of online commemoration. The main points have been that the videos, via their rhythmic strategies and content, support official framings of the war as just and necessary, and that they attempt to create a bond of commonality between the dead or 'post-vulnerable' soldiers and the receivers. Looking at the comments this attempt is a topic of dispute and fierce discussions or arrhythmic/géno-textual rhythms thereby transform the arena of commemoration into a political space of democratic struggle. Following this we have argued that YouTube as a media arena enables the creation of a democratised memory practice where official justifications of war can not only be affirmed but also disputed and scrutinised via all sorts of discursive and affective investments.

Are these democratic practices celebrating hate speech? Are they fundamentally dishonouring the dead soldiers as many of the reactions to the critical outbursts claim? Potentially but not necessarily. The divergent comments are democratic in the sense of Rancière, but also occasionally articulate trans-individual communal expressions of sympathy and empathy beyond political differences. As an online memorial practice the tribute videos on YouTube and their comments therefore break with the traditional war monuments' focus on national unity and establish a more democratic situation characterised by public and affective commemorative arrhythmia.

NOTES

1. As argued by Christian Borch (2005) this interest in differential repetition as important social forces that connect and position bodies in more-than-representational ways actually seems to be a pivotal point both in the early sociology of Gabriel Tarde, in Gilles Deleuze's writings, in Lefebvre's 'rhythmanalysis', and in, we might add, the theories of the affective turn.
2. Original text: 'Må Gud være med våre tapre soldater I kampen for frihet'.
3. Original text: 'Gud velsigne de danske tropper, Gud velsigne vores lnd, Gud give os ærefrygt for de snde b'værdier som synes glemt'.
4. Original text: 'Gud er død'. Comments to 'Danish soldiers fighting in Helmand' (2 April 2008).
5. Comment to 'Heltene' (2 July 2007). Original text: 'et barn der går I Taleban fordi nato myrdede hans far har ike nogen familie? Eller fædre der melder sig I Taleban fordi de fik deres børn eller nogen tæt på dem dræbt?'.
6. Comment to 'Til ære for de danske soldater der faldet i krig' (25 March 2008). Original text: 'Hvad med de uskyldige civile ofre? Skal de ikke også mindes??'.
7. Original text: 'når jeg bliver 19–20 vil jeg kæmpe for et fritland hvor børn og kvinder kan gøre hvad de vil'.
8. Comments to 'Danish soldiers fighting in Helmand' (2 April 2008).
9. Original text: 'pff!!! Gud xD du crazy'.
10. http://jp.dk/indland/article2166582.ece (accessed 27 May 2014).

REFERENCES

ANDÉN-PAPADOPOULOS, K. 2009. US Soldiers Imaging the Iraq War on YouTube. *Popular Communication*, 7, 17–27.
APPERLEY, T. 2010. *Gaming Rhythms: Play and Counterplay from the Situated to the Global*, Amsterdam, Institute of Network Cultures.

ASHPLANT, T., DAWSON, G. & ROPER, M. 2004. *Commemorating War*, London, Transaction Publishers.

BLACKMAN, L. 2012. *Immaterial Bodies. Affect, Embodiment, Mediation*, London, Sage.

BLAIR, C. & MICHEL, N. 2007. The AIDS Memorial Quilt and the Contemporary Culture of Public Commemoration. *Rhetoric & Public Affairs*, 10, 595–626.

BORCH, C. 2005. Urban Imitations: Tarde's Sociology Revisted. *Theory Culture Society*, 22, 81–100.

BURGESS, J. & GREEN, J. 2009. *YouTube*, Cambridge, Polity.

BUTLER, J. 2009. *Frames of War. When Is Life Grievable?*, London, Verso.

CANETTI, E. 1960. *Crowds and Power*, New York, Farrar, Straus and Giroux.

COULDRY, N. 2010. *Why Voice Matters*, London, Sage.

CRARY, J. 2013. *24/7*, London, Verso.

DELEUZE, G. & GUATTARI, F.L. 1987. *A Thousand Plateaus*, Minneapolis, University of Minnesota Press.

GRIDER, N. 2007. Faces of the Fallen and the Dematerialization of US War Memorials. *Visual Communication*, 6, 265–279.

HENRIQUES, J. 2010. The Vibrations of Affect and their Propagation on a Night Out on Kingston's Dancehall Scene. *Body & Society*, 16, 57–89.

HESS, A. 2009. Resistance Up in Smoke: Analyzing the Limitations of Deliberation on YouTube. *Critical Studies in Media Communication*, 26, 411–434.

HESS, A. 2010. Democracy through the Polarized Lens of the Camcorder: Argumentation and Vernacular Spectacle on YouTube in the 2008 Election. *Argumentation and Advocacy*, 47, 106–122.

KAPLAN, A. & HAENLEIN, M. 2010. Users of the World, Unite! The challenges and Opportunities of Social Media. *Business Horizons*, 53, 59–68.

KNUDSEN, B.T. & STAGE, C. 2012. Contagious Bodies: An Investigation of Affective and Discursive Strategies in Contemporary Online Activism. *Emotion, Space and Society*, 5, 148–155.

KRISTEVA, J. 1974. *La révolution du language poétique*, Paris, Seuil.

LE BON, G. 1895. *The Crowd. A Study of the Popular Mind*, New York, Dover Publications.

LEFEBVRE, H. 1992. *Rhythmanalysis*, London, Continuum.

LEFEBVRE, H. & RÉGULIER, C. 1992a. Attempt at the Rhythmanalysis of Mediterranean Cities. *Rhythmanalysis*, London, Continuum.

LEFEBVRE, H. & RÉGULIER, C. 1992b. The Rhythmanalytical Project. *Rhythmanalysis*, London, Continnum.

MEYROWITZ, J. 1997. Tre paradigmer i kommunikationsforskningen. *Mediekultur*, 13, 56–69.

MOUFFE, C. 2000. *The Democratic Paradox*, London.

PROTEVI, J. 2009. Rhythm and Cadence. Frenzy and March: Music and the Geo-bio-techno-affective Assemblages of Ancient Warfare. *Theory and Event* [Online], 13. Available at: http://muse.jhu.edu/login?auth=0&type=summary&url=/journals/theory_and_event/v013/13.3.protevi.html (accessed 13 November 2014).

RANCIÈRE, J. 1999. *Disagreement*, Minneapolis, University of Minnesota Press.

READING, A. 2011. The London Bombings: Mobile Witnessing, Mortal Bodies and Globital Time. *Memory Studies*, 4, 298–311.

ROBERTSON, R. 1995. Glocalization: Time-space and Homogeneity-heterogeneity. *In:* FEATHERSTONE, M., LASH, S. & ROBERTSON, R. (eds.) *Global Modernities*, London, Sage.

SCANNELL, P. 1988. Radio Times: The Temporal Arrangements of Broadcasting in the Modern World. *In:* DRUMMOND, P. & PATERSON, R. (eds.) *Television and its Audience*, London, British Film Institute.

SILVERSTONE, R. 1994. *Television and Everyday Life*, London, Routledge.

SMITH, C.M. & MCDONALD, K.M. 2011. The Mundane to the Memorial: Circulating and Deliberating the War in Iraq through Vernacular Soldier-produced Videos. *Critical Studies in Media Communication*, 28, 292–313.

STAGE, C. 2014. Online A-liveness: A 'Rhytmanalysis' of Three Illness Blogs Made by Rosie Kilburn, Jessica Joy Rees and Eva Markvoort. *In:* SANDVIK, K. & CHRISTENSEN, D.R. (eds.) *Mediating and Re-Mediating Death*, London, Ashgate.

STURKEN, M. 2007. *Tourists of Memory*, Durham, Durham University Press.

WAHLBERG, M. 2009. YouTube Commemoration: Private Grief and Communal Consolation. *In:* SNICKARS, P. & VONDERAU, P. (eds.) *The YouTube Reader*, Mediehistoriskt Arkiv 12, Stockholm, National Library of Sweden.

WETHERELL, M. 2012. *Affect and Emotion*, London, Sage.

Title	Upload	Length	Views
ISAF 9—Æret være deres minde http://www.youtube.com/watch? v=DOvG2seHQm4&feature=related	9 July 2010	4.00	5,004
Martin Hjorth http://www.youtube.com/watch? v=qa4L9i-2fVs&feature=related	6 October 2008	2.04	4,498*
Danish Dragoons http://www.youtube.com/watch? v=2P33CP4cSTM&feature=related	15 April 2008	3.41	4,354
Never forge thttp://www.youtube.com/watch? v=-t9dzlFfJXk&feature=related	20 October 2008	3.52	4,269
danske soldater http://www.youtube.com/watch? v=XRGfnY4bH7c&feature=related	19 February 2009	3.05	4,166
Dan Gyde—Begravelsen http://www.youtube.com/ watch?v=YMSbuRokuBs& feature=related	17 December 2008	4.50	4,103
Vi mindes de Danske soldater der gav deres *liv for fred* http://www.youtube.com/watch? v=_edpDMxIGZs&feature=related	9 February 2009	2.22	4,016
The fallen Danish soldiers http://www.youtube.com/watch? v=-7R3cX69wzs	19 November 2009	5.11	2,982
Tribute to danish soldiers http://www.youtube.com/watch? v=6gQwR70J8pY&feature=related	27 October 2009	3.06	1,692
Til ære & minde om de faldne danske soldater http://www.youtube.com/watch? v=gqp3FXi8nsg&feature=related	5 June 2010	4.27	1,412
De faldne danskere i Afghanistan http://www.youtube.com/watch? v=Qxc1n1yHSOc&feature=related	27 May 2009	4.12	1,302
Danske soldater http://www.youtube.com/watch? v=doSeM7Xcs4I&feature=related	29 January 2009	3.05	1,301*
Til ære for de faldne http://www.youtube.com/watch? v=baM-q6spOQM	3 December 2010	6.25	193
Minde film—Til ære for soldater & pårørende http://www.youtube.com/watch? v=zcqDBru5r_0&feature=related	6 January 2011	2.05	53

* Data for videos collected 31 May 2011 rather than on 28 April 2011, as for the other videos.

6 Media Witnessing from Chora

In this chapter we investigate mediated vulnerability of bodies in danger of being killed by snipers from places of current and past violent conflicts. Live streaming either in the immediacy of the events or recorded livestreams of past events re-uploaded—is analysed as a prominent form of witnessing from city-spaces transformed into chaotic 'chora' warzones. We show how witnessing has to communicate the un-communicable, and we discuss how the truth claim of witnessing both places it beyond and within politics.

In this final chapter of the book we consider two scenes of conflicts in Europe: one from the recent European past and one from the European present. The siege of Sarajevo and the war in the Balkans are considered two of the most atrocious conflicts in continental Europe since World War II. These violent conflicts that occurred in the heart of Europe between 1992 and 1996 reintroduced the continent's citizens to the horrors of concentration camps, ethnic cleansing, systematic torture, and persecution of inhabitants due to their ethnicity. The 44-month long siege of Sarajevo, during which 11,000 people were killed and 50,000 wounded, was broadcasted daily in Western media and thus became a visually mediated televisual event. Because of this mediation and associated global notoriety, the besieged city has subsequently become a favourite topic in globital memory (Reading, 2011: 299). In this chapter we scrutinise both professional (journalists') and user-generated audiovisual clips that have been posted on YouTube and which bear witness to the vulnerability of the citizens of this war-torn area of the recent past.

But before beginning our survey of mediated images of vulnerability in conflicts of the recent past, we would like to include an event that is developing as we write (May 2014). Europe is once again witnessing conflict, this time in Ukraine. A wave of protests (known as Euromaidan) against the Ukrainian state has been sweeping the country since November 2013. This was when the then prime minister suspended the signing of the Association Agreement, which would have brought Ukraine closer to the European Union (EU). During subsequent months the conflict has escalated. There have been many claims and counter claims about the brutality of both the Ukrainian erkut special police units and Russian-sponsored activists, who played a big part in the annexing of the Crimea region in February 2014, and the subsequent protests in Ukraine's Eastern Provinces. As a former Soviet Republic from 1922 to 1991, some of Ukraine's citizens maintain strong ties to Russia.

Like the conflicts in the heart of Europe mentioned earlier, the situation in the Ukraine is highly mediated, only in this instance it is not only the broadcast media which portrays the citizens' vulnerability in the face of what could become a destructive civil war or herald the return of the cold war; this time the media is also in the hands of the citizens who are live-streaming their experiences alongside the eyewitness testimonials of the professional journalists. We now look at how eyewitness accounts have become political tools of vulnerability and an integral aspect of both the recent conflict in Sarajevo, and the continuing conflict across the Ukraine.

The two cases have some conspicuous similarities. First, they share the same geopolitical situation: both are former Eastern bloc regions seeking a (new) post-communist European identity. Second, in both cases citizens, journalists, and unarmed activists soon found themselves in the crossfire as police and military loyal to one side or another began to turn their weapons on perceived opponents. This creates affectively tense spaces for both the people inhabiting these areas and the people witnessing the events through media. However, the situations also differ on important points as illustrated in Table 6.1.

The two forms of witnessing are—at least from a contemporary point of departure—different in terms of the immediacy of the event. In the Ukrainian case, the event, eye-witnessing, and the reception tend to collapse into one moment, while in the Sarajevo case the ones witnessing are most often distanced in time, although present in space, to the atrocious events as they are remediated. Although the focus of this chapter in both cases is on digital media and easy access to simple mobile recording devices and uploading facilities, there is a qualitative difference in use of these technologies in the two cases. In the Ukrainian case witnessing is eye-witnessing as events unfold, whereas witnessing in the Sarajevo case means bearing witness to uploaded testimonials. In the paragraph on witnessing this distinction is elaborated further.

Table 6.1 Media witnessing in Ukraine and Sarajevo

	Ukraine 2014	Sarajevo 2007–2011
Time	Livestreaming	Re-uploading
Space	Being there	Being there
Event-transmission-reception	Instantaneity (simultaneity of transmission and reception) Immediacy (simultaneity of an event and its reception)	Instantaneity
Witnessing	Eye-witnessing	Bearing witness

WITNESSING IN SITU

In concordance with the general theme of this volume, which sets out to explore the political potentials of vulnerability, it seems appropriate to include vernacular media witnessing in politically tense situations. It is now widely recognised that visual footage and the digital mobile witnessing of citizens in situations of catastrophe (the Indian Ocean tsunami in 2004, Hurricane Katrina in New Orleans in 2005, the Earth Quake in Haiti in 2010), terror (9/11, the London bombings in 2005), war (Abu Ghraib in Iraq, Afghanistan), uprisings/revolutions (Iran, Egypt, Tunisia), civil wars (Syria, Ukraine?) play a significant role in mobilising opinion around issues. In this chapter we continue what we initiated with the analysis of Neda's assemblage capacities in Chapter 2, only here we consider primarily media witnessing at places of past or contemporary tensions and conflicts. In our Ukrainian case we look at witnessing as an utterance of 'being there' as events unfold, while witnessing in the Sarajevo case means bearing witness to globital memory of a historical recent past. Our two cases represent two kinds of witnessing: eyewitness testimonies based on first-hand knowledge of present vulnerabilities and secondary witnessing as bearing witness to past vulnerable bodies. In both cases the witnessing manifests digitally as uploaded video shots on the networking site YouTube. We argue that digital witnessing facilitates affective mobilisation around politically tense issues, and that it does not only offer the potential to change the present, but also the past. In this we disagree with John Durham Peters's statement that 'the past in some sense, is safe. The present, in contrast, is catastrophic, subject to radical alterations' (2009: 37). Digital witnessing is not only able to create events in the present but can also affect perceptions of the past in circumstances of non-closure and open-endedness. We subscribe to the argument that to witness is to be an 'event-generator' as witnessing transcends time and offers alternative futures both for situations that are current and those that are past.

WITNESSING

The witness has gained a new social and political significance with the advent of digital media that enable ordinary citizens to communicate/upload on social media platforms with ease. To understand the importance of 'media witnessing', a term canonised by Frosh and Pinchevski (2009), we first consider the characteristics of the act of witnessing and, from there, consider how new media might alter some of the traditional assumptions about testimony.

When considering witnessing as a form of communication it can be considered at three levels: the agent bearing witness, the utterance itself, and the audience who witness (Peters, 2009: 25). First, one must determine *who* qualifies as a witness. Paul Ricoeur (1972) and John Durham Peters (2009) argue that witnessing is tied to the body of the survivor. The witness has seen or heard something that he and she must report. The dialectics between the perception and experiencing of an event and the telling of the event requires that any testimony needs to be interpreted, according to Ricoeur. One only qualifies as a witness if one was present at a certain singular event the argument goes. Media scholars' interpretation of witnessing is considerably wider. It encompasses everybody listening to others' testimonies as well as those bearing witness digitally to atrocious events of the past (Frosh and Pinchevski, 2014).[1] New media scholarship thus argues that we have progressed from a narrow interpretation of the witness as the individual or individuals who testified the one core event, to a much broader definition of those who are *touched or affected* by an event to the extent that they bear witness by sharing their experience in daily conversations, through the digital sharing of talk, photos, or productions and circulation of more articulate responses. *Thus, witnessing both includes eye-witnessing and witnessing that testifies an affectedness resulting in an utterance bearing witness to something atrocious.*

Second, one must determine the frames and general semantics of witnessing. Ricoeur puts forward the argument that the testimony is an utterance that asserts something in a space of struggle (1972: 110–111). By this he did not mean that witnessing is the inherently political practice that Ashuri and Pinchevski determine it to be (Ashuri and Pinchevski, 2009: 135) but more that witnessing can be implied in a truth–falsehood dichotomy. Witnessing is not equivalent to partaking in political discussions even though witnessing always involves the assertion of something in a space of struggle. Witnessing is not mundane according to Peters. He thus refutes the old claim by Ellis that we all are witnesses to atrocities due to mass media. Instead, Peters claims that witnessing only happens in states of emergency, states of exception. Ricoeur considers three overall theoretical framings to understand witnessing; law, theology, and Holocaust. In the court the witness must testify in the name of the truth. In a theological frame the witness is supposedly willing to sacrifice his/her own life for a cause. The passion that a witness invests in a cause matters in order to qualify the witness as a witness, *but* it does not automatically qualify the witnessing. Ricoeur adds that the cause one is willing to die for has to be *just*: 'The witness is a man who has identified with the just cause that crowds and men in power hate but for which he risks his life' (Ricoeur, 1972: 115, our translation). These two frames give birth to two subject positions: that of the 'eyewitness' and that of the 'martyr'. The last frame, that of Holocaust, gives birth to the witness as 'survivor'. What is important here is the role witnessing plays in politically tense situations. Ricoeur's witness is one who balances between the theological, the above political, and the political sphere of different positions, conflicts of interest, and values, and of the ability to move crowds. Witnessing witnesses the immediacy of the absolute that is beyond politics and to which we need to give voice, but witnessing also gives rise to criticism and struggle because there is no manifestation of the absolute without the crisis of the false testimony and thus without the political decision that divides between the sign and the idol. *Witnessing thus is to be found both inside and outside of the political realm but cannot exclusively find itself within one of the realms.*

Third, the Holocaust frame of witnessing points to a significant paradox in witnessing that is important to our current argument around vulnerability and affect. *Witnessing is tied to the body of the survivor and the witness is caught in a double obligation: one must witness because silence is not an option, and at the same time, witnessing is impossible because the magnitude of the event exceeds ordinary channels of expressions.* Witnessing thus reports the affective imprints of extraordinary events. This often takes the form of silence, broken language, omissions, repetitions, and so on or the exaggerations and excesses that can become expressions of an individual psychic experience of Holocaust. As Dori Laub states, the testimony of the eyewitness survivor of Auschwitz may describe an uprising in which prisoners set fire to the camp and four chimneys go up in flames, while historians know that only one chimney blows up (Felman and Laub, 1992: 61). This inaccuracy may disqualify his or her testimony in the eyes of the law but not as a survivor, according to Laub (Felman and Laub, 1992: 61). The testimony testifies the unimaginable and the fictitious number of four chimneys translates the magnitude of the event: Jewish resistance to the overwhelming power of the Nazis in Auschwitz, which testifies to the historical truth of Jewish resistance and of human resistance towards totalitarian power in general, even in extreme cases where life is reduced to existence (Kelly, 2001: 1).

Witnessing means being an affected body communicating something atrocious that you can only partly render. We look on our audiovisual material as forms of witnessing and forms of broken utterances. We focus especially on how the absolute is witnessed and on how speechlessness is incorporated in the witnessing utterance. This means we look for traces of affect such as muteness, repetitions, broken language, shakings, omissions, and so on. It also means that we try to identify expressions of discrepancies between seeing/listening and grasping, because it is between these gaps that witnessing mobilises viewers and listeners. The aesthetic qualities of the audiovisual material such as 'realness', excess, index, haptic response, and rawness (Barthes, [1980] 1982; Foster, 1996; Marks, 2000; McCosker, 2013) mobilise affectively through an experienced immediacy between referential event, its recording, and reception, and through direct encounters with an unframed reality. Deleuze calls unframed images of raw reality 'pure images', in order to distinguish them from what he describes as sensory-motor clichés. If our conventional schemes break down, pure optic-sound images appear that render the 'thing in itself' either as beauty or as atrocity (Deleuze, 1985: 32).

Immediacy and rawness of witnessing has two important consequences that must be taken into consideration: (1) The immediacy provided by livestreaming seems to confirm the broad definition of witnessing outlined earlier in which we can all become witnesses of exceptional situations. It also seems to turn us all into eyewitnesses who can be virtually present at atrocious events. This signifies a rupture with Ricoeur's conception of the two-sidedness of witnessing, which divides the process into a sequence of experience followed by a sequence of communication. With the immediacy of livestreaming, the two sequences merge. (2) Being an eyewitness as a result of encountering an unframed experience changes the mobilisation impact of witnessing. Thus, it is the very character of the unedited visual material that legitimises its value as witnessing of truth, in contrast to false witnessing or strategic witnessing found in the political realm. The unedited character of the audio-visual material is what guarantees truth and what mobilises affectively around a felt injustice, an unheard atrocity that is able to attune viewers and mobilise them to react to the situation of the vulnerable eyewitnesses.

THE SEMIOTICS OF CHORA

The witnessing we look at takes place in urban landscapes that suddenly transform into warzones. In our specific cases, Sarajevo between 1992 and 1995 and around Maidan Square in Kiev in February 2014, unarmed protesters, activists, and ordinary citizens (in Sarajevo) suddenly find themselves the targets of snipers; what was only a few days previously an everyday urban space is transformed into a hostile environment. To characterise these spaces in transition from the everyday to the hostile, we use the concept of 'chora' taken from the semiotic psychoanalyst Julia Kristeva. Our aim is to explore the relationship between affect, bodies, and places by means of this concept.

Davidson et al. (2011) propose the term *affective ecologies* in order to understand the complex relationship between places, bodies, and affects. They define affects as 'a form of allure or attention, which provides the emotional "glue" that drive bodies to assemble into collectives' (Davidson et al., 2011: 6), and they highlight two characteristics of places that we explore in our cases. On one hand, they point to the fact that places have affective capacities because they are imaginary at the same time as they are material and real. The imaginary capacities of places are how attachments have been performed in the past or how they might develop in the future. The imaginary capacities of a place have to do with how bodies remember, recall its history, or dream it to be otherwise. On the other hand—and this relates it to Kristeva's chora—ecologies (places, affects, and bodies) 'are always in a state of emergence, hovering on the verge of unpredictability' (Davidson et al., 2011: 6). As ecologies are places–bodies–affects in motion and change, chora is the space from which change and rupture originate. It is, however, important for us to stress that the change-rupture quality of chora does not necessarily make it a space of ethical care or positive political development. Changes and ruptures can represent the rise of promising as well as totalitarian futures.

Tarde describes the social as a nervous system that basically consists of affective processes of imitation, contagion, and propagation (see the Introduction). The work of psychoanalyst and linguist Julia Kristeva on semiotic processes and chora could add to the exploration of biosocial processes of places in transition and at the same time qualify analytically the affective power of witnessing. In the previous chapter, we have already mentioned Kristeva's useful distinction between phéno-text and géno-text in order to look at rhythms and ruptures in audiovisual communication. Chora as concept has also been touched on in the field of geography. In geographical thought according to Olwig (2008) and Kymäläinen and Lehtinen (2010) Plato's concept of chora is introduced in the *Timaeus* in order to explain the passage from the intelligible to the sensible, that is from the perfect world of ideal forms to the imperfect world of change and becoming. Kymäläinen and Lehtinen point to two manifestations of chora: deconstructive architecture as in Parc de la Villette in Paris, which uses non-functional devices to create half-places, third places, or middle-places (2010: 254), or place changing from the perspective of living and embodied subjects.

Kristeva, meanwhile, conceives chora as the matrix, the womb, and the receptacle in which creation takes place (Isar, 2009: 40). Although it is a structural phenomenon, she places it within the genesis of the child before the emergence of mirroring, imitation, and identification, and the mastery and performance of language. As we saw in Chapter 5 Kristeva distinguishes between two modalities, the symbolic, and the semiotic, in all systems of signification including the non-verbal. The dialectics between the two modalities are constituent of the subject and no utterance or form of representation is exclusively one or the other. Chora is a space in the psychic economy that is characterised by its emptiness, meaning that it is a space in transition between a *no longer something* to a *not yet something else*, hence its designation as receptacle or womb: a place of birth—but again a birth of the new, which bears no promise of improvement in itself. The chora is traversed by energetic charges, and separates the inner and outer, and 'the me' and not me (Kristeva, 1974: 23). The semiotic runs through the chora as primary process traces and as indices of the psychic past understood as the maternal body that subjects can remember but to which they cannot return. Desire is what structures this space, but it is a desire that is not possible to represent.

How does Kristeva characterise the semiotic drives in the chora apart from them being a receptacle of energetic charges? Chora is basically a rhythm that is destructive and creative at the same time. It has strong similarities with Lefebvre's concept of arrhythmia that is both disturbing and disrupting, for example a city's eurhythmic and polyrhythmic flows, as well as capable of motivating creative invention (see Chapter 5). In chora we have vocal or kinetic rhythm structured by oral and anal drives, and the two drives that characterise 'life' in chora are the incorporation or oral assimilation that we leave aside here and *the rejection* that we find in Kristeva's famous theory of the 'abject'. Before being like someone, 'I' am not, I separate, reject, ab-ject that is to say I am threatened by annihilation (Kristeva, 1980: 21). Kristeva connects the drive of rejection to new birth: 'It's alchemy, that transforms death drives into jerks of life, of new significations' Kristeva, 1980: 22, our translation) and to her general theory on creativity in language that is based on the disruptive force of primary energies (the géno-textual) in relation to established structures of communication (the phéno-textual). From an affective perspective, warlike situations transform cities into choras, destructive and productive spaces at one and the same time. When a city for example is turned into a chora of drives, it is an expression of a narcissistic crisis, that appears either when the Other (the regime, the Law) is too severe (e.g. in totalitarian states) or when the Other is too weak (failed states lacking legal-political institutions). In the urban space transformed into a warzone, the places themselves become chora—no longer something and not yet something else.

In the case of Sarajevo, contemporary witnessing commemorates how the everyday space of a city transforms into a warzone. As for Kiev and Eastern Ukraine, violent confrontations are occurring and the risk of civil war is realistic: The subjects experience on a daily basis the kind of narcissistic crisis that chora represents. In both cases eye-witnessing means being a vulnerable body exposed to the Other's too severe punishment. The unarmed protesters, the activists, and the civilians find themselves in a former familiar space, which at the same time is unfamiliar as they are now potential targets for sniper fire. Visibility in such spaces makes the bodies vulnerable. Once visible, bodies become targets (Virilio, 1988; Thompson, 1995) and at the same time eyewitnesses with the potential to stream unedited visible evidence and the possibility of resurrection as heroes, martyrs, and seers of the horrifying truth: how a democratic state can so quickly return to a situation of authoritarian rule when those loyal to the powerful exercise their legitimate right to kill. Such scenes hit at the heart of the Western democratic dream and raise the prospect that if such a situation can arise in one state, it could happen elsewhere. The uploading of eyewitness testimonials in the Sarajevo case revitalises a conflict that is clearly not yet over, and it is our argument that the eyewitness style of uploaded videos trigger affect anew.

In Ukraine the chora characteristic of the urban spaces transformed into battlefields is apparent as we write this chapter, while it is the many indexical traces of the atrocious past in the form of in situ memorial sites (Vrbanja Bridge, Markale open-air market, the bullet holes in buildings, the tunnel in Dinji Kotorac, etc.) and the few official monuments to the siege that give the urban space in Sarajevo its chora characteristics. Sites such as the National

Figure 6.1 Entrance to the Tunnel Museum, Sarajevo

and University Library of Bosnia and Herzegovina, with its 1.5 million volumes of Muslim, Serbian, and Croat common heritage, which was attacked and destroyed by Serbian forces in 1992, and the tunnel transformed into a tiny museum that is run as a private enterprise, have become memorial sites in place of official monuments (Figure 6.1). The relative absence of official monuments itself signifies the non-closure of the past, and in doing so prolongs the space's chora character.

METHODOLOGY

From the two scenes of conflict we analyse two kinds of witnessing. From Sarajevo we look at a core material of 37 YouTube videos selected from a search on the term 'Sniper Alley'. We look at viewer ratings and at actual viewers' responses to the various forms of witnessing. Both journalists and ordinary citizens have uploaded YouTube videos. In the case of the Ukraine we have focused on user-generated anonymous live streaming from the start of the conflict around 20 February 2014. We have also studied more journalistic material from two groups of broadcasters—Spilno.tv and RT, Russia Today—as these are prominent examples of broadcasters using livestreaming from conflict zones. Spilno.tv is a group of Ukrainian streamers who perform media activism as they stream live from hotspots. The streamers' productions are widely used by news agencies such as the BBC, Al Jazeera, CNN, and the Ukrainian News channels. Its political 'adversary' is broadcaster RT, an international news channel, and an all-digital Russian TV network that also streams live from conflict zones.

In the following we analyse (1) the kinds of witnessing with a particular focus on the formal-aesthetic characteristics of the unedited-ness (chora) of the material, with reference to documentary film theory (Nichols, 1991; 1994; Bruzzi, 2000); (2) the bodily positionings of the witnesses, the degree of affectedness from chora (forms of enunciation) in the audiovisual utterances; (3) how the encounter with chora and the raw imagery is framed and reframed visually and linguistically; and (4) the affective mobilising impact of mobile and livestreaming witnessing from chora.

SNIPER ALLEY ON YOUTUBE

The 37 videos can be divided into two main categories of witnessing. Either witnessing is performed by vicarious footage that involves re-uploading of already made footage. Or witnessing takes the form of self-produced material commenting on the past events.

In both of these categories we find three documentary modes in use: the *expository* mode, the *observational* mode, and the *performative* mode. The *expository* mode is the classic documentary form with images of the world and a voice-of-God narrator telling you what to think, believe, and find meaningful about that world. Here we find news documentaries produced by well-known production companies and news channels such as Journeyman Pictures and Al Jazeera. But we likewise find user-generated web-witnessing videos, for example Glenn Campbell's *Sarajevo Sniper Alley (standup sample)*, 2010 (Figure 6.2), and cestima's *Snipers view in Sarajevo*, 2008. Taking a closer look at these two audio-visual utterances, the affective mobilisation impact leaps out because reactions are antagonistic: 'Also, you could see this and then tell who was sniper!!!! Idiot from USA . . . USA NOOB!! You are idiotic prick . . . that were not SERBIAN snipers, that was muslim forces, or you can call them Mujahedin snipers . . . My aunt, and many Serbs were killed by their shots, so FUCK YOU and your statement!!!' (1mrle); 'i love sentence when u say: to pick of civilians . . . they were aiming mostly for soldiers . . . why would they aim civilians . . . ? waist of ammo, time and no real reason to do it . . . its just muslim propaganda' (vladan891). Glenn Campbell stated that he had never had so many hate mails in his life as he got after his 27-second-long news-footage-like presentation of contemporary Sniper Alley as the 'most dangerous place' in Sarajevo with 'radical Serb forces shooting at everything that moved'. 'You had to move at an enormous speed because the Serbs were shooting at everybody'. In 2012, two years after uploading the video, Glenn Campbell

Figure 6.2   Screenshot from *Sarajevo Sniper Alley (standup sample)*

writes the following: 'Surprisingly, my most popular video on YouTube is this 30-second bit from Sarajevo last year. Not sure why. I get a lot of hate mail about it, too! (see video comments)'. Campbell's witnessing clearly antagonises the viewers, both because his legitimacy as a witness is contested and because his testimonial lacks authenticity markers.

Snipers view in Sarajevo is a very short video: 0:47 with a female voice-over commenting on what she is seeing from the top of Mount Trebevic. Cestima, the commentator, is positioned near the Jewish Cemetery, the Serbian artillery position with its view over Sniper Alley from the south. On the soundtrack it is possible to hear the wind and other tourists' voices, and these background sounds fill gaps between the voice-over of the female presenter[2] who denounces Serbian snipers (perpetrators) killing civilians (victims). During the documentary, the presenter pans her camera from east to west and backwards highlighting particular places of note using deictic markers: Holiday Inn (*that* yellow building *there*) and Sniper Alley (*that's* Sniper Alley). In doing this, the narrator creates intimacy and spatial co-presence between herself and the viewers. The unedited characteristics of this short video are mainly its instantaneity, and the fact that the viewers perceive what cestima perceives framed clearly through her voice-over. This creates solidarity between the viewers who are distanced—both concretely and metaphorically—from the perspective of the victim-civilians. As a witness, cestima incarnates the former perpetrators' perspective at the same time as she denounces it. Her witnessing distributes guilt and victim-hood but it does not give voice to the dead, mute, or the survivors. There is absolutely no trace of chora in the video-witnessing as the recording body finds itself on top of and removed in time from the conflict.

The violent and antagonistic comments on these two videos are attributable to many factors. The witnesses bearing witness are not eyewitnesses (a trivial fact), nor do they bear witness of their own affectedness. This is a feature disqualifying the two tourists as witnesses. Additionally, the positioning of the testimonies on YouTube locates them in a space of political struggle and that is the reason why they are so violently attacked. This feature qualifies their testimony as a perfect example of witnessing, which is capable of reopening spaces of struggle or atrocious events. Finally—and this is connected to the idea of the proper witness as an eyewitness—the testimony has to bear traceable features of the magnitude of the event and the encounters with chora. It has to try to render pure images and give voice to the grey zone. The two testimonies try to give voice to victims, civilians, and the vulnerable bodies targeted by Serb forces, but they do so only through denouncing the perpetrators and not through affective sameness with the vulnerable others. For this reason the videos create antagonistic interactions (where vulnerability and victimhood become discursive objects of struggle), rather than a space for attaching receivers affectively to the atrocities related to the chora-site.

Lots of the witnessing material related to Sarajevo on YouTube is uploaded found footage. In these samples there is a high use of the *observational*—classic fly-on-the-wall—perspective in which a selected part of reality, more unframed than in an expository mode, is presented. These observational mode videos mainly recycle core scenes from the siege: killings and wounding of civilians on the street (e.g. *Snipers kill people in Bosnia*).[3] Primary cues of affect are provided by the speed of the moving bodies and their sudden immobility if shot; the real sound—sudden shots; people screaming when they are hit. One video titled *sarajevo 1993 daily bread lottery*[4] is interesting for its witnessing qualities. The time and date of the recording—13:40, 25.2.1993—shown on each frame of the clip, the graininess and pixilation of the video images, and the scarcely audible, real sound of the moving, recording body and the background noises from the street all bear witness in an indexical style, while the digital dissemination provides the opportunity for repeated eye-witnessing. From a window high above street level, the camera pans over the snow-covered city showing cranes and rooftops, it then zooms in on a queue apparently in front of a bakery; the snow continues to fall, and two bodies are captured running away from the shop. Why do they run? Is the way back home dangerous to traverse, or is it just kids playing? There is no answer as the video suddenly stops. Although the image content of the video is apparently trivial, and it lacks the drama of civilians shot on the street, the viewer is drawn into this video (213,915 viewers) by its indexical quality: its visible recording time/date, the graininess of the images, the near muteness of the scene, and the depiction of an everyday rhythm that, on closer inspection, are exceptional. Under the headline of daily bread lottery and with the image of the queue, the hunger of the citizens under siege is evoked and felt through this short eye-witnessing testimonial. The commentaries on this clip manage to recapture some of the ambience of the siege ('Never forget, never forgive', UploadedL; 'I can't believe that my mother walk to get that bread when we was in Sarajevo on that time', Mostarac 233).

The *performative* mode of documentaries has, according to Stella Bruzzi and Bill Nichols, a double function: On one hand, the performative mode is a suggestive way of evoking the moment, the memory, and the place in the viewer's mind. It has less to do with the referential world as the viewer experience is filtered through artistic staged devices. On the other hand, the performative mode can be critically constructivist, as the documentary can become a part of the situation it aims at depicting. It could be argued that the latter point describes all the videos uploaded at YouTube: They are all interpreted as utterances in an ongoing conflict, and they are all performative by being able to trigger affects which is what our two American tourists experience to their own astonishment. At a more specific level, we can detect the performative in more detail. Two kinds of witnessing stand out here: the rather artistic web memorial produced in the form of still images of wounded and mutilated bodies, bombarded houses, burnt-out cars, and landscapes in ruin accompanied by an edited musical soundtrack of elegies. Another kind consists of videos where the camera itself becomes involved in the conflict: the recording body becomes part of the scene. The most obvious example is when the camera body itself is hit. This happens in the *KLA Camera MAN gets shot by Serbian Sniper 50 cal.*[5] (876,079 views), by far the most viewed video of all, a so-called death on direct. We now take a closer look at journalist Philippe Bouffon's video that shows Bosnian snipers on top of a 30-storey building shooting Serbian snipers.[6] The video is an extract (3:01) of the report *Sarajevo sniper la mort au bout du fusil* (25:56) that we look at in greater depth.[7]

The author/journalist Philippe Bouffon has made many documentaries for the journal *Envoyé Spécial*, as well as for French and international news channels. *Sarajevo sniper la mort au bout du fusil* depicts Göran, a Bosnian 'soldier', who happens to be in the middle of a conflict he did not ask for and that he does not want. He fights 'the animals', or the Chetniks, as he calls the pro-Serb armed units. But it is not so much in the depictions of the ordinary guy becoming a soldier-hero whose fears and tears the viewer gains knowledge of and feels sorry for. For the audiovisual utterance to be an eye-witnessing testimonial that mobilises affectively we have to look at the formal-aesthetic levels in the videos. *Sarajevo sniper la mort au bout du fusil* has a strong affective potential (and has a very high number of views) because it shows and not only tells the everyday experiences of inhabitants and fighters in Sarajevo during the siege. As a documentary, and not live-streaming images, the affective impact on viewers' bodies is transmitted through the body of the journalist as camera bearer acting as a mediator between the chaotic chora place and the viewers in their familiar spaces. Bouffon's own body becomes vulnerable, 'Often they took me for a target' (0:54), and[8] this vulnerability is evidenced by tilting images and seconds of camera immobility. One of the major points in this performative documentary is that the camera not only depicts what is moving but because it is handheld, it also follows the body and so is often forced 'to run', to hurry from A to B because the invisible front lines in the middle of the city are constantly changing. When the city transforms from a homely and familiar space to an 'unheimlich' space, a chora space, it is visible in disjunctions such as a cow and some hay, children in Dobinja playing with heavy weapons, tombs scattered about, and also through the changes to everyday rhythms. Either the streets and the warzones/front-line zones are empty or the people move very fast. 'Go,go,go,go, come on, come on, hey, hey', as Göran commands Bouffon to move quickly from one floor to another in order to prevent being hit. The constant rhythmic oscillation between acceleration and deceleration, and the sudden stops and starts as the body falls down and gets up again, characterise life on the front line, and the viewer experiences this existence vicariously through the journalist as camera bearer. The viewer is here invited to affectively share the exceptional experiences of the Sarajevo citizens during the siege through the journalist as a vicarious body at risk.

Two significant findings are manifest in the Sarajevo material. The non-simultaneity of event and witnessing is compensated for through the uploads of found eyewitness footage which can (re-)attune viewers' bodies rhythmically to past events. In order to mobilise viewers affectively without dissent, elements in the formal-aesthetic levels (again rhythmic pulsations of life in a warzone) of the audio-visual testimonies have to be in play. If the formal-aesthetic layers are not in play, antagonistic dissent appears immediately to de-legitimise the witnessing.

KIEV LIVE

For the case of the conflict in Ukraine we investigate three different examples of digital witnessing: (1) one from the street level showing unarmed activists and citizens in 'battle' portrayed by an anonymous source, supposedly other citizens documenting the current situation; (2) a news production that uses livestreaming strategically, which is made by Spilno.tv, a pro-Ukrainian news channel, that in their own words are performing a 'streaming revolution' (as a parallel to the Twitter Revolution mentioned in Chapter 2); (3) another piece of news production made by the Russian channel RT—Russia Today—that likewise uses live streaming as a strategic tool in their news production.

The eyewitness testimonials on YouTube of the current conflict in Ukraine and especially those uploaded around February 2014 often follow a similar script to the video *Снайпер стреляет по митингующим Майдан Украина по людям без оружия с щитами,* 2014.[9] On a city street, a small group of people can be seen slowly moving forward (Figure 6.3).

They can be identified as civilians due to their hesitation and their apparent unease with this state of emergency. Nevertheless, they do have some protection. Their heads are covered with helmets in a variety of colours, and they carry billboards, steel gates, and other makeshift shields. There is a lot of noise: people shouting and gunshots. When gunshots are heard the small crowd stops, crouches, and waits for the opportunity to continue to move forward. Suddenly a body in the crowd is hit, falls immediately and violently to one side, loses the shield, and hits the ground. One of the crowd crawls over to him to try and move him away while still protecting himself. Many wounded bodies are dragged away by the legs, under the arms, and by the arms and legs. The bodies are treated roughly as those moving them panic with the sound of every gunshot. Being hit, trying to escape if you get wounded, calling medics (they appear from time to time in easily recognisable neon orange and white), getting stretchers, and the effort of rescuing wounded people and removing corpses are very much the content of these videos. The predominant difference between the audiovisual utterances we have just analysed and the current eye-witnessing testimonials on YouTube from Kiev, is that the latter present live streaming images that tend to converge the communication process—event–transmission–reception—into one at the time of their upload. McCosker (2013) argues that livestreaming images intensify attention and affective engagement because of their unedited raw characteristics and because they de-frame the events. This argument

Figure 6.3   Screenshot from *Снайпер стреляет*

supports the truth claim of eye-witnessing according to Ricoeur, and if we continue in the same vein, we can say that the telling and witnessing of the eyewitness in the mobile digital utterances is substituted by the showing of images that *speak for themselves*. We would add, however, that it is the mediated rhythmic synchrony established between vulnerable bodies, which suddenly find their everyday surroundings have become a warzone, and viewers' bodies, which produces a feeling of sympathy. Following the rhythm analysis in the previous chapter the affective vibrations (Henriques, 2010) created by the irregular rhythm of snipers shooting is somehow transmitted to the distant receivers. This sameness is, of course, constructed upon a fundamental difference: The harrowing events are happening to the bodies in the imagery and not to the viewer, but it *could happen to the viewer*, and the horror of this experience is what is felt bodily.

Similar to the situation in Sarajevo during the siege, it is noticeable that the Kiev civilians avoid organised armed personnel units who are acting on behalf of the state, in this instance, the democratically elected Ukrainian government. As mentioned earlier, the frightening aspect of this is that a democratic regime can transform into a sovereign state, which then shoots at its own unarmed people. The anonymous uploader MegaPRONICK is one sender of an audiovisual utterance.[10] The unedited character of the imagery is particularly apparent in the unframed showing of bodies being hit by gunfire and then falling as the 2:42-minute-long video proceeds. The enunciation position of the recording body is present in the limited perspective it has from its position behind two windows. There are clips of a small group of moving bodies at street level and a few scenes from a courtyard, showing people dragging bodies away. The camera is drawn to the dramatic shifts in body-positions at street level: bodies falling; bodies lying down signalling for help; bodies crawling away obviously hurt; bodies being dragged away; bodies gliding down roofs, carried away on stretchers. But there are no attempts to show the origin of the gunfire. The body eye-witnessing here only focuses on the immediate impact of the gunfire coming from beyond the field of vision. And we see the eyewitness, who is looking down on the action—documentary style—shift between looking more closely (zooming in) and taking more distance (zooming out) to document the scenes. With the focus on the victim bodies, the unknown character of the perpetrators is highlighted. It is as if the chora space itself hits and hurts. We can say that the eyewitness is not interested in revealing and denouncing guilty parties but only in documenting the impact of these actions on civilians. The viewers are exposed and attuned to the mobility–arrest pulsation, the rhythm of the zoom in and zoom out, and the various victim body-positions in the imagery, which afford the bodies with a palpable vulnerability.

We now turn to two news journalist sources: the Ukrainian news channel Spilno.tv and RT, Russia Today, both of which use live streaming in their news reports, but from different political hotspots and from different political angles. Spilno.tv is performing media activism and is also using videos from non-professional live streamers and is thus part of a global movement in countries where citizens are critical towards mainstream media, for example Midia Ninja in Brazil. Spilno.tv's viewership grew to 16 million during the first two months of the conflict in Ukraine. The reason for the station's success in attracting viewers may be found in its affective mobilisation as seen when it presents a particular project and then tries to recruit new 'members'. Looking at a typical presentation video[11] we have identified four main strategies used by Spilno.tv:

1. Relying on the fact that live streaming has a *truth* claim, the immediacy of the absolute, according to Ricoeur: This is derived from a combination of traditional journalistic virtues and the eye-witnessing position journalists gain when they stream from current violent political events. So, for example, in the case of the Ukrainian conflict Kolya Savchenko, age 21 could prove that the 'green men' in Slavyansk were the same people as in Crimea before its annexation (e.g. Russians; 3:19).
2. Using a relatively simple rhetoric of *war*: Streamers are recruited as warrior-journalists using their technology to *shoot events* that perform the same political task as hard power (guns, institutional power). Streaming is presented as a way of creating a new political arena that politicians have to take seriously. Streamers stream events as they unfold following the belligerent way of thinking: We will defeat them or they will defeat us. The 'shooting' activities of the journalists put the streamers' own bodies at risk and expose as well as use their bodies as a political tool. Eleven streamers were wounded during the first few months of the conflict in Ukraine as Ukrainian police forces were ordered to shoot at the streamers. 'We showed it life as they did it. They shot our guys' hands to make them drop their cameras' (0:59).
3. To take part in a *digital revolution* that will disseminate and spread all over the region: Russia, Belorussia, and Kazakstan: 'Streaming is a unique mobilising resource. Because when people are seeing what's happening at a specific location, they have a desire to be part of it' (4:18), as Bogdana Babich, founder of Spilno.tv, says. In this revolution vernacular, witnessing and more professional witnessing converge.
4. *Streaming is media activism and post-1989 identity making*, and it has now become an activity of national Ukrainian interest: Babich argues that '[i]t's clear that Ukraine has been part of a script. We understand that. We understand that we are not the subject. We are not the players, we are being played' (2:21). Media activism is offered as a platform for Ukrainian nationalist agency against foreign influence.

THE JOURNALIST BODY AT RISK

In the *Uncut live report by RT from Kiev during Maidan shooting*[12] produced and uploaded by Russia Today, an official Russian news agency, journalist Alexey Yaroshevsky's affective mobilisation of viewers is used in spectacular ways to attract audiences to the channel. The live report is from the Maidan Square on 20 February 2014. A truce decided by President Viktor Yanukovych, who was democratically elected in 2010 but interpreted here as corrupt and authoritarian, and two of the opposition leaders Vitali Klitschko and Arseniy Yatsenyuk came into force on 19 February 2014, but it never really occurred. Journalist Alexey Yaroshevsky (AY) was sent out to report from an area that should be calm under the truce.

The stream begins with AY standing in the middle of the screen in a blue bulletproof vest with 'press' written on it. The scenery unfolds behind AY with people wearing gasmasks crossing the street, the cracking sound of shots, small explosions, sirens, smoke, water cannons (Figure 6.4). As the shooting intensifies, AY turns his back to the viewers and at a certain point exclaims, 'Wow' (2:40). As the time to start his report nears, he begins to blink nervously. A substantial part of the video is dedicated to the technical set-up prior to the streaming of events: The crew members fix their microphones in place, the format and aspect ratios for the recorded images are adjusted, and there is a sound test. It is six minutes into the news clip before the journalist begins his report. Prior to this he appears as the mute witness in a scene over which he has no control.

Figure 6.4   Screenshot of Alexey Yaroshevsky witnessing from Kiev

The truth claim of this eye-witnessing report lies in the body placement of the journalist who is in front of a scene that he denotes and points to. His body, in particular, remains unaffected and cool. For the major part of the news clip, he is mute and does not make the radical rhythmic changes we would expect from a body in peril. Occasionally he shifts between facing us and turning his back to us. He is positioned in the centre of the image and overshadows the scene that we, as viewers, see as fluid shadows. During this time we experience the situation through his nearly mute body and an occasional technical comment regarding the recording. There are a few exchanges in Russian between him and the technician about image adjustments as we are invited into the news production suite. These strategies are used exclusively to heighten *the legitimacy as eyewitness* of the journalist. This legitimacy is used to report a pro-government and pro-Russian (Yanukovych) biased view on the conflict in Ukraine. He calls the anti-government protesters 'rioters' and 'right-wing Nationalists'. The more neutral namings of the adversaries in the conflict such as pro-Russian separatists and pro-Ukrainian protesters were not used. His explicit discursive framing more easily passes as the truth due to the eye-witnessing positioning of his body, his muteness, and not least his will to risk his personal safety. Most of the commentaries beneath his report (80 in all) revolve around his personal risk taking that is seen as professionalism: 'Alexey Yarochevsky has to be one of the calmest reporters out there'; 'Alexey Yaroshevsky keep doing what you do best brother!'; 'Alexey Yaroshevsky is pro'; 'Big balls. Well done'; 'lots respects to you, Alex Yarochevsky! Thanks you for letting the whole world know what really happens. You are the BEST!'. Only one person comments indirectly on the discursive framing of the clip: 'It's almost comical to hop on BBC then onto Russia Today and it's like two different worlds. I'm confused as to what the truth actually is.. Are the right wing factions still rioting then?'.

The uncut clip from RT shows that the back-stage information, the live streaming, and the bodily risk taking overshadow the content and truth seeking of eye-witnessing reports. The affective attunement of the viewers' comments about this clip revolves around the courageous journalist, and only one questions the different worldview viewers get on various other news channels. His legitimacy as an eyewitness is due to his bodily engagement in the events, and consequently viewers oversee the ideologically biased (pro-Russian) framing of his report.[13] We could say that he uses affect strategically in order to sustain a politically biased argument about a situation. The argument is led from above, but it is masked as coming from a grass-roots perspective. The affective attunement is used to conceal or overshadow an argument about the world that is biased, and looking at the reactions, it clearly works. The viewers overlook the discursive framing of the scene. The Russian journalist performs as a witness, but frames as a partner in the conflict. According to Ricoeur, the journalist is a false witness to the political struggle to which his testimony relates, because he conceals the politically biased representation of the conflict via mediated vulnerability.

CONCLUSION

We have pursued three dialectics of witnessing, the first one being the one between eyewitness and witness, the second one being between witnessing being able to touch the immediacy of the absolute at the same time as being interpreted within a much more mundane given frame of struggle, and thirdly that witnessing has to bear traces of the magnitude of the event (it is uncommunicable) at the same time as the witness is obliged to bear witness. To witness is to give voice to vulnerable bodies—or in Anne Cubilié's words, 'from within this "grey zone" between human and nonhuman, life and death' (2005: 3). Live streaming is here seen as an important form of witnessing.

The witnessing happens at specific places in states experiencing exceptional circumstances or in transition. Places that change significantly from everyday places to warzones. In our Sarajevo case, the city becomes something beyond atrocity, whereas in Kiev, and other sites in Ukraine, a chaotic chora time, no longer something and not yet something else, is beginning. In our reading of the affective mobilisation possibilities of digital material from these two conflict arenas, the places and their affective ecologies are important. Through the digital material, perceptual shocks from the arrhythmic chora (shots, bodies falling, etc.) hit the viewers' bodies, which can then become attuned rhythmically with the bodies in situ. Witnessing that bears traces of the magnitude of the event (livestreaming, rawness) can attune viewers' bodies to and mobilise around vulnerable bodies elsewhere, both in space and time.

Through the changing rhythms of the former everyday places that have become chora places of transition, digital witnessing gives voice to the dead, the dying, the wounded, the exposed, the suffering bodies in the grey zone between the living and the dead. Thus, voice is given to victims of civil wars and violent political conflicts because their suffering seen through the digital livestreaming is documented as a truth claim beyond politics. To witness is different from just making a (political) statement, as witnesses can decide who should be perceived as the vulnerable bodies and who are to be called legitimate victims. The witness is capable of seeing the victim (in a nearly theological sense) beyond politics, which is why the position as witness is so acclaimed. But witnesses' truth claims immediately fall into a political struggle that confirms former antagonisms (the adversary parties in the Balkan civil war) or that creates new opponents (pro-Russians and pro-Ukrainians in the conflict in Ukraine). RT's use of livestreaming to frame a biased report on the current conflict in Ukraine shows that viewers tend to overlook or minimise the discursive framing of a situation and instead focus on the more affectively arousing elements. This clearly exposes the dangers of affective mobilisation that neglects political complexities. The image of unarmed citizens being targeted by snipers can transform an everyday space into a warzone and can evoke affective sympathy, as live streaming is particularly effective at transmitting what it 'feels like'. But the political discussions of who are perpetrators, allies, bystanders, and victims still tend to be fiercely antagonistic and reconfirm old nationalist agendas. Looking at the comments on the Sarajevo material, there seems still to be no consensual interpretation of the conflict in the Balkans even 20 years after the siege. In the two cases considered in this chapter, the affects aroused by vulnerability do not seem to produce new significant forms of understanding or common affective ground, but rather reproduce well-known power geometries and identity positions.

NOTES

1. It is open to discussion whether the best way to give voice and justice to victims of atrocious events is to widen the concept of witnessing as a way of widening the memory of the events or whether we should hold to the insurmountable distinction between the first-hand witnesses and the ones who have followed events at a distance or have only been told of them after the fact. Gary Weissman's book from 2004, *Fantasies of Witnessing, Postwar Efforts to Experience the Holocaust*, is born out of his own dilemma as a descendant of a holocaust survivor and *not* being able to feel the horror when he visited a concentration camp. Weissman opts for a historical understanding of the Holocaust, the only possible, and warns against the widening of memory and witnessing because it could represent a denial of the last survivors.
2. The script is as follows: 'This is where snipers, Serbian snipers, would pick off civilians and it is as you can see the perfect vantage point of just killing people. That yellow building is the Holiday Inn, that's Sniper Alley, Holiday Inn is where journalists were staying during the war, you can hear the [inaudible chant] in the background'.
3. http://www.youtube.com/watch?v=ZJKZ8QrdJpo (accessed 19 June 2014).
4. https://www.youtube.com/watch?v=OeDaObvbE0s (accessed 19 June 2014).
5. https://www.youtube.com/watch?v=KgxFZf9Gtzc (accessed 19 June 2014).
6. https://www.youtube.com/watch?v=vFNH12xXtrc (accessed 19 June 2014).
7. https://www.youtube.com/watch?v=6a1ogbCrQEg (accessed 19 June 2014).
8. Our translation of 'Plusieurs fois ils me prennent pour cible'.
9. https://www.youtube.com/watch?v=ZaLvEFghWw4 (accessed 19 June 2014).
10. https://www.youtube.com/watch?v=ZaLvEFghWw4 (accessed 19 June 2014).
11. https://www.youtube.com/watch?v=PZksh5RnRRU (accessed 19 June 2014).
12. https://www.youtube.com/watch?v=-eI9ircmiBc (accessed 19 June 2014).
13. This could also be due to the fact that adversaries of pro-Russian perspectives do not watch RT.

REFERENCES

ASHURI, T. & PINCHEVSKI, A. 2009. Witnessing as a Field. *In:* FROSH, P. & PINCHEVSKI, A. (eds.) *Media Witnessing. Testimony in the Age of Mass Communication*, New York, Palgrave Macmillan.
BARTHES, R. [1980] 1982. *Camera Lucida*, London, Vintage.
BRUZZI, S. 2000. *Documentary. A Critical Introduction*, London, Routledge.
CUBILIÉ, A. 2005. *Women Witnessing Terror: Testimony and the Cultural Politics of Human Rights*, New York, Fordham University Press.
DAVIDSON, T. K., PARK, O. & SHIELDS, R. (eds.). 2011. *Ecologies of Affect. Placing Nostalgia, Desire, and Hope*, Ontario, Wilfrid Laurier University Press.

DELEUZE, G. 1985. *Cinema 2, L'IMAGE-TEMPS*, Paris, Editions de Minuit.

FELMAN, S. & LAUB, D. 1992. *Testimony: Crisis of Witnessing in Literature, Psychoanalysis, and History*, New York, Routledge.

FOSTER, H. 1996. *The Return of the Real*, Cambridge, MIT Press.

FROSH, P. & PINCHEVSKI, A. (eds.) 2009. *Media Witnessing. Testimony in the Age of Mass Communication*, London, Palgrave Macmillan.

FROSH, P. & PINCHEVSKI, A. 2014. Media Witnessing and the Ripeness of Time. *Cultural Studies*, 28, 594–610.

HENRIQUES, J. 2010. The Vibrations of Affect and their Propagation on a Night Out on Kingston's Dancehall Scene. *Body & Society*, 16, 57–80.

ISAR, N. 2009. *Chora*: Tracing the Presence. *Review of European Studies*, 1(1), 39–55.

KELLY, O. 2001. *Witnessing beyond Recognition*, Minneapolis, University of Minnesota Press.

KRISTEVA, J. 1974. *La révolution du language poétique*, Paris Seuil.

KRISTEVA, J. 1980. *Pouvoirs de l'horreur. Essai sur l'abjection*, Paris, Seuil.

KYMÄLÄINEN, P. & LEHTINEN, A. 2010. Chora in Current Geographical Thought: Places of Co-design and Re-membering. *Geografiska Annaler: Series B, Human Geography*, 92(3), 251–261.

MARKS, L. U. 2000. *The Skin of the Film Intercultural Cinema, Embodiment, and the Senses*, Durham, Duke University Press.

MCCOSKER, A. 2013. De-framing Disaster: Affective Encounters with Raw and Autonomous Media. *Continuum: Journal of Media and Cultural Studies*, 27, 382–396.

NICHOLS, B. 1991. *Representing Reality. Issues and Concepts in Documentary.* Bloomington and Indianapolis, Indiania University Press.

NICHOLS, B. 1994. *Blurred Boundaries. Questions of Meaning in Contemporary Culture*, Bloomington, Indiana University Press.

OLWIG, K. R. 2008. Has 'Geography' Always Been Modern? *Choros*, (Non)Representation, Performance, and the Landscape. *Environment and Planning A*, 40, 1843–1861.

PETERS, J. D. 2009. Witnessing. *In*: FROSH, P. & PINCHEVSKI, A. (eds.) *Media Witnessing. Testimony in the Age of Mass Communication*, New York, Palgrave Macmillan.

READING, A. 2011. The London Bombings: Mobile Witnessing, Mortal Bodies and Globital Time. *Memory Studies*, 4, 298–311.

RICOEUR, P. 1972. L'hermeneutique du témoignage. *Archiv de Filosofia*, 42, 35–61.

THOMPSON, J. B. 1995. *The Media and Modernity. A Social Theory of the Media*, Stanford, Stanford University Press.

VIRILIO, P. 1988. *La machine de vision*, Paris, Galilée.

Epilogue
Vulnerable Power

We begin the epilogue by discussing our claims in the book with an imaginary challenger: the political scientist and philosopher Hannah Arendt via her main arguments in the book *On Revolution* (1963). Over six chapters we have shown how bodily vulnerability plays an increasing role in digital global media networks, in relation to illness blogging, digital protest assemblages, charity, green activism, war commemoration, and digital witnessing in conflict zones, and how it—under certain circumstances—is able to *mobilise affectively as a political energiser* and *to open the future as an event maker of the virtual*. We have also stressed that this mobilisation and virtualisation is not in itself a positive political force that can motivate empowerment and emancipation, although this may be the end result as was the case in the first four chapters, it can also motivate antagonistic struggles and produce figures of alterity and nationalism, as was partly the case in the last two chapters of the book.

Let us now imagine how Arendt would respond.[1] According to Arendt, the recognition of the bodily vulnerability of those affected by poverty, suffering, tyranny, and misfortune has played a significant role in many revolutions. In the case of the French Revolution, Arendt argues, it was when the poor joined the revolution in order to get better conditions that the movement became doomed. From Arendt's perspective, the rule of necessity means the end of politics instead of the installation of a new body politic. Even though one could disagree with her interpretation of the American Revolution, which Arendt portrays as a success compared to the French Revolution in the eighteenth century, it is noteworthy how Arendt links this success with the fact that *freedom* was the aim of the American Revolution. The American revolutionaries reacted towards slavery not because they were moved by pity or by a feeling of solidarity with their fellow men but because they were 'convinced with the incompatibility of the institution of slavery with the foundation of freedom' (Arendt, 1963: 61). The slave as someone to feel sorry for is not the issue here, because only an abstract generalisable principle of freedom makes slavery a political issue.

The French revolutionaries, on the contrary, did not seek freedom but the *happiness of the people*. As in all other revolutions, except the American, compassion as an 'innate repugnance at seeing a fellow creature suffer' (Arendt, 1963: 61) was a key catalyst of decisions and actions. Three features are predominant in her understanding of compassion that could prove useful for a discussion of the affective and political potential of vulnerability. Compassion is 'stricken in the flesh' (Arendt, 1963: 79), which distinguishes it from pity that keeps its sentimental distance. Compassion thus is a passion that touches the flesh exactly like affects. Second, compassion is, in contrast to reason, only capable of comprehending the particular and individual and has no capacity for generalisation. And, third, when the one touched in the flesh by compassion sets out to change the world, he or she will avoid the wearisome processes of persuasion, negotiation, and compromise and 'lend its voice to the suffering itself, which must claim for swift and direct action, that is, for action with the means of violence' (Arendt, 1963: 77). Arendt thus argues that the men of the American Revolution remained men of action and reason from beginning to end, whereas the French revolutionaries raised compassion to the rank of supreme political passion and virtue. The French Revolution therefore failed when the Jacobins, under the leadership of Robespierre, seized power, because they were not concerned with the republic, the government, the institutions, and the constitutions— that secure general principles and rights—but only with the people and their natural goodness.

In brief, mediated vulnerability itself, as well as the affective compassion it ignites and the actions following passionate engagement, would not imply a new body politic according to Arendt. On the contrary, such vulnerability stays within a private realm or it results in violent actions short-circuiting the political. Arendt's point is therefore that compassion as an affect cannot be trusted as a proper catalyst of positive political processes. We to some extent agree with that, because mediated vulnerability in itself seems to offer no generalisable solutions to be implemented in law or institutions, but we would like to add two important qualifications: the first, pragmatic; the second, more a principal.

First, we argue that the lack of generalisable potentials is not important from a pragmatic point of view, where we would have to acknowledge that political processes are filled with affects, desires, fascination, attractions, and repulsions. In this sense affects are not necessarily constructive guidelines for making law, but they are important facilitators of the attention, visibility, cognitive transgression, discussion, and struggle that sometimes motivate standpoints and policy-making. And for this reason, vulnerability is already—and should be treated as—political whether one could criticise this from a theoretical-normative perspective. By arguing that vulnerability is constantly being politicised, we have thus used a broad understanding of 'the political' inspired by Chantal Mouffe, who defines 'the political' as the 'dimension of antagonism which I take to be constitutive of human societies, while by "politics" I mean the set of practices and institutions through which an order is created, organizing human coexistence in the context of conflictuality provided by the political' (2005: 9). We have not primarily analysed how affect motivated by mediated vulnerability can or should be part of 'politics' in the sense of institutions and lawmaking, which seem to be of primary concern to Arendt, but, rather, how it is an unavoidable part of the everyday sociopolitical processes of mobilising, changing, moving, reforming, and sensitising bodies in relation to conflicting notions of how the challenges of illness/health care, political violence, global inequality, pollution, war, and regional conflict should be dealt with and acted on and thus how affects are pragmatically part of the political that creates the foundation for institutional politics as well. Therefore, we have chosen to focus more on how vulnerability can play a political role in attuning and mobilising citizens around topics rather than on theoretically denouncing it as a-political per se.

Second, vulnerability *can* actually be deployed as a more general political category to guide states and policies, as Judith Butler (2004) has argued, because these can be more or less supportive of the idea of vulnerability as the condition all humans have in common. We are depending on each other to survive, and on the others to not abuse the vulnerability of the singular body/organism. In this sense a totalitarian state overlooks vulnerability, whereas a democratic state would often acknowledge it to a higher degree. This qualification is more fundamental than the first as it simply installs the recognition of vulnerability as a core principle of politics. An objection, which Butler also deals with, would be that 'vulnerability' is often used strategically (e.g. to legitimise the war on terror), as we have also shown in Chapters 4 to 6, and that we therefore need to be constantly aware of the reasons why certain bodies may be mediated as vulnerable. In this way our quest for an analytical framework that acknowledges common vulnerability and affects as political principles is in harmony with Arendt's view of politics as the reign of generalisable principles, but it also tries to avoid the Arendtian scepticism towards politicising particularities.

In our book we have thus taken a more explorative approach to 'political affect' by arguing (1) that the political and affects cannot be separated—especially not in an era of new digital media, (2) that affects cannot always be trusted as catalysts of positive political changes and therefore need to the critically discussed, but (3) that they nevertheless are capable of sometimes opening up spaces of existence for new voices, attachments, and mobilisations, which should be acknowledged. We thus share Arendt's normative interest in not idealising affect and vulnerability as the main road to proper political change but pragmatically maintain that one must instead analyse the political shapes affect can take, how it spreads, if it avoids the exploitation of human vulnerability, or if it uses vulnerability strategically for unjust causes.

We have thus approached mediated vulnerability as a truly vulnerable form of power, in the sense that it attunes, energises, and virtualises political processes and conduct (it is a form of power) but in ways that are unpredictable and often balance between the constructive and destructive, the excessive and positively transformative (its ability to control effects is shaky and vulnerable).

In the chapters we investigated 'vulnerable power' by showing how crowding, assembling, seducing, staging the sublime, creating rhythmic vibrations, and witnessing chora in relation to mediated vulnerability are important contemporary ways to saturate the political by energising citizens and opening spaces for imagining new futures. However, we have also maintained that these processes should always be critically scrutinised by asking if and/or how mediated vulnerability gives voices to otherwise marginalised positions, as was the case in the chapters about Eva Markvoort's illness blog and the documentation of Neda Agda Soltan's death, or simply reproduces established discourses and hierarchies as in some of the commemoration videos analysed in Chapter 5 and conflict videos in Chapter 6.

Another question discussed has been whether or not the affective processes are characterised by an *agonistic* ethos in which differences can coexist, as in the comments to the commemoration videos in Chapter 5, or rather as *antagonistic* struggles in which differences seem to motivate violent aversions towards other positions as in some of the comments to the videos in Chapter 6. Furthermore, we have continuously discussed whether or not mediated vulnerability stimulates political actions characterised by *action, long-term involvement*, and *structural political solutions* or the opposite. In the charity cases in Chapter 3 we clearly saw an urge to act and be part of long-term projects (e.g. the Kibera project) instead of short-term processes of donation. In Chapter 4 on green activism, the involved key figures did become important in longer processes of environmental mobilisation, and in Chapter 1 it was obvious that ill blogger Markvoort succeeded in attaching more people (structurally) to solving the problem of organ donation by signing up as donors.

But whether affect and mediated vulnerability offer the key to positive structural changes is a reoccurring discussion and an 'Arendtian doubt' can be detected throughout the chapters. Realistically this question can only be answered by following the longitudinal effects of our cases and how they are assembled with new parts and processes over the coming years. We can, however, conclude with certainty that digitally mediated vulnerability, and the affective processes it generates, is increasingly important, powerful, and unpredictable political forces of mobilisation and virtualisation. Instead of idealising the rationality of politics, we must therefore scrutinise and constantly evaluate how politicisations around vulnerabilities occur and whether they help shape sustainable, caring, and inclusive worlds.

NOTE

1. Luc Boltanski (1999) is likewise discussing Hannah Arendt as he develops the concept of 'politics of pity' in *Distant Suffering, Morality, Media and Politics*. He formulates a politics that is based on a sentiment that at one and the same time keeps a distance and difference between the unfortunate and the spectators of the misfortune and obliges spectators to engage morally in the destiny of the unfortunate. Boltanski proposes a humanitarianism that works at a distance through media, but that engages sentimentally by evoking pity in viewers.

REFERENCES

ARENDT, H. 1963. *On Revolution*, London: Penguin Books.
BOLTANSKI, L. 1999. *Distant Suffering. Morality, Media and Politics*, Cambridge: Cambridge University Press.
BUTLER, J. 2004. *Precarious Life. The Powers of Mourning and Violence*, London, Verso.
MOUFFE, C. 2005. *On the Political*, London and New York, Routledge.

.

Index

Milton Keynes UK
Ingram Content Group UK Ltd.
UKHW022108141024
449569UK00031B/1828